Sacrifice

IN GREEK AND ROMAN RELIGIONS

AND EARLY JUDAISM

[THE HALE LECTURES]

Sacrifice

IN GREEK AND ROMAN RELIGIONS AND EARLY JUDAISM

by

Royden Keith Yerkes

*Sometime Professor
of Theology
in the University
of the South*

WIPF & STOCK · Eugene, Oregon

Wipf and Stock Publishers
199 W 8th Ave, Suite 3
Eugene, OR 97401

Sacrifce in Greek and Roman Religions and Early Judaism
By Yerkes, Royden Keith and Wach, Joachim
ISBN 13: 978-1-60899-933-0
Publication date 9/1/2010
Previously published by Charles Scribner's Sons, 1952

TO
WALLACE EDMONDS CONKLING

FOREWORD

Sacrifice, as one of the major forms of expression of religious experience, has not, until now, received as much attention by students of religion as it deserves. Yet it has been in all ages and under very different skies, the culminating act in man's worship of the Divine. The two great cult communities whose religious ideas and institutions have so profoundly influenced our own civilization, the Greek and the Hebrew, both were sacrificing communities. The careful investigation of the nature and role of sacrifice in Greece and in Israel which is undertaken in this volume prepares the way for thorough study of the Christian notion of sacrifice.

Dr. Yerkes is well known in the Episcopal Church of America and in the Anglican community as a scholar, an educator and a spiritual advisor to many. It is an honor and pleasure for me to introduce this work of his, a fruit of several decades of labour, to a wider public.

JOACHIM WACH

April 24, 1952

PREFACE

The incentive to this study came over forty years ago when a young graduate student was introduced to the subject by Morris Jastrow who, despite his vast knowledge in the field, was becoming increasingly uncertain about the origin and significance of sacrificial rites. The gift theory, as proposed by E. B. Tylor (*Primitive Culture* ii, 375) in 1874, does not explain sacrifices wholly or partly eaten by worshipers, although it does enter into later interpretation of sacrifices. The theory of a common meal with the gods, as proposed by W. Robertson Smith (*Religion of the Semites* 226–227 in 2nd edition) in 1889, leaves the holocaust unsatisfactorily explained, but this theory was a step in the right direction. Both these theories assume that some concept of deities preceded worship and leave the rise of the concept of deity unexplained, except upon the basis of Tylor's animism. Sir James G. Frazer, in his exhaustive studies in *The Golden Bough*, left no doubt that sacrificial rites can be traced to a period long anteceding any concept of deity. He concluded that these rites arose from purely magical practices, thus leaving the concept of deity still unexplained. Jastrow himself leaned to the opinion that all sacrifices were developed from divination rites, especially hepatoscopy as practised in Babylonia. Burning the corpse of the animal used in the rites seemed the most fitting disposition of what had been used for a quasi-supernatural purpose. The young graduate student began to accumulate and explore references from Semitic and Greek and Latin sources in the endeavour to ascertain how far all proposed theories were right and how far they were unsatisfactory.

Change and circumstance, including two world wars, have interrupted the work. During many years of teaching in the field of theology, the explorer was delayed in the examination of the mass of material furnished by inscriptions. Certain questions kept obtruding themselves. Why was sacrifice used by early Christians to interpret the work of Jesus? Why was it adopted to explain the ideal of the Christian life? How came it to be the dominant explanation of the Christian Eucharist? Why are men so divided upon this question today? Students of the history of religions are, for the most part, not interested in these questions; those who are interested in these questions appear not always to be acquainted with the history of religions. What seemed needed was not a book on sacrifice, but a series of volumes.

In the passing decades heavy teaching duties left little hope of completing the task. From a mass of notes, material has been selected to assist in giving a bird's eye view of the subject, as illustrated by Greek, Latin and Hebrew sources, without being too superficial, in the hope that it may be of value to more thorough pursuit of the subject.

My classmate BURTON SCOTT EASTON read the manuscript and spent many hours in discussion of the subject; he insisted that this work should be published. His recent death makes this expression of gratitude purely formal.

My former student PROFESSOR ROBERT E. DENGLER has given valuable service for which he is peculiarly fitted, by checking notes and references, pointing out errors and making suggestions which facilitated the completion of the work. His tiresome labour of love can be understood by those who use the notes.

I deeply appreciate the enthusiastic interest of DOM GREGORY DIX, O.S.B., who gave much time to reading portions of the manuscript and discussion of details. His generous offer to have the book presented by the English press came the day after I had accepted the invitation to deliver the Hale Lectures.

To PROFESSOR JOACHIM WACH I tender thanks for his careful reading of the manuscript and his making many helpful suggestions. It is difficult to find words to acknowledge his eager willingness to give the foreword to the book.

The material in Chapter XII is compressed. I am hoping to be able to use this material in a second volume which will treat the subject from a theological and liturgical point of view.

The invitation to deliver the Hale Lectures of 1951 came as a complete surprise. For this great honour I am deeply indebted. To the Trustees of the Hale Foundation, and especially to the chairman, DEAN ALDEN DREW KELLEY of the Seabury-Western Theological Seminary, I proffer thanks.

I am happy that my former student, who is now my Bishop, has given me permission to dedicate this book to him. His constant friendship for over thirty years has given me more inspiration than he will ever know.

ROYDEN KEITH YERKES

The Feast of the Annunciation 1952

ABBREVIATIONS

BIBLE VERSIONS

MV	Masoretic version of the Old Testament
LXX	Septuagint
LV	Latin version (Vulgate)
DV	Douay translation into English
AV	Authorized version of 1611
RV	Revised version of 1881–1886
JV	Jewish Publication Society version of the Old Testament

ENCYCLOPAEDIAS AND COLLECTIONS

CE	Catholic Encyclopaedia
DB	Hastings' Dictionary of the Bible (5 volumes)
EB	Encyclopedia Biblica
ERE	Hastings' Encyclopaedia of Religion and Ethics
JE	Jewish Encyclopedia
SIG	Dittenberger: *Sylloge Inscriptionum Graecarum* 3rd edition
Michel	*Recueil d'inscriptions grecques*

TRANSLITERATION OF HEBREW WORDS

Consonants and vowels are rendered, as nearly as possible, by English consonants and vowels with at least approximately the same pronunciation.

The following signs will be used to render Hebrew consonants for which no single English consonant is an equivalent.

dh to render *th* as in *this*

ch pronounced as in German, by placing the tongue as if to say *k*, and aspirating as in *h*.

to designate Hebrew *ayin*. There is no similar sound in English. The nearest approach is that of g in *sing*, which is not silent, but is about as much softer than ordinary g, as g is than *k*.

TRANSLITERATION OF GREEK WORDS

Consonants of Greek words occurring in the text are rendered as nearly as possible by English consonants and vowels with the same pronunciation. The *e* in Greek, as in most languages, is pronounced as long *a* is pronounced in English. In the notes Greek words are given in Greek letters.

TABLE OF CONTENTS

Chapter I. CONTRAST BETWEEN MODERN AND ANCIENT MEANINGS OF SACRIFICE

From generation to generation words vary in spelling, in pronunciation and in connotation. Discoveries and inventions, new contacts, new customs, new social, economic, political and religious conditions, new ideas—all subject words to processes of transformation which often reverse their original meaning.

The word *doctor* is a familiar instance of this process. Originally the word meant *teacher,* and connoted extraordinary learning, tested by examination, in some field of study. In present-day popular use it has become synonymous with *physician* or *surgeon,* neither of which was originally called doctor.[1] Almost every American college now uses the word to describe recognition of prominence or sheer perseverance in some field of public or semi-public activity, while some institutions bestow the title as a subtle endeavour to secure financial friends. The word never means teacher and does not necessarily connote learning in any subject.

This process is abundantly illustrated in religious vocabularies. The words *religious* and *spiritual* have so many vague connotations that one should define them before using them. The word *service,* once denoting an act or group of acts performed by a subordinate for a superior, came to describe solemn rites performed by humble devotees in honour of a superior being or god. In modern religious use the word describes almost any aggregation of noises made within four walls devoted to the purpose.

2. MODERN POPULAR USE OF THE TERM *Sacrifice*

The word *sacrifice* has likewise undergone complete transformation of meaning. The general and popular use of the term today, with a few esoteric exceptions, is wholly secular and describes some sort of renunciation, usually destruction,[2] of something valuable in order that something more valuable may be obtained. One may sacrifice duty for pleasure or pleasure for duty, or honesty for gain or gain for honesty. One may sacrifice an eye or a limb or a life for one's country or for some other country. One may even sell stocks "at a sacrifice." The modern secular connotation of sacrifice, as a noun or as a verb, may be analyzed as follows:

1. That which is sacrificed may be material (e.g., a fortune or a limb) or it may be immaterial (e.g., pleasure, honesty, fidelity, reputation).

2. It must be of some value to the person making the sacrifice. One does not sacrifice a pebble or a button or the hair shorn from one's head by a barber.

3. The sacrifice is constituted by renouncing or giving *up* the valuable thing. He who makes the sacrifice is, by his act, deprived of the use of that which is sacrificed.

4. The sacrifice is *by* somebody, *of* something, and *for* something, but never *to* anybody. In fact, it is usually destroyed. The honesty is not given to anybody; the soldier's arm does not become the possession of the country. If, perchance, that which is sacrificed does become the possession of some other person—such as the fortune which may be sacrificed—the new recipient is a subsequent fact, but never a factor, of the sacrifice.

5. Because of the basic importance of deprivation and destruction, the idea of sacrifice always denotes sadness and some sort of misfortune. It is always "too bad" that the sacrifice had to be made; it would have been so much better if the boon could have been secured without it. Therefore, we desire to make our sacrifices as small as possible; only a fool sacrifices more than is necessary, and the sacrifice is senseless if the boon can be obtained otherwise.

6. Because of the natural desire to obtain as much as possible for as little as possible, we frequently compare the cost of the

sacrifice with the value of the boon obtained. We are familiar with the statements, "He sacrificed a great deal for very little," or, "He obtained much for little sacrifice."

7. The boon for which the sacrifice is made is presumably of greater value than that which is sacrificed, or at least it seems so. This boon may or may not be shared by the one making the sacrifice. If he shares the boon he has in reality made a bargain purchase [8] by giving up what he thinks of less value than that which he obtains. In what is called "the supreme sacrifice" the sacrificer gives up everything and obtains nothing; he does not share the boon.

So completely does this popular and secular concept of sacrifice obtain that many suppose it to be the basic and original connotation of the term. With this assumption men frequently approach the interpretation of sacrifice in ancient religions and, in particular, the sacrifice of Jesus. In ancient religions the sacrificer gave up the animal which, in turn, gave up its life. From these two acts of deprivation sacrifices are explained. The explanation almost invariably proceeds from the death of the animal, which is a necessary fact and is therefore supposed to be a factor of the sacrifice.

From the first Christian days the word *sacrifice* was applied to the work of Jesus. In earliest writings no endeavour was made to explain this application. Latin writers began to explain the death of Jesus as a sort of supreme sacrifice in which he gave up everything in order that others might profit without giving up so much. Since all sacrifice seemed regrettable but inevitable, two distortions of Christian tradition resulted.

From the inevitability of the death of Jesus in his work of sacrifice, men have conceived all sorts of grotesque and immoral theories of a "doctrine of the atonement." The idea that the death of Jesus was regrettable gave opportunity for flowering of sentimentality which has been especially luxuriant in western Christendom in the last three centuries. In Protestantism it has been nourished by emotional revivalism and theological subjectivism, and in Romanism by the cult of the Bleeding Heart and the Five Wounds, of the Stations of the Cross, of the Mater Dolorosa and all their kith and kin. On Good Friday both Romanism and Protestantism seem to try to forget Easter Day and to concentrate upon the sufferings of Jesus as if they were ends in themselves instead of steps to a mighty victory.

3. ANCIENT CONCEPT OF SACRIFICE

The connotation of the modern secular concept of sacrifice is the very opposite to that of the term in all those ancient religions which formed the milieu of early Christianity and furnished the vocabulary with which early Christians expressed their ideas and their ideals. Despite many differences of detail, certain common features characterize sacrifice in the Hebrew-Jewish, the Greek and the Roman civilizations.

1. The word had no secular significance whatever, but strictly described religious rites and things. It is one of the few words which were not transferred from secular to religious use, but from the beginning expressed what we may call spiritual ideas.

2. The word never connoted reluctance or deprivation or renunciation or sadness or inevitability grimly accepted. Sacrifices were occasions of greatest joy and festivity and thanksgiving, and were gladly performed as expressions of the attitude of men to their gods.

3. Sacrifices were always as large as possible; the larger they could be made, the greater would be the accompanying joy and festivity.

4. They were offered *by* men *to* their gods; a sacrifice not offered to some person was inconceivable. The stress was upon the *giving* and not upon giving *up*.

5. While they were offered to procure boons from the gods, they were frequently offered after the boon had been received, and as expressions of thanksgiving.

6. The death of the animal, while a necessary fact prelimi-

nary to the sacrifice as it is necessary to the preparation of a roast of meat for dinner, was not a factor of the sacrifice any more than it is a factor of the dinner. The animal had to be killed for the purpose, as any animal has to be killed before it can be eaten. Slaying for sacrifice was naturally performed with solemnity proper for the occasion, but no significance was ever attached to the fact that the animal had died.[4] We never hear of death *qua* death effecting anything. This cannot be emphasized too strongly, since it is the point of departure for all the modern erroneous explanations of sacrifice.

The contrast between the two concepts of sacrifice may be tabulated as follows:

	Ancient	*Modern*
Field of use	Wholly religious. Never used secularly.	Almost wholly secular; transferred to religious use.
Purpose	Solely a cultic act.	Never a cultic act.
Size of sacrifice	As large as possible.	As small as possible.
Recipient	Always offered *to* a god, thus indicating a recognition of superiority.	Never offered *to* anyone.
Performance and accompanying emotions	Always performed with joy; came to be identified with thanksgiving.	Always performed with regret; accompanied by sadness.
Significant emphasis	Emphasis on giving and action. Deprivation, while a necessary fact as with all giving, never a constituent factor of the sacrifice.	Emphasis always on giving *up* and on deprivation.
Death of the thing sacrificed	Wholly incidental and never with any inherent or significant meaning. A fact but never a factor in the sacrifice.	Signifies the "supreme sacrifice." A necessary factor in all sacrifice.

4. ETYMOLOGICAL ORIGIN OF THE WORD *Sacrifice*

The word *sacrifice* derives from Latin, which gives more than forty other words from the same root *sac,* one of the few roots not adopted by metonymy or analogy from physical use to describe spiritual processes. From the beginning it denoted the relation of certain physical objects or acts to invisible and intangible powers for weal or woe, by which primitive man regarded himself surrounded. Gracious powers he would fain please that they might hover near him and preserve his life and health. Malevolent powers were to be coaxed or driven away.

Men thought of these powers as resembling themselves and therefore to be pleased or averted by doing something for them or to them. One gladly prepares a sumptuous meal for an honoured guest or, not gladly but faithfully, pays exorbitant tribute to a skulking blackmailer. About the only possessions of the average man of old were food and clothing. To the welcome guests of the upper air the food was sent, sublimated into smoke that it might the more easily reach its destination; for chthonic spirits the food was usually buried or burnt on an underground altar.

Any object which had been given to a god by repetition of prescribed words and with a prescribed ceremony was called *sacer,* which was used long before the period of classical Latin to describe buildings, trees, men and women, animals and vegetables, gold, incense and days and years, whether the objects so described were to be consumed or to be used as accessories in worship or related in any way to such use.

This process of devoting things to the use of a god was described by the phrase *rem divinam facere* (to make a thing belong to a god) or by the single word *sacrificare* or its kindred *consecrare,* both of which were equivalent to our concept of hallowing or sanctifying or devoting. Objects so set apart were *sacra. Sacrificium* was referred to such objects as were for the immediate use of a god, principally animal or vegetable food. The word was employed both substantivally and participially to describe the objects so offered or the act of offering them.

The original connotation of sacrifice was first any ceremonial act to or in the name of a god; later it might refer to the thing upon which the act was centred. Latin was the first language to coin a blanket term to describe all such offerings or acts. Neither Greek nor Hebrew had such a term; both denoted particular kinds of offerings or acts by special phrases.

The fact that sacrifice is a peculiarly religious term necessitates the understanding of the significance of religion in human culture.

Chapter II. THE SIGNIFICANCE
OF RELIGION

Many theories have been proposed to explain the origin of religion. Ardent devotees have sought this origin in some sort of direct call from a deity to primitive worshipers; the call almost always took the form of a human voice and was usually accompanied by the epiphany of the god. Non-devotees have naturally rejected this suggestion and have turned to animism or totemism or taboo or magic or hepatoscopy or some other primitive social practice. A favourite homiletic supposition is that man is possessed of what is called "the religious instinct" and worships because he cannot help it.

The theory of a primitive call and epiphany of a god is purely hypothetical and belongs to the realm of faith and not to that of knowledge. The theory of descent from an earlier social practice carries the story one step farther back but makes no contribution to the question of the real origin of religion.

Whether there be such a phenomenon as instinct is for psychologists to decide. The term is used to denote those common animal acts which do not have to be learned by the individual and from which the individual can be restrained only with great difficulty, if at all. Simple observation indicates how religious any man would become without much conditioning teaching, and also how readily individuals lay aside every kind of religious practice. "The religious instinct" seems to be a phrase coined to express the conclusion that we do not know how religion started.

2. OBVIOUS FACTORS OF THE ORIGIN OF RELIGION

The first human individual fared forth, like every living thing, with instinctive acts or tendencies directed to two ends: self-preservation and self-continuation. The trite proverb, "self-preservation is the first law of nature," probably lies at the base of most of the phenomena of physical life. This, in turn, arises from the inevitable necessity for every individual, animate or inanimate, to adjust itself to the environments in which it is set.

Contact between any two beings results, even in the inorganic world, in the automatic adjustment of each and frequently causes serious alteration in the behaviour of both. The very continuation of life depends upon contact with beings which have the power to sustain it and to destroy it. Life is contingent upon the proper reaction of the living thing to potentially destructive factors. Vegetable life finds its sustenance in the inorganic world; animal life can be sustained only by substances which were themselves once alive. Every ounce of food which an animal eats has once lived, and the atoms which supported that other life pass to support the life of him who eats them. If he does not become food for some other animal, his sustaining atoms are disorganized and passed back to the earth from which they came and from which succeeding vegetables take them. Animal life is preserved only by life. The function of the individual in nature seems to be to play his short and unconscious part in maintaining the rhythmic process and to provide other individuals to continue it when he is gone.

Every individual functions in a certain place, at a certain time, and with a limited amount of energy. Thus we may speak of finiteness of space, of time, and of energy. Within the limits of that finiteness the individual must perform his short, monotonous task of continuing the life principle and passing into oblivion. In some "higher forms" of animal life, contact with environments is more complex. For instance, the reactions of nerve systems and sense perception enter into adjustments and make the life of the individual more variegated. He may live a little longer, although not so long as some trees. His life may seem a little more diversified; he may slightly extend the radius of his activity; he may be possessed of a little more energy. Eventually he is a victim of his threefold finiteness and passes into oblivion.

When the human individual appeared on the scene he became possessed of potentialities of knowledge and choice denied to other forms of life. These, in their development, have brought about the ever deepening and widening gulf between man and all other forms of creation. Both potentialities have their counterparts, possibly their roots, in animal life, but the rigid finiteness which constricts the animals has kept them within definite and recognizable bounds from which man has at least commenced to make his escape.

The knowledge of the animal seems limited to its own sense percepts of concrete things.[1] Man not only can conceive abstract ideas and reason from them; he can, by the aid of communication and tradition, transcend the bounds of space and time and share the knowledge of those who are thousands of miles removed from him, as well as that of hundreds of generations which preceded him. Man's experiments are no longer pure trial, as are animal efforts; proceeding from reasoned premisses, they are planned and directed to reasoned expectations. The finite, rudimentary knowledge of the animal gives rise to fear; man knows not only that the dangers of life are dangers; he knows why they are dangerous and he can reason methods of avoiding them. Thus begins his conquest of fear, which has only just started. Man, by his knowledge, can often avoid having to adapt himself to environments; he can adapt the environments to himself and make the wilderness and solitary place rejoice, and the desert to blossom as the rose. Finally, knowledge for man is no longer merely a means to physical comfort; it can become an end and joy in itself.

Animal choices seem to be restricted to concrete things as means to life and comfort. The principle of these choices is the immediate convenience of the chooser; the incentive is some physical appetite or emotion. Despite the fact that all men act upon this basis in infancy, and many remain close to the infant plane throughout life, the mature man undoubtedly has the potentiality of saying, "No," to emotional urges and can make his choices upon the principle of remote values at the expense of immediate convenience as, for instance, in the payment of insurance premiums. The incentives to his choices can be abstract and altruistic values, such as courage or honesty or culture or the welfare of others. For the attainment of these values he is willing to suffer inconvenience and pain and loss. His choices, like his knowledge, can transcend the bounds of space and time; they can reach to faraway places and to remotely succeeding generations. Nor are they confined to his own energy; he has so learned to co-operate with the powers of nature that he can freely choose objects which reach beyond his power of attainment; he can choose and plan methods by which others may attain them.

3. PROGRESS AND DEVELOPMENT OF HUMAN ACTIVITIES

The development of the activities of human culture is analogous to the pattern of the biological history of the individual, recapitulating the biological history of the race and passing imperceptibly to successive forms unpredictable from the first stage, but retaining an identity from beginning to end. Such is the story of languages, of arts, of sciences and of all the elements of civilization. The speech in which each of these activities is described and discussed retains vestiges of the early forms of the activity. Astronomers still speak of the rising and the setting of the sun without taking the trouble to note that they do not mean by these terms what early astrologers meant, albeit both groups of men refer to the same event, but with different interpretation.

In religion, with which we are here concerned, men have progressed, as they have progressed in physical sciences, by discovery after discovery, from rude beginnings to noble achievements. It must have given men a shock to learn that the gods did not eat beef and mutton and pork; but by that discovery men passed to nobler concepts of religion. Men who prayed earnestly for removal of eclipses, and saw their prayers invariably answered in a few moments, must have been taken aback by the discovery that eclipses disappear without prayers; but thus they began to understand both prayer and eclipses.

Equally shocking was the discovery that space is limitless and matter indestructible, but by this discovery men made such progress in science that they find it difficult to resign themselves to the conclusion that, after all, space is limited and matter destructible. We have all smiled at the naïveté with which mediaeval scientists sought to transmute metals; after spending millions of dollars we learn that the transmutation of elements releases energy and may transform our way of living.

Our quest for knowledge and our consequent regulation of choices have had a strange history. What we once thought was knowledge has often proved to be erroneous opinion; nevertheless, men continue undaunted in their search. Men of science proceed upon the assumption that the power which moves the stars causes the atom to cohere, and they seek to understand it and to co-operate with it. Men of religion proceed upon the assumption that the Power which moves the stars can mould human character, and they seek to understand it and co-operate with it. Both groups have required centuries to arrive at these conclusions.

4. THE BASES OF RELIGION

Religion has gradually developed in three phases of its activity —in worship, in beliefs and in behaviour, which have been alliteratively styled cult, creed and conduct, corresponding to the affective, the rational and the volitional sides of man's nature. In all of these the development has been from the particular to the universal, and from the universal back to the particular. One facet of the religious ideal is the blending, converging and balancing of these three sides of man's nature in such a fashion that, in the words of philosophy, "all his potentialities are actuated." Each of these stories merits a separate study. The present study is concerned with cult and with a single element of it.

The understanding of worship, as of all religion, requires clear distinction between the obvious and the implicit, between natural and symbolic, between direct and analogic. Failure to make this distinction has occasioned much difficulty in discussions of religion.

The obvious meaning of a thing proceeds directly from the physical nature of the thing and may always be apprehended by the individual from direct sense percept of the thing. The implicit meaning is not directly perceptible to the senses but requires the aid of knowledge and reason. The obvious meaning of a photograph is that of any other piece of paper; implicitly that piece of paper bears to a certain person a relation which it bears to no one else.

The symbolic meaning of a thing does not inhere in the physical nature of the thing but is traditionally attached to it by analogy; it therefore may be apprehended only by one who knows the tradition. A salute to a flag has no natural significance; symbolically it is full of significance which can be understood only by those who have had some instruction.

The transmission of ideas, through centuries of history, has passed from a stage which was originally obvious and onomatopoeic to one which is wholly symbolic. Every individual must experience this transition before he can share the tradition of the race. Objects were primitively described by imitation of the sounds and motions which they made, as the infant still speaks of a "bow-wow" or a "choo-choo." The sounds made in adult communication have no relation to the things they describe, except as symbols. The same sounds may, in different traditions or in the same tradition, have totally different symbolic meanings. The sound indicated by the letters d-a-n-k have a different meaning in English from the same sounds in German. Writing is doubly symbolic, referring not to things, but to the purely symbolic sounds used to indicate the things, and sometimes attempting to indicate different symbolic meanings for the same sounds as, for instance, *rain, rein* and *reign* in English.

Learning any language involves education in the tradition of that language.

When two persons of different traditions meet, and neither understands the tradition of the other, their only means of communication are basic sounds and motions of obvious meaning which served in good stead before the parting of traditions and which developed differently in differing traditions. The adult of any tradition, if his vocabulary is confined to such basic sounds, is described as "a case of arrested development." We are happy when the one-year-old says, "Bow-wow"; we are sad if he still has to say it at twenty-one.

The acts and language of religion form no exception to this rule. Originally their meaning was obvious and physical. In the course of centuries they have become symbolic, analogic, traditional. They can be understood only by him who has been instructed in the tradition. Religion also provides cases of arrested development which must be treated with the clemency which is extended to all such cases without allowing them to impede normal development. Cult, creed and conduct all exhibit instances of arrested development, both in individuals and among groups. Difficulty arises when these become too numerous and try to impede development.

For preservation of the tradition which makes spiritual cultivation possible, some social unit is necessary. The prolongation of human infancy [2] to within approximately a quarter of man's natural life formed the basis of the family, the first social unit, which was related to its component individuals somewhat as those individuals were related to their component members, or those component members to their constituent cells. Members of a family share physically and socially the same life which must be preserved and continued. The union of families developed the clan and the tribe as larger units which shared the same life. Strangers might be admitted to any of these groups, but only by some ceremony such as mingling their blood with that of the members of the group to which they were admitted. Blood was always regarded as the seat and source of life. With enlargement of the social unit came common participation in the acts which had to do with preserving and extending and enriching life.

All the activities of civilization proceeded from man's endeavours to supplement or complement his finiteness. Our ancestors were compelled to forage for food and to be on the alert lest some animal choose them for food. The visible and tangible things of the earth constituted man's first acquaintance with his environments. Those which served his purpose or assisted in attaining it were friendly; those which thwarted that purpose or threatened his life were inimical. The study of the ways of these visible and tangible environments and the knowledge of proper relations with them gave rise to arts and sciences.

5. THE RISE OF RELIGION

Early in his history man became aware of invisible and intangible powers with which he must needs reckon. Life itself was the first of these imponderables which made him wonder. He entered it without consultation or consent as to time and place and manner. He matured mysteriously and became possessed of hunger for a mate. He had to cope with illness and accidents which threatened to remove him from life and thus awakened fear. He watched the waning of his powers and realized that he must leave life as he had entered it, without consultation or consent as to time or place or manner. He saw others leave it and wondered where they had gone and whether they could still help him or hinder him in his endeavours to cling to life. These wonder moments of life—birth, maturity, mating, sickness, accidents, death—made man aware of some sort of Power with which he simply had to reckon. It was futile to try to resist that Power: could he learn to co-operate with it?

He saw the Power at work around him in the lives of other men, in animals and trees, in wells and springs which needed no refilling like cisterns but came to life without his help. He saw it in the warmth and light of the sun, in the moon and stars which moved across the sky and guided his steps at night, in rivers and seas without which he could not live but which constricted and menaced him, in storms and earthquakes which embodied invincible force.

He saw the powers at work unequally in different individuals and different species. Some men were stronger and more clever than he, and some were his inferior. The powers were at work within him and also outside him. It was futile for him to try to resist them; could he learn to co-operate with them? The study of the ways of these invisible powers, and the endeavour to effect co-operative relations with those that were friendly and to avert the harm which could be wrought by those that were inimical, gave rise to philosophy and religion.

From his animal ancestry man brought the desire to know the causes of all things and events which concerned him. His new equipment of knowledge and choice extended the range of these phenomena; thus he was started on the elaborate quest which has resulted in civilization. In the centuries which have intervened we have classified and departmentalized our knowledge and practice; the range of the efforts of any single individual is more limited than it was with primitive man. Nevertheless, every phase of our cultural progress—artistic, scientific, social, economic, political, military, literary and religious—is still based upon the effort to understand the processes of cause and effect in order that we may set into operation those causes which produce desired effects and that we may neutralize or avert those causes which produce effects which are undesired. What we now call religious rites were not so classified by primitive man, but were indiscriminately mingled with all the acts and practices of life.[3] Early interest was not in *why* effects were produced, but in the fact that they could be produced.

Primitive man did not distinguish clearly between causes which were visible, audible and tangible and those which were invisible, inaudible and intangible. The latter simply gave him more wonder and perplexity and possibly more uncertainty in his efforts, as they do for us. Science and religion both derive from what we now call magic, by which we describe the planned processes in which the sequence of cause and effect was erroneously imagined. Magic was a primitive, unformed philosophy underlying many acts, some of which became scientific operation and others religious rites.[4]

6. THE RISE OF WORSHIP

The first endeavours to understand cause and effect were by way of trial and error. Methods which, to primitive reason, seemed effective were continued and developed. When the invisible powers began to be regarded as possessing knowledge and choice, those acts by which men sought contact with them were considered as addressed to them. This marked the beginning of religious rites—of worship. At some time in the distant past, men began to perform acts of worship, as they began to speak articulately, to use fire and tools, to wear clothing, to write, to barter and to engage in all the activities which, taken together, make for what we call civilization.

Ancient Greeks gave to these rites the name *ta hiera*, "the sacred" (things or acts); Latin coined the word *sacrificium* which, in the plural form *sacrificia*, served the same purpose. Many early practices, which antedated religious concepts, developed into *sacrificia* or acts of worship. Not all rites can be traced to the same origin, any more than all languages can be traced to a single group of fundamental sounds or experiences.

As no two peoples are alike and no two languages are alike, so no two rites are alike. Among early peoples we find a great variety of uses, many addressed to the same purpose, and all undergoing constant transformation by isolation, by translation, by synthesis, by separation, and by sublimation.

(1) The same rite may come to have totally different significance with groups of worshipers who are isolated from each other. For example, among the Greeks the holocaust was always a horrible rite of aversion; among the Hebrews it became the greatest rite of adoration.

(2) A given rite will undergo many changes if it is transferred to a different climate or to a different culture or to a different group in the same culture. When rites are copied or imitated or deliberately spread, as in missionary activity, they sometimes become hard to recognize as definitely related to or descended from an original. Christian baptism in the twentieth century in the north temperate climates bears little resemblance to the same rite in the first century in sub-tropical regions.

(3) The fusion of two rites invariably effects changes in both and sometimes produces a third which is unlike either. Geographical proximity of two rites, without formal fusion, will produce the same result, whether the two rites are parallel or seemingly contradictory. Fusion of the ancient Hebrew *pesach* with the *mazzoth* rite produced the modern *passover* which is reminiscent of both and unlike either.

(4) Two parts of the same rite may be disunited and become two entirely different rites. The early Christian initiation rite has become, in western Christendom, two distinct rites separated by several years, performed by different officials and given entirely different explanations.

(5) Religious rites are persistent and preserve many details of ceremonial long after the real or obvious reason for them has been outmoded or forgotten. Devotees will then find some analogous or symbolic reason for continuing them rather than break forcibly with tradition. The stole, as a priestly symbol, has so changed its significance that few even know its origin in pagan religions. Sublimation, effected at different tempo by different groups, explains many religious schisms; divisions are, for the most part, ceremonial and social rather than intellectual. After the schism has been effected, intellectual rationalization proceeds to accentuate it and to make the schismatics more divergent.

Of rites which may be properly called religious we find many which cannot be traced to any single source, but which all have to do with efforts to apprehend the invisible Power or powers which men recognize as part of their environment. Some of these were strictly group rites; others were of primary concern to individuals as related to their groups. They are not always carefully separated and are found in various combinations. The chronological order in which they arose will always be a subject of conjecture. These rites are:

(1) A sacred communal meal
(2) Solemn burning or burying of a sacred object
(3) Rites of fertilization
(4) Rites of exorcism and incantation
(5) Divination rites and oracles
(6) Rites at the wonder moments of life
(7) Rites performed with reference to departed persons

Chapter III. EARLY DEVELOPMENT OF SACRIFICE

The common meal, probably a by-product of the prolongation of human infancy, has always been an agent in maintaining the unity of the group. It is for anthropologists to determine its origin and history; it had become a fixed institution before the development of religious rites. The members of a family, sharing the same life, shared likewise in the invigoration and preservation of that life.

Primitive man did not distinguish nicely between life and the atoms and molecules which support it. To him the life of that which had been eaten passed into the eater, together with all the desirable qualities which that other thing had possessed. The fleetness of the deer, the endurance of the camel, the might and fertilizing power of the bull could now be his. A way was opened for man to compensate his finiteness and to become more than mere man.

Early in human history, after the appearance of articulate speech and infant reason, members of a family or of a clan or of a tribe exhibited one more distinctively human characteristic by meeting together to share the power or the courage or the fleetness or the endurance or the wisdom of what they were eating. The common sharing of the same power served to bind them more closely together. Not only were they kinsmen by blood; they had become kinsmen by sharing the power which was greater than they because it would compensate their finiteness.

It was inevitable that the meal should become ceremonious. The tendency to ceremony seems to find its root in man's animal nature. He does the same thing in the same way. He puts the same arm first into his coat; he walks in the same track until he has beaten a path; he holds his fork the same way and tries to teach that way to his children; he has the same form of greeting and reply. This tendency to ceremony is bound to be exhibited when men are engaged in a deliberate group act.

They sit in the same order; the same one leads; each does the same thing and says the same words. Otherwise the act could not be a group act; it would be an aggregation of conflicting individual acts.

The common meal would soon come to be held on stated occasions as life became more routine. It would also be resorted to when human finiteness was more acute, as before going on a trek or striking camp, or before entering a battle or after the successful performance of these acts, or after failure, that they who had failed might lay greater hold on the Power.

2. VALUE OF EXPLANATION OF EARLY SACRIFICE

At first men did not reason about the Power; it was that which compensated their finiteness and gave them courage to dare and strength to do. Long before they reasoned about it they had become possessed of a rite which later, like all familiar acts and objects, would demand explanation. Cult, or worship, was the first element of religion to appear. After cult was well established, creed arose, first as explanation of the worship and then, as time continued, as making certain demands upon the lives of devotees.

While cult may retain at least a faintly recognizable integrity among many groups, each group will have its own explanation, and the proposals, almost as numerous as the groups, will sometimes be almost contradictory. This has always been true and still obtains in modern religions. Christians, for instance, agree pretty generally upon a rite which they call baptism. Upon the amount of water to be used their opinions differ; upon the explanation of the reason for the rite and the effects of its use they go from one extreme to the other in contradiction. We must not expect men, in the morning of their thinking, to exhibit any more similarity than they do when reason is more highly developed. We are therefore not surprised at the varieties of explanation of the sacred meal.

In many parts of the world have been known clans or tribes

which maintained a tradition of descent from a particular species of plant or animal. Every individual of that species was therefore a sort of brother to every member of the clan or tribe. From American Indians came the word *totem* [1] to describe that individual; for instance, the bear might be the totem of such and such a tribe, and every bear was held in particular regard by each person in the tribe. In some instances, the regard was such that no one in that tribe would eat bear meat. In other instances, the bear would be solemnly and ceremoniously eaten upon an occasion set apart for the purpose.

The investigation of totemism is strictly the work of the anthropologist. Its mention in a study of this kind is necessitated by the fact that some maintain that the idea of a god was evolved from the idea of a totem and that honours to a god were but a form of magnification of honours to a totem. The eating of a sacrifice offered to a god was accordingly explained upon the basis of eating the god and thus incorporating his qualities. It is maintained by some and contested by others that every tribe of people has retained vestiges of original totemism and that therefore totemism is a true ancestor of religion.

Scholars differ upon the thesis of the universality of early totemism. Totemistic practices are widely variant and totemism itself is a social philosophy rather than a religious tenet. Moreover, it is not necessary to suppose that the social and religious development of every people has been mechanically identical. After the entrance of human intellect and will upon the scene, it is impossible to make accurate prediction of the succession of stages of progress, unless one is in possession of all the factors of choice.

All that we can say is that totemism is a social state in which many peoples have once probably lived and some have surely lived. It is certainly one form which the eating of the sacred meal may have taken. It seems, however, to have been a sort of social excursion rather than a definite step in religious development. Since it was preceded by earlier social forms of life, it cannot be regarded as the origin of religion or of anything else.

Nor need one have any shame or misgivings if it be discovered that his ancestors were once totemistic. They were probably worse than that in days which preceded their totemism.

A commonly accepted explanation of the origin of sacrifice is that it was first a method of feeding the gods, which were imagined as possessed of the desires of human beings. This suggestion assumes that worship and sacrifice were necessary corollaries of the conviction that the gods were personal beings; it assumes that some sort of reasoned creed preceded the cult and thus violates the natural process which is becoming increasingly better recognized, viz., that the order of development of religious activities was cult, creed and conduct.

The Power or powers, with which primitive man desired to come into contact, were originally not personified; they were forces with which he had to cope. The Greek Zeus was originally simply the sky; the Hebrew Yahweh was possibly originally the "feller," the force which was exhibited in the destructive processes of nature such as storms, thunder and earthquakes, before the power of which the things of nature were helpless; the earth was the great source of life especially when it was united with the power of the sun. Vestiges of this primitive concept are found in all ancient records. Archaeological discoveries of ancient cult sites and accessories indicate that early worship was not iconic; the powers were not regarded as persons.

It was not hard for man, with his infant reasoning, to conclude, since eating the food effected some sort of union with the powers, that part of the food must come into contact with the powers themselves. Since these powers were chiefly of the upper air, the food which went to them was that which had passed into the smoke of the fire which roasted it. This may well have been the incentive which made almost all peoples come to think of their powers as real persons with proper names, life histories, dwelling places, natural needs and wants, peculiar habits and all other marks of human beings or persons.

It was therefore quite natural that the common meal, in which union with the powers was sought, should develop into a banquet at which the powers were honoured guests, or into a sumptuous meal given entirely to them and not even shared by the devotees. Thus would easily arise the concept of sending food to them; the only known method was to sublimate it into smoke which would obviously go up to the deities and satisfy their wants. Thus can we understand the very name given by ancient Greeks to these powers, *theoi,* which by many scholars is derived from the root *thu* (smoke); *thuein* would mean *to make smoke* and *theoi* would be *receivers of smoke.*[2]

Instead of the desire to feed the gods being the origin of sacrifice, feeding the gods may have been but a later explanation of already familiar rites, rising after personification of the deities had occurred. This would be in keeping with a well-recognized rule of doctrinal and ceremonial development. The reason for the pious continuance of given rites and ceremonies and cult accessories is seldom, if ever, the reason for their origin. It is genuine rationalization, and rationalization may be good as well as bad; in fact, it is good if it is reasonable and sensible.

One may find oneself possessed of a habit and may not know how it arose. One may find oneself in certain environments or engaged in a certain occupation. As far as he knows, "It hath ever been thus." He may find himself also face to face with the opportunity of choosing to continue or to break with this of which he has become conscious. If he continues, it may be from sheer inertia or from intellectual or moral laziness; or it may be because he sees in his habit or occupation certain values of which its originators did not even dream. The reason for the commencement of the habit or the occupation was probably obvious; the reason for continuing it is purely or partly symbolic.

The personification of deities would occasion some confusion in thinking and expression among men of rudimentary reasoning powers, as it does among more intelligent folk. Such expressions, from the morning of civilization, must be evaluated, not in the light of our sophisticated method of premiss and conclusion, but from the point of view of uncivilized men who were just beginning to grope in the realm of thought. A single instance of this process will suffice.

In the whole eastern Mediterranean world, where our civilization seems to have had its beginnings, the wild bull[3] was identified with invincible might and with fertilizing power by men who loved life and longed to increase and to strengthen it. In Babylonia, in Syria, in Palestine, among the Hebrews, in Egypt and in the whole Aegean world he struck fear and wonder into men's hearts. We must think not of the comparatively tame bull of the farmyard herd, but of the fierce, huge monster which roamed untrammelled in the forests, was the source of death to luckless ones, and became the source of life to those who learned to meet and handle him. From the beginning he seems to have been considered as peculiarly possessed of the power of fertilization—the mysterious, awesome, coveted power of creating life. To eat of bull meat would be to appropriate the power of the bull and might easily be expressed as "having the bull within one."

When the power which was resident in the bull had become personified and therefore called a *theos* (which we translate *a god*), he who had eaten of the bull might easily think of himself as having eaten the *theos*. In fact, the word *entheos,* meaning "a *theos* in (one)," or "in a *theos,*" was actually used to describe a participant in such a feast. Such participation was frequently accompanied by frenzied revelries, and the verb describing this condition was *enthousiazein,* meaning "to become *engodded.*" From this stem comes our word enthusiasm and all its cognate words. Eating the god was therefore not the origin of sacrifice; it was a later explanation of its effects. Sacrificial rites constituted the origin of the phrase "eating the god."

3. THE BASIC ELEMENTS OF ALL WORSHIP

The word *sacrifice,* which means "to make a thing sacred" or "to do a sacred act," was used in Latin to describe various rites which arose from the common meal when that meal was held, not for the ordinary purpose of satisfying hunger, but for the purpose of entering into union with the mysterious Power or powers which men felt within them and about them as life itself, and which they recognized in all their environments as both menacing and strengthening the life which they loved and to which they longed to cling.

In the course of a long time men began to direct their thoughts to these powers and their workings, and tried to explain the rites, which had become ceremonious. Still later, the powers were gradually personified. We must think of this personification, not as conforming to an act of Parliament or as the result of a majority vote, but as a tendency which probably required centuries for development. The process may have been faster in one group and slower in another; it was doubtless uneven among members of the same group. During this period we may expect to find words and phrases and sentences which posited the powers as persons, and others which pictured them as blind forces.

From the common meal have arisen such concepts as eating the gods, eating with the gods and feeding the gods. When men had come to regard the gods as persons, the custom arose of reserving certain portions of each meal to be sublimated into smoke which would arise to the upper air and thus reach the deities.

Three kinds of rites have developed from the sacred meal and from these three rites have grown three different sacrificial concepts.

(1) In some rites the meal was wholly eaten by the devotees.
(2) In others part of the meal was eaten by the devotees and part burnt for the gods.
(3) In others the meal had disappeared entirely; all of the food was burnt.

The second became the commonest and best known of all rites.

Chapter IV. ADDITIONAL RITES CONNECTED WITH SACRIFICE

Many rites, besides that of the sacred communal meal, have contributed to the development of sacrificial concepts. They are so primitive that no chronological study of their early history can be made. We cannot even decide whether they arose in succession or contemporaneously. They appear among all early peoples but were more extensively practised and more highly developed by some than by others. In early days they were not classified but were confused and overlapping. However, for purpose of studying them, we may group them into four classes:

(1) Prophylactic rites of exorcism and incantation.
(2) Divination rites and oracles.
(3) Rites performed at the "wonder moments" of life.
(4) Rites performed with reference to departed persons.

It would be impossible and irrelevant, in a study of this kind, to attempt to examine these rites in detail. Their interest here arises from the extent to which they have influenced group sacrificial rites. They all proceed upon the assumption that anything, visible or invisible, which moves of its own accord, that is, without being moved, is living and therefore marked by some degree of unpredictability. Sun, moon, and stars, trees, rivers and varying springs, winds, lightning and thunder, floods and rain, animals of all kinds and human beings are obviously possessed of something which makes them function as they do. Life and all apparently automatic motion are naturally confused by the elementary mind.

I. EXORCISM AND INCANTATION

All things in our environments seem possessed of the power to work harm; some, if we co-operate with them, can also work for good. Harm is that which enfeebles or threatens the existence of life; good is that which invigorates or prolongs life.

Hence arises the natural query with every new contact: What is the proper method of dealing with this that it may work good? If such a method cannot be found, the thing is definitely harmful. If the harmful thing is not possessed of life it must be recognized and avoided. If it is possessed of life, its presence is to some degree unpredictable. One must be on the alert for such powers to master them or to drive them away. The approach of a physical thing can be noted, and he who is stronger can master it or drive it away; he who is not stronger may summon the assistance of his friends to help in the struggle. If it is non-physical, invisible, or comes from the upper air, or from under the earth, its presence may be wholly unpredictable and unnoticed until it has commenced its evil work. The poor victim can only seek for some means to neutralize the evil influence and drive it away before it works further harm.

A philosophy such as this underlies the innumerable prophylactic rites which every primitive religion exhibits, sometimes in abundance, and of which vestiges have survived in the highest religions of civilization. Such rites constituted almost the basis of early Roman religion. Popular Greek religion never was rid of them. The elaborate incantations of Babylonia would seem to provide for every imaginable contingency. They crept into late Judaism and emerged with full force into much popular, and some official, Christianity.

Sometimes the rite was one of simple magic, indicating that the harm was supposed to come from some impersonal cause. At other times a rite would deal with nameless demons to be exorcised with foul-smelling, nauseous concoctions. In Babylon these goblins had proper names; they were thought of as persons. In Persia they were marshalled under the authority of a prince of demons, Angra Mainyu, who later became the Jewish Satan and was finally admitted, with all his noisome horde, into Christianity, where he has remained, with varying influence, to the present day. Sometimes gifts of food were offered to these unlovely folk to divert their attention or to purchase their departure. At other times beneficent deities were called upon, with appropriate sacrifices, to assist in their discomfiture. It was inevitable that this lower, popular stratum of religion should retard and discolour spiritual development, and even influence the interpretation of sacrificial acts. Such was the case in Rome; such has been the case in Christianity.

The reasoning of all primitive men, and of many who are not so primitive, is *post hoc* equals *propter hoc*. Such men cannot be blamed, therefore, for supposing that, if the sacrificial invocation of deities had secured aid in expelling demons, the sacrifices themselves may have produced the desired result. Ceremony is essential to civilization; if not protected and directed, it tends to follow the line of least resistance and become ceremonialism. They are always in the minority who keep their attention concentrated upon symbolic values. It is easy for men in every stage of development to be content with the ceremony.

2. DIVINATION AND ORACLES: HEPATOSCOPY

In nothing is man's finiteness more acutely recognized than in the realm of time. To transcend the limitations imposed by space and to augment his restricted energy, man can call upon the help of his fellows and of the animals which he and they have tamed; he can devise vehicles and engines which will carry huge loads across land and water, but never has he been able to penetrate the future with certainty. To verify the validity of his choices he must wait until the consequences have ensued; he frequently learns of his mistakes only when it is too late to rectify them. These trite observations were quite as plain to our remote ancestors as they are to us. Modern man is gradually resigning himself to his ignorance of the future and trusting to faith in what he calls "the laws of nature."

Primitive man was not so complacent. He had not learned to generalize or to analyze in his thinking and he may easily be pardoned for concluding that the Power or powers which enabled him to overcome the limits of space and to achieve apparently impossible results would somehow guide his choice and save him from error. The range of these powers must extend into the future; mayhap he could obtain some inkling of what that future held in store.

From the skies he learned to discern the portents of the weather for the morrow. Falling leaves from the trees were harbingers of a drop in temperature. Flights of migratory birds announced the advent of spring and autumn. Winter and summer were heralded by the sun in his travels close to the southern horizon or far up in the sky. Nature was full of omens of the future if man could learn to read them.

He brought from his animal ancestry his sense of cause and effect; his endowment of knowledge and choice enabled him to pursue the study of causality much further. He knew, as we know, that no such phenomenon as a pure accident exists, but that every event is the result of causes, known or unknown, and also a factor or an agent in producing subsequent events. Gathering clouds portend approaching rain; later it might be reasoned that the personal power which produced rain had sent a warning of its plan. Any unexpected or inexplicable phenomenon was a "sign of something."

Eclipses of the sun and of the moon, conjunctions of planets, the positions of planets in the sky, lightning and thunder, earthquakes, unexpected flights or cries of birds, appearances of unfamiliar birds, unusual behaviour of men or of animals, as, for example, a sneeze—these and hundreds of other phenomena were predictive of unusual events and were subject to interpretation by those who knew how. Learned ones could gain this knowledge and obtain fame as seers of the future.

In addition to these unarranged omens which "just happened," obtruding themselves involuntarily upon men's notice and challenging interpretation, are found many others which may be called arranged or prepared. The purpose of these was to assist in answering questions which had to do with making decisions. The great majority of the decisions of life are "Yes" or "No." Into any decision must enter not only knowledge of the past, but whatever indication that knowledge might give toward saying "Yes" or "No." Before planting or going on a journey or striking camp or entering a battle and before making the multitude of minor decisions of life, common sense would impel men to avail themselves of every possible aid. Recourse was had to many processes which soon grew into rites. Most, if not all of them, had their origin in days when the powers had not yet been thought of as persons; after these powers were personified, rites became more elaborate.

Widespread employment was made of the examination of vital organs, particularly the liver, of animals. The liver is the bloodiest organ of the animal, containing one-sixth or more of the total blood of the body. The well-known identification of blood with life is seen in the Teutonic names of the organ, as *liver* in English. It was always regarded as the seat of life, therefore the seat of the soul and the organ of emotions. No two livers are alike, as no two noses are alike. The difference in size and shape and configuration of an animal liver was resorted to as indicative of the answer to pending questions. The practice was well known in Greek and Roman religions, where it ante-dated the days of Homer, but its most elaborate and extensive development was in Babylon and Assyria where the liver was carefully studied in every detail and noted by professionals for whom handbooks were meticulously prepared, that they might make no mistake in their decisions.[1]

It has been suggested that the original purpose in killing an animal was hepatoscopy, or examination of the liver, and that, because this was a serious and therefore a solemn rite, the car-case could not be disposed of casually but must be eaten or burnt with appropriate ceremonies. It would seem more natural to suppose that the discovery of the extraordinary peculiarities of the liver was made in the course of preparing an animal for the sacred meal.

The constant, sturdy opposition of all Hebrew and Jewish religious leaders[2] to divination of all sorts indicates that the practice was known in Israel. The repeated prescription to burn "the caul above the liver" [3] voices direct opposition to hepatoscopy. The selection of Matthias by casting lots,[4] a mild form of divination, assumes such a practice among early Christians, whose cult officials soon came to be known as the clergy, i.e., "those chosen by lot."

The other "prepared process" of ascertaining answers to questions was the oracle, the oldest form of which seems to have been casting lots. It is well known that an old tradition of early Hebrew days referred to a sacred box which was taken on marches and consulted before battle; it contained two stones which are supposed to have been *yes* and *no* stones, one of which would be drawn from the box at the time of inquiry.[5] In the later form of the tradition both the box and the stones had grown considerably in size, and on the stones Yahweh had written the ten commandments. This would be a natural development of the fact that from the box their ancestors had ascertained the will of the Power for their decisions. Throughout the pre-exilic days of Israel were prominent individuals who were supposed to have some special means of learning the will of Yahweh and who were consulted at times of decision.[6]

Oracles of various kinds were well known in Greece, where the most famous was, of course, that of Apollo at Delphi to which recourse was had for assistance in decisions of all kinds. In its historic days consulters provided a sacrifice before presenting their inquiries. The priestess, from within a sacred cave, would babble incoherent sounds in answer to questions. These would be translated (sometimes in verse) for the inquirer. The translator, in earlier days before the erection of the elaborate temple, probably took his stand in front of the cave from which the priestess spoke. His earliest name seems to have been "He who speaks in front of" (the cave), which, in Greek, would be *prophētēs.*[7] If the priestess of the oracle was the one who spoke the will of the god, the prophet, in turn, was he who interpreted it to the inquirer. Interestingly, when the Hebrew sacred writings were translated into Greek, *prophet* was used to render the

Hebrew word for one who both spoke and interpreted the will of Yahweh.

A common homiletic error today proclaims that modern man seeks to do the will of God but that primitive men sought, by sacrifice, to impose their will upon that of the gods. Such a statement indicates unfamiliarity with divination and oracular rites which expressed men's constant alertness to ascertain the will of the gods in order that their choices might be rightly made. A fundamental assumption of all early rites is that the Power is greater than the devotees and therefore must be obeyed by them; to disobey would incur the greatest peril.

3. RITES PERFORMED AT THE "WONDER MOMENTS" OF LIFE

Reference has already been made to those events in human life whose cause, invisible, untraceable, irresistible, presses home man's finiteness and leaves him to wonder at his weakness. He, cannot help concluding that he is in the presence of powers which, however near they come, remain inaccessible but produce unalterable changes in him and his environments. From earliest days the approach of these powers was met with rites which inevitably became religious. The events are, of course, (1) birth, (2) maturity, (3) marriage and pregnancy, (4) sickness and accidents and (5) death. The rites connected with any one of these would require a volume for study. Their importance here arises from their relation to and influence upon sacrificial development.

Birth rites, the world over, concern reciprocal relations between the new-born child and the group into which he has been born. They have much to do with removal of taboos incurred by the fact of birth and with official recognition of the infant as the newest member of the tribe. Taboo,[8] which came into English from Polynesia, connotes a curious combination of the eerie, the inexplicable and the traditionally forbidden. Things and acts and words can all be taboo by nature or may become taboo by contact. The essence of the idea is "Don't touch it (or don't do it, or don't say it) lest some dreadful thing happen." Bold and foolish and punishable is he who deliberately violates it. For him who violates it unwittingly or involuntarily may come some relief if the taboo incurred can be removed.

Blood was, by primitive people, hedged about by innumerable taboos which have not all been entirely forgotten. Many peoples retained a tradition of strong scruples against shedding blood, that is, letting it run on the ground; all sorts of means were devised for preventing this at sacrificial meals, possibly lest the life which it contained be allowed to escape. This may have been the origin of pouring it upon the portion to be burnt, that the life might return to the Power whence it came. Even touching blood was taboo for many folk.

The birth of an infant brought into the world a living thing freighted with taboos which, unless they could somehow be removed, would forever ban him from association with the family or tribe. Simple exorcisms might serve to rout malevolent powers lurking about the child or the room where he was born, but these would not suffice to remove the blood taboo, which could be neutralized only by careful performance of increasingly elaborate ceremonies. Not only must the child be so purified; his mother and all who had assisted at the birth must likewise be cleansed from taboos. Water, fire, blood, salt and many other familiar articles figured singly or in combination as accessories. The father of the family or the proper official of the clan or the tribe must certify the purity (that is, freedom from blood taboo) of child and mother and friends. A name was frequently given to the child upon this occasion. After all were purified—and this process sometimes extended several days—the group could join in a sacrificial feast.

The arrival of a child at puberty or adolescence was plainly due to the working of a Power which effected serious changes within him. While an average age of puberty would soon be learned, the exact time of the Power's beginning to work was unpredictable and therefore beyond human ken and influence.

It was natural that, when the Power commenced to work, appropriate rites should mark the event.

By those whose training in religious studies has been upon a background of modern purely individualistic concepts of religion, the necessary association of puberty rites with the erotic urge has been credited with being the real origin of what is called "personal religion" which, for some, exhausts the meaning of religion. Because "conversion" (marked among a few primitive peoples by attainment of a sort of mystical experience) frequently occurs at the time of puberty, it is often traced to a development of puberty rites. Such an assumption leaves out of consideration the fact that primitive "first mystical experiences" quite often occur several years before puberty or as long as twenty-five years after it. Moreover, such experiences have to do, not with the relation of an individual *qua* individual with a Great Power, but with the relation of the individual as a member of a group—a family, a clan or a tribe—with the Power particularly associated with that group. That this Power always has a proper name justifies the inference that it is already conceived as personal. It is not surprising that these experiences occur at puberty, for this is the time at which the mind, as well as the body, begins to mature. It is also a fact that these experiences are not common elements of maturity rites but are confined to certain peoples.

Maturity rites which are common among all peoples are concerned with equipping the adolescent to function properly as an adult member of the group. The lad must take his place as hunter or fighter and thus assist in furnishing food for the group and warding enemies from it. The lass must learn to prepare the food and to furnish new members for the tribe.

The association of the conception of children with cohabitation was definitely not primitive; even among peoples developed above the state of primitive savagery, conception is attributed to the waves of the sea or to the working of the spirit of the earth which originates vegetable life. Among some peoples are found indications that organization was originally matriarchal rather than patriarchal. In many women's rites having to do with childbearing, the males did not participate. Appreciation of the fact of paternity was a later development of the process of civilization.

Maturity rites have principally to do with assumption of responsibility and equipment to discharge it. The adolescent child must therefore be initiated not only as a member of a tribe, but as a producing member rather than a mere consumer. He must learn to fend for himself in performance of tribal duties and functions. He must be equipped not only to eat of the common meal, but to provide and prepare it and have his own part in the liturgy or common act of sharing it.

They who insist that primitive maturity rites were primarily social rather than religious lose sight of the fact that this nice, modern distinction was wholly unknown in the morning of man's development, and is observed only after religion has come to be thought of as a purely personal affair. All rites were social, and the Power with which they were concerned was not assigned specified departmental duties. Men's relations with one another were governed by the Power which ruled them all, whether that Power was specially invoked or not. Distinction between religious and social rites has wrought harm to both and cannot even be considered by students of early history.

That maturity rites were never considered quite as important as birth rites will probably explain the paucity of information upon them. It will also probably explain their relative shortness and simplicity as compared with longer and more elaborate rites at birth. Nevertheless, maturity rites must be recognized as forming a factor in the development of sacrificial concepts.

The mating[9] of a male with a single female, or of a female with a single male, is well known among animals, especially among birds. So also is the preliminary process which has extended into courtship. It is not surprising that these were known among some primitive human peoples and apparently absent from others. Very early in man's civilization, however, promiscuity was frowned upon, and cohabitation became a privilege to be fought for and jealously guarded when obtained. For many centuries, however, that privilege was not confined to one person.

Strict monogamy has never been the natural practice of man. Today it is coming to be regarded more and more as temporal rather than factual. A man may have many wives and a woman may have many husbands, but the laws of many nations require that these be had in succession and not contemporaneously. Islam, which limits a man to three or four wives, says nothing against concubinage. Christian churches all officially sanction strict monogamy, but all find ways and means for not taking the term too literally.

Whatever may have been the early influence of matriarchy, the tendency among all peoples has been to regard patriarchy as the basis of organization, although in early patriarchies the descendants of one wife were carefully distinguished from the descendants of another. Therefore monogamy became the rule for a woman long before it became the ideal for a man.

While sharing of wives, especially with guests, has not been unknown in the distant past, it has automatically become a disapproved practice. A man's wives soon became his most cherished possessions; his was the sole privilege of associating with them. He would win them by wooing them or by bargaining for them or by fighting for them, or by all methods together, and he would defend them and guard them for his own. They only could provide new members for his family or clan, and each could ordinarily provide only one new member at a time. The pregnancy of a wife was naturally a cause for rejoicing.

The linking of conception with cohabitation was doubtless retarded by the simple fact that the succession was not infallible. The Power did not always work within the woman. This was a misfortune to be bemoaned by the luckless one. It might be due to some taboo which she had unwittingly broken; it might be the result of harmful powers working upon her. Even if she finally conceived, the next nine moons held innumerable dangers in store to threaten the life of the child. The Power might start its work but not bring it to fruition; demons might beset the woman when she was off guard. Women had their own rites to provide for such emergencies; no woman had done her duty until she had borne a child. The tribe itself might be concerned and resort to rites of exorcism or incantation or omens or invocation. Something must be done to remove the shame of the one who was unable to do her duty.

Once more we must guard against the supposition that rites were carefully classified and performed with modern appointment and precision, or that nice distinctions were made so that this rite was performed separately for this purpose and another for another purpose. Rites could easily be fused and the synthesis would produce the seed of a new rite.

The two important events of nuptials were, of course, the betrothal and the consummation. Among some peoples the former was more emphasized, and among others the latter; by some peoples both events, together with the long or short intervening period, were marked by elaborate ceremonies. Old taboos had to be removed and new ones established; purificatory and prophylactic ceremonies of various kinds served to prepare the bride and groom for their new life and to protect the commencement of it. Omens and oracles must be consulted. The outstanding rite of all was the feasting—the common meal, embellished with details proper to the occasion. Some of these details were mirthful; some were religious; they might be separated or they might be mingled. The influence upon sacrificial concepts is obvious.

The untoward events which impaired or threatened the life of man must be traced to sufficient causes. These causes were not hard to find when we remember the universal belief in malevolent powers — demons and goblins, "Ghoulies and beasties and things that go bump in the night." Throughout one's life one was never safe from their attack. The victim of them was, of course, taboo while the disease remained. The approach to these powers was partly prophylactic and partly purificatory. The demons must be either frightened or cajoled away. Omens and oracles would give aid in discovering the kind of demons with which one had to deal. Exorcisms and incantations, sometimes elaborate and intricate, were applied; nauseous and noxious potions were administered. Some demons could be easily banished; others put up a stiff resistance; still others won the victory and the victim's life was forfeit. The shaman, the medicine-man, the priest of the tribe was the obvious consultant and practitioner in dealing with these malicious and invisible powers.

A biblical illustration of this process may be seen in the leprosy laws of Leviticus.[10] Leprosy (which means *whiteness*) was considered a definitely curable disease; it included far more than the modern disease called by the same name. Any unexpectedly appearing white spot on the skin was called leprosy. The victim must immediately present himself to the priest who decided whether the spot was trifling or serious. If it was serious the victim must be quarantined a week. At the expiration of that time he was again examined by the priest and pronounced well or quarantined for another week, at the expiration of which he was examined again. If the spot remained or had grown the victim must remain under taboo. If he became white all over he was no longer spotted and therefore no longer taboo. All diseases might linger throughout life and leprosy was no exception. The normal case, however, seems to have been expected to clear up at the end of the second or third week of quarantine. When the priest decided that the disease had been healed or arrested the fortunate victim then underwent elaborate purificatory ceremonies and was quarantined for another week, after which proper sacrifices were offered to mark the fact that the patient was no longer taboo and could associate once more with his fellows. Leprosy could be in a garment or in a house or in the walls of a house and must be treated in much the same way.

The important fact to note is that no sacrifice could be offered by the patient while he was taboo. The sacrifice was never a means of removing the taboo; it was the normal act of worship.

Taboo was always an impediment to sacrifice and therefore incongruous with it. Failure to notice this simple fact has resulted in much homiletic and devotional distortion.

Among undiscriminating and unintelligent persons the notion might easily have arisen that the rites produced the cures; distinction would not be made between sacrifice and other rites. This would account for lower concepts in popular circles and these lower concepts would undoubtedly exert some influence. Gravity, in religious ideas as in anything else, tends downward.

From earliest days care has been taken of the bodies of the departed. Fundamental to all rites was the belief that the life-power resident in the departed had obviously escaped from the body. Questions of all kinds were bound to arise and to demand attention; they could not be brusquely dismissed. What had happened to the escaped life-power or spirit? It had manifestly escaped many times previously in sleep and had returned to resume its residence; would it return again? If it did not return, or until it had returned, would it roam at large and disembodied, or would it take its residence in some other object, or possibly in the womb of some wife and impregnate her? If it roamed at large would it have some malevolent influence until it found a suitable habitat? It had possibly left the body because of unsuccessful conflict with demons of sickness or accident; were those demons still lurking about?

Endeavours to meet these problems gave rise to various kinds of rites. A few of these rites were fundamental; the majority varied so greatly as to seem dissimilar. Common to all rites were exorcisms and incantations for purificatory and prophylactic purposes. Not only must the corpse be purified; every person and everything which had come into contact with it must be cleansed. Rites of purification continued well after burial.

Contact with a dead body incurred a taboo very difficult to remove and disqualifying for all religious rites. St. Luke (10:30ff.) tells a story of a priest and a levite on the road to Jerusalem (probably to officiate at sacrifice). From a distance they saw what must have looked like a corpse lying on the roadside. Their law rigidly pronounced uncleanness or taboo upon anyone who touched the dead; rather than incur the penalty of uncleanness they passed by on the other side.[11]

In some religions, for instance, the Persian, the individuality of the soul was believed to continue after death. Such a belief would necessitate prophylactic rites to fortify the departed in his final struggle with evil demons and thus aid him in winning happiness.

In Greece, care for the dead and the cult of the departed were highly developed. In earliest days burial seems to have been the usual mode of disposal; in Homer cremation is known, in classic days tombs abound. Tombs of heroes (the great departed ones of the past) were marked by frequent cultic rites. Offerings of food were made but, since the heroes dwelt not with the gods of the upper air but in regions under the earth, the offerings were not burnt on regular altars but stuffed into a hole in the ground or placed on specially constructed low altars for the purpose. These offerings and altars and ceremonies were all described by special words in Greek, but in Latin they would all come under the general word *sacrificia*.[12]

Among the majority of peoples, either before burial or after burial or at both times, occurred a solemn feast. This could be held only after proper purifications. Interpretations of such feasts have varied, but they were plainly concerned in some way with the soul of the departed. Once more the sacred communal meal appears; this time it was more than usually laden with purifying rites. Synthesis of feast and purifications served to produce additional sacrificial rites.

Chapter V. BLOOD AND BLOOD RITES

The laconic biblical statement, "The blood is the life," [1] expresses a conviction not only of ancient Hebrews and later Jews, but of all mankind from the dawn of culture to the present days of scientific study. It represents one of the first results of human reflection and may therefore be expected to underlie primitive human practices and rites.

To think of blood as the seat of life was an obvious conclusion from observing that loss of blood entailed weakness; loss of too much blood meant loss of life. We are familiar with the phrase "bleeding to death." If blood is the seat of life, men cannot be faulted for having concluded that it is the life principle. If it is the life principle it ought to be a vehicle of life. It might even be the source of life.

An old Greek myth [2] told of the mutilation of the divine patriach Ouranos by his son Kronos. The blood thus shed was received by Gaia who, by its influence, conceived and bore the giants. Another similar myth [3] traced the origin of men to a rain of blood drops falling from Zeus. Both these stories find the source of human life in the blood of a god.

It is commonplace knowledge today that blood transfusion, or administration of blood plasma, will renew life and its powers when all other hope is gone. This is the scientific development of a tradition, common to man from early days, in which therapeutic value was attributed to blood administered as a potion or applied externally to those suffering from leprosy or epilepsy and to those who were weak from the infirmities of old age. [4] The same rationale prompted many primitive men to wound themselves and let the blood drop or flow over the body of a departed one, or over his grave after burial, even repeating the acts on weekly or monthly or annual memorial days, in hope of continuing and strengthening the life of the soul which had escaped from the body and might return to its old abode. [5] A classic instance of belief in the power of blood to invigorate departed spirits is the story of the visit of Odysseus to Hades. Before the spirits could talk with him he must administer the blood of a sheep slain for the purpose, pouring the blood into a prepared trench.[6]

Greek tradition from Argos [7] records a practice of the seeress of Apollo. Once a month, at nighttime, she sacrificed a lamb and tasted of the blood in order to come under the power of the god and prophesy. The sacrificial blood was evidently the means of superinducing the frenzy under which she spoke her oracles.

Among primitive blood rites should be mentioned the old and gruesome rite of the taurobolium [8] which seems to have originated in Persian regions. It was adopted into the rites of Magna Mater in Asia Minor and thence made its way to Rome. In outline the ceremony was as follows: Over a platform punctured with holes a steer was slain. Under the platform stood a neophyte upon which the fresh blood dripped. The neophyte literally bathed himself in the blood, rubbing it into his mouth, eyes, ears, etc. The whole ceremony was accompanied by appropriate songs and music. In the course of centuries appeared many elaborations of detail and explanation.

Originally the taurobolium illustrated the same primitive philosophy which underlay the sacred meal. The qualities of the life of the victim were supposedly transferred to him who ate of it. The taurobolium, like the sacred meal, was a process of transferral of life. The life strength of the steer, located naturally in the blood, enveloped one by bathing him and by passing into him through his mouth. From the blood bath he emerged confident that his was now the invincible might of the bull. In later centuries this interpretation was sublimated into spiritual concepts; he who bathed in the blood of the bull emerged with a new life which would be immortal.

This ancient and persistent ceremony forms a gory illustration of the old thesis that life, with all its qualities, inheres in the blood and can literally be communicated.

2. THE BLOOD COVENANT

It is not surprising that blood, which from earliest times was identified with life and the life-soul, should be instrumental in effecting ties of union not otherwise achievable. To share the same blood was to create the strongest kind of bond one could conceive.[9] Two members of different families in the same tribe became brothers by the blood rite. A stranger was admitted to membership in the tribe by the blood rite. A solemn oath received strongest fortification by the blood rite.

Participation in the rite might be mutual or common; men might share one another's blood by sucking it or drinking it pure or mingled with wine, or they might drink in common the blood of a slain animal. They might prick their thumbs or arms and smear the blood upon a stone. In these and many other ways men made the blood compact which could not be broken.

We are apt to think of these as eerie, barbarous rites devoid of spiritual content. If so, we forget that they who performed them were striving, in the best way they knew, for that solid union in which alone is strength. Blood, to all ancient men, was symbolic, never of death, always of life. Blood and life were synonymous. For two persons to share the same life implied innumerable privileges and duties. For two persons to share one another's life bound them together as one. The tasks, the joys, the insults and the enemies of one were those of the other. These men may have been uncouth, but they knew the value of fidelity and they knew how to produce it better than many modern men who are more sophisticated and more selfish.

A Greek story[10] told of seven men who conspired to beleaguer the city of Thebes. To strengthen their oath they cut the throat of a bull over a black iron shield into which the blood flowed. Then, dipping their hands into the blood, they swore mightily to Ares, Enyo and Phobos, the war gods, to unite their efforts to raze the city. This rite implies a later stage in thinking, that of personal gods to whom the participants can pledge themselves. An old blood rite which once linked men together is, by this time, adapted to link these men with their gods, the powers which will gladly aid them, but which can harm them if they do not obey. Once the blood is shared in common, the task is pursued to its fearful conclusion.

We are here on the threshold of religion. In religion, men always think of the helping powers as other than themselves. To neglect or oppose these powers is to court disaster; to co-operate with them and do their will is to come to the fullness of life, whatever that may mean at the time. It is but a step from the blood oath of man to man to the oath of men united with their gods.

One cannot help wondering what was the disposition of the carcase of the bull after his blood was drained for the oath. It may have been eaten as a sequel to the oath, the gruesome features of which must surely have cast their shadow on the meal. On the other hand, it may have been burnt as a holocaust. Whether by burning or by eating, the disposition of the carcase would be a natural conclusion of the oath ceremony.

3. THE BLOOD TABOO

Every environment of man is a potential menace to his very existence; this is as true of the invisible powers as of the material things with which man comes into constant contact. Some of these environments are also potentially sustaining of that very existence which they menace. It is for man, by experiment and tradition, to learn how to meet these environments. To those which are sustaining he will turn for the help he needs, remembering all the while that these can harm him if he treats them not aright. To those which seem to lack all power of sustenance he will oppose himself with every care to avoid or neutralize the harm which they can do. From the realization of the potential harm in all environments is born what men call fear, of which the animals are never rid, and which appears unexpectedly in all human activities.

There are, however, two kinds of fear. One proceeds from the knowledge of potential harm, coupled with the further knowledge that the harmful thing resists or seems impervious to all gestures of affiliation or compact. This is the fear which is best known to us and, with some, exhausts the meaning of the word. Few are they who are not affected by this instinctive fear.

Acquaintance with life, however, reveals an amazing number of environments whose sustaining power is greater than their power to harm or at least as great as that power. With these one enters into friendly relations, the benefit of which may eclipse the fear of their capacity to harm. This may lead to carelessness in behaviour, and carelessness portends disaster. When experience was young, tradition short, knowledge fragmentary and the dangers of life uncertain, one could not afford the carelessness of forgetting the fear of potential harm while experimenting with or practising methods of strengthening friendliness. This fear is altogether different from the terror of certain evil; it seems to be the root of awe for the power which is potentially favourable, albeit great enough to slay.

Awe prompts the attitude toward the taboo of many things which are feared as capable of unknown and indescribable harm but reverenced for their capacity for appreciated and recognized blessing. Therefore we find, among some peoples, a horror of blood which, instead of being eaten for any purpose, is disposed of in some other way which will indicate proper reverence for it but will avoid the slightest taste of it.

The blood taboo was common among primitive peoples and left its influence upon religions of people of higher culture.[11] It extends from the prohibition to eat or touch or look upon blood to the prohibition of even glancing at raw flesh (sometimes called living flesh[12]). Those who were so unfortunate as to have to come into contact with such articles were themselves taboo and must be purified by appropriate rites.

The Hebrew-Jewish tradition contained a number of instances in which practices and rites known to other Semitic peoples were specifically forbidden. All specific prohibitions imply the existence of the forbidden act or practice. This principle will appear many times in the course of our study; it is illustrated by the rigid taboo upon the eating of blood. How soon this was established we do not know, but there are clues that the rigidity of the custom dates from exilic days.

In I Samuel 14:31–35 is a story of a victory over the Philistines, after which "the people flew upon the spoil and took sheep and oxen and calves and slew them on the ground; and the people did eat them with the blood." This was so horrifying to some that they reported the affair to Saul who lectured them against the practice. Ezekiel (33:25) lists eating blood among the sins for which Jerusalem had been destroyed. Deuteronomy (12:16, 23) contains a flat prohibition against the practice. These instances seem to indicate that the prohibition was known in late pre-exilic days although not always observed. In post-exilic literature the prohibition is often repeated.[13] The rigid faithfulness with which orthodox Judaism has always adhered to it possibly dates from the time of the exile. Jewish interpretation of this includes meat cooked rare.

It is interesting that, among the few traits of Judaism which nascent Christianity tried to continue, was this same prohibition,[14] which seems to have been taken very lightly by the Church. Islam also prohibits the eating of blood.[15] This is not surprising; a Jewish practice which ran counter to both Christianity and primitive Arabism would commend itself to Mohammed and his followers.

4. BLOOD IN PURIFICATORY AND APOTROPAIC RITES

The use of blood in purificatory and apotropaic rites is widespread among peoples of barbarous and higher cultures. Rites found in Polynesia, Africa, South America and Arabia can hardly be accounted for by a theory of contact and influence. They must proceed from some common primitive concept. Because life power is the most potent and the most mysterious

force known, blood, the vehicle of life, becomes the best prophylactic against unknown dangers which threaten men. The
greatest of the dangers is death. We need not be surprised to
find blood used to break drought, to neutralize the horror of
slaying man or beast, to withstand epidemics and to frighten
away the "things that go bump in the night."

Blood may be smeared on a tree[16] or poured at the roots of
a tree[17] to break drought and bring rain. It may be sprinkled
on the leaves of a tree which is about to be felled in order to
counteract the anger of the tree spirit.[18] It may be smeared on
members of a tribe[19] before they are permitted to look at a
stranger, or it may be smeared on the stranger himself.[20] When
one has killed another man his blood may be made to trickle
on the ground from a gash made in his chest.[21] Blood may be
smeared upon weapons after one has killed a dangerous beast
such as a panther in order to counteract the anger of the soul
of the beast.[22]

Among some tribes fornication and adultery were considered as sure omens of disaster which might be averted by killing
a pig and pouring his blood into a furrow dug for the purpose.[23]
In a South American tribe the blood of slain children smeared
on the face of an idol would avert disaster.[24]

Blood sprinkled or smeared on the door posts of a king's
house at the time of his installation would protect the new
ruler from harm.[25] Again, blood smeared on door posts might
prove efficacious in combating an epidemic, as of cholera.[26] A
Mohammedan rite in Arabia furnishes an excellent illustration
of the fusion of two rites and their incorporation into a later
religion. An annual commemoration was made at the tomb of
a certain prophet named Salich. At the end of the rite blood was
smeared on the door posts of the tomb.[27] Since Islam rigidly
bans sacrificial rites we must look to pre-Islamic days for the
origin of this custom. In all these apotropaic rites the animal
whose blood was used could be solemnly eaten after the rite.
Akin to these door post rites is a strange custom apparently
inherited by the Hebrews from an earlier culture. At the time

of the Pesach feast the door posts and lintels of their houses must be sprinkled with the blood of the lamb which was to be eaten for the feast.[28]

All these rites would come under the general heading of Latin *sacrificia*. One can easily see how some sacrifices were thought of as apotropaic or purificatory, and how, in later days, when ethical considerations became important, the moral taboo of sin could be removed only by a blood rite, after which a sacrifice might be offered. One can also understand the confusion of the blood rite and the sacrifice, although that confusion seems never to have existed in the minds of the leaders who compiled the regulations.

5. BLOOD RITES IN THE OLD TESTAMENT

It is not surprising that the Old Testament, which is so definitely set against eating blood, makes elaborate provisions for the disposal of the blood of animals used for sacrifice. These provisions are always preliminary to the sacrifice itself. Only he who is *en rapport* with God can offer sacrifice. Taboo of any kind—of forbidden contact, of sickness and, after the development of ethical interpretation, of sin—automatically disqualified one for worship. The removal of the taboo was accordingly a necessary preliminary for any worship. Because taboos might be unwittingly incurred, it was much safer to have the preliminary cleansings before every sacrifice. In this precaution the Hebrews differed little from other peoples. The juxtaposition of the preliminary rite and the sacrificial rite issued in the fusion of the two into one religious act.

The familiar phrase "blood of the covenant" occurs twice, once in the tradition of the establishment of the covenant between Yahweh and the people,[29] and once to recall the fact that such a covenant was established by blood;[30] the blood shed at circumcision was regarded as effecting such a covenant.[31] The blood used at the consecration of a priest is called the "blood of consecration." [32] Only a blood rite can cleanse a place in which murder has been committed.[33] A blood rite is necessary to cleanse a house from leprosy.[34]

The elaborate use of blood for pre-sacrificial purification is more specifically codified by the Hebrews and Jews than by any other people. The blood of the animal to be sacrificed is "sprinkled" on the worshiper,[35] and on the new priest at the time of his consecration.[36] It is "sprinkled" before the sanctuary,[37] around the altar,[38] on the altar,[39] at the base of the altar,[40] on the side of the altar,[41] on the horns of the altar,[42] before and on the "mercy-seat," [43] and sprinkled or poured on a burning sacrifice.[44]

This pre-sacrificial purificatory blood rite is frequently explained by the phrase which has been translated as "making atonement." [45] The "atonement" rite was preliminary to the sacrifice proper. Sin is not regarded as removed or forgiven by sacrifice. The fact of sin disqualifies one for worship of any kind. He who incurs taboo, ceremonial or moral, has automatically alienated himself from God and is thereby rendered unworthy to worship. This is especially serious when the taboo has been incurred unwittingly, or when one does not know whether one has incurred taboo or not. The conventional translation of the term describing this condition is "sins of ignorance" which prevent one from showing oneself "boldly at the throne of grace." [46] When these disqualifications have been purified by the blood rite the worship can proceed apace. The use of the word *atonement* in English to translate the title of these rites is interesting and confusing.[47] Its discussion can well be reserved for the proper place under Hebrew sacrifices.

Chapter VI. PROPITIATION AND CONCILIATION

The *Iliad* of Homer opens with a description of a scene after the Greeks had sacked some of the outlying villages of Troy. Among the prizes of the booty, Chryseis, beautiful daughter of the priest of Apollo, was claimed by Agamemnon, leader of the Greeks. Her father, Chryses, approached the Greeks with the promise that, if they would return his daughter, he would pray Apollo to make them victorious against Troy; if they refused, Apollo would wreak his vengeance upon them. Agamemnon refused and Chryses addressed this prayer to Apollo:

> Hear me, thou of the silver bow, thou who surroundest
> Chryses and sacred Cilla, Tenedos' mighty ruler;
> Smintheus, if ever I roofed a temple with which thou wast pleased,
> If ever I burned to thee fat thighs of goats and of oxen,
> Grant this request: May Danaeans pay for my tears by thine
> arrows.[1]

Apollo answered the prayer by sending a pestilence to the Greek forces. In consternation the Greeks appealed to Calchas the seer to divine the cause of their misfortune. Calchas discovered that the plague was the work of Apollo, who was angry at the outrage to the priest. After long argument, Agamemnon consented to return the maid to her father. The Greek embassy, headed by Odysseus, escorted Chryseis to the old man who straightway prayed Apollo to stay the pestilence. Immediately after the prayer, the Greeks offered a large sacrifice to Apollo. When the priest had solemnly burned the thigh pieces on an altar, they poured abundant libations and held the sacred feast.

> Then the youth of the Greeks, after their all-day feasting,
> Sang a fair paean with music, beseeching far-darting Apollo,
> Hear and be gracious. He, when he heard their song, was
> delighted.[2]

The customary, familiar interpretation of this scene describes Apollo as a whimsical, irascible, vindictive, and cajolable deity who gladly placed his might at the disposition of sacrificers and restrained it in return for hekatombs. In this interpretation two important facts are neglected. (1) While the pestilence is definitely pictured as the result of Apollo's anger at the wrong done to his priest, that wrong was righted, not by the sacrifice, but by the return of the maid to her father. The wrong had to be undone before any sacrifice could be offered. (2) The word *hilaskesthai*, here translated *beseech*, is almost invariably rendered *propitiate*, which is always assumed to mean *appease, remove the anger of*.

The word *hilaskesthai*, or one of its variant forms, *hilassesthai* or *hilattesthai*, is frequently used without any thought of appeasement. In the *Odyssey* Nestor is described as planning a sacrifice of a heifer in order to worship Athene as a mark of gratitude for her guidance of Telemachus. The word used for *worship* is *hilaskesthai*.[3] The same word is used by Aeschylus as the equivalent of *invoke*.[4] Apollonius of Rhodes uses the same word in the same way.[5] Without any question this worship is considered as pleasing to the gods; conversely, neglect of it was displeasing and might result in divine anger. When a god is thought of as angry because of this neglect, men might try to worship him, thinking the worship would be pleasing and thus avert his anger by repairing a neglect. Failure to promise hekatombs might bring temporary defeat.[6] Sacrifice was sometimes rejected[7] and sometimes accepted without granting a request.[8] If divine anger had been aroused by disobedience to the god's will, sacrifice was no surrogate for obedience. It could not even be offered until the sinful act had been corrected. Then, and then only, could the god be worshiped. Sacrifice could propitiate divine anger only if that anger had been kindled by its neglect.

It is not suggested that this subtle rationalization was a process in the minds of the Trojan heroes. Since the word *hilaskesthai* was frequently used with the simple connotation of offering worship, and since this worship could not be offered if the devotee had incurred some ceremonial or moral taboo, this may be another instance of the fusion of the preliminary removal of the taboo and the offering of the worship; thus a single word came to describe the whole process. In the instance which has been given in some detail the return of the girl was the necessary prelude to the sacrificial feast, which is described as a very happy affair.

Propitiatory rites, however, were well known in Greek popular religion for chthonic deities, for malevolent sprites of the underworld and for ghosts of departed ancestors and of ancient heroes. Such rites were not addressed to the gods of the upper air, the Olympian deities whose stories form part of well-known mythology and whose gladsome public worship is so abundantly described in poetry and prose. The best collation of sources for the study of these rites was first made more than forty years ago by Miss Jane E. Harrison, who thus contrasts them with the better known Olympian worship:

> It is clear then that Greek religion contained two diverse, even opposite, factors: on the one hand the element of *service* (*therapeia*), on the other the element of *aversion* (*apotrope*). The rites of *service* were connected by tradition with the Olympians, or, as they are sometimes called, the Ouranians; the rites of *aversion* with ghosts, heroes, and underground divinities. The rites of service were of a cheerful and rational character, the rites of aversion gloomy and tending to superstition.[9]

The difference between these two elements of Greek religion is marked by the difference between the cults. The worship of the Ouranian deities was always in daytime; that of the underground powers always at night. Sacrifice to the Olympians always culminated in a glad meal; no one so much as tasted offerings to underground powers. After blood rites, and other lugubrious ceremonies, the bodies of the victims were burnt or buried or stuffed into a hole or cast into the sea or into a river. Victims for sacrifices to the Olympians were called *hiereia*; those to chthonic powers were *sphagia* or *holokausta* (or *holokauta*). The altar on which sacrifices to Olympians were burnt was a *bomos*, built high from the earth; when *sphagia* were burnt they were burnt upon an *eschara* built as close to the ground as possible, or in a trench dug for the purpose. The verbs describing the worship of the deities of the upper air were *thuein* (with reference to the burning) and *hiereuein* (with reference to the portions which were eaten); those describing the cult of chthonic powers were *sphagiazesthai, enagizein* and *holokautein*.[10] Our uniform translation of the groups of Greek words by victim, altar and sacrifice entirely loses the contrasting distinctions between the rites.

This ritual distinction marked a further distinction between the purposes of the two worships. Olympian deities were, for the most part, friendly, and their worship was that of awe and adoration. They could do incalculable harm if they were angered, and failure to worship was an inevitable source of anger; such anger could be turned away by the performance of neglected rites. If the anger arose from another source, as from ceremonial or moral taboo (murder always incurred taboo of the worst sort), the taint must first be removed by appropriate purificatory rites. The gladsome worship could then follow: choice parts of the victims were placed upon the altar fire and sublimated into smoke to ascend to the upper air; the remaining parts were eaten in a joyous meal with music and dancing. Communion with these gods was a source of joy and thanksgiving.

Chthonic powers were usually malevolent. With a few exceptions,[11] the common use of sphagiastic rites (if this necessary word may be coined) was for the placation of ghosts and evil sprites like the Keres who could cause disease, old age and death, or for the aversion of blights and sterility, or for combating harpies and other destructive powers. The rites were performed in almost absolute silence. Dark, dismal and gruesome they were and finished as soon as possible to achieve their terrifying purpose. These were the Greek uses of the holocaust, the rite in which the victims were wholly burned.

These distinctions may be analyzed as follows:

Factors	*Thusiai*	*Sphagia*
Time	day	night
Victims	*hiereia*	*sphagia*
Altar	*bomos*	*eschara*
Rite	*thuein, hiereuein*	*enagizein, sphagiazesthai*
		holokautein
Disposition of	Part eaten, part	Burnt, buried, cast into
victims' bodies	burnt	water
Recipients	Olympian deities	Chthonic powers
Prime purpose	Service and com-	Placation and aversion
	munion	
Accompaniments	Music and dancing	Silence

2. ROMAN RITES

The examination of the rites of the Roman cults is important and difficult.[12] It is important because of the profound influence of Roman civilization upon the western world which it dominated for so long a time. It is difficult because of the many culture strains which were adopted and adapted by the Romans in their own life. The process was not merely one of synthesis. Foreign rites were always recognized as such; tradition always gave greater importance to the older rites.

(1) The life of the Latin agricultural peoples in ancient Italy laid the foundation for Roman civilization. (2) The Etruscans, those strange, possibly Semitic[13] people who moved into Italy from the north, introduced religious elements which were blended very early with those of the ancient Italic stock. (3) The Greek cults, which were introduced by way of Sicily and South Italy, exerted much influence, but were almost always recognized as foreign. (4) The cults of Asia Minor, introduced at the time of the Punic wars, were only partly naturalized. (5) The stream of foreign cults which found their way to Rome in the days of the Empire furnished the religious medley which marked the milieu in which Christianity was born. To speak of that which is strictly Roman, one should confine oneself to those elements which came from the earliest stratum. These

elements maintained themselves throughout the centuries of Roman history; they were recognized as Roman *par excellence* and as claiming the principal devotion of the State.

Fowler's definition of religion as the "effective desire to be in the right relation with the Power manifesting itself in the universe" [14] is not only one of the most satisfactory definitions proposed; it is *the* dominant motif of Roman religious life. It appears in the early Italic people who sought for contact with the powers which controlled physical existence and social communication of every kind. These people were already agricultural, but definitely barbarous. The powers which they approached were those with which we are already familiar—the mysterious, impersonal life-giving and death-dealing powers which they met on every side. The former they sought to keep kindly; the latter they sought to drive away. Their rites were what are called magical; not until much later were these powers thought of as personal and they never attained the lively individual character of Greek gods. The notes of propitiation and aversion were always uppermost in Roman cults.

We need not be surprised, therefore, that the sacrificial or sacramental meal shared with the gods was never developed among the Romans. The development of this religious custom into a fixed cult is contingent upon the development of that concept of deity which is called anthropomorphic and which pictures gods as persons requiring the same kind of sustenance as the men who gave them tendance. Without the growth of this concept the common meal loses its significance as a religious ceremony. The sacred meal, however, did not disappear entirely. It was observed at the annual *Feriae Latinae* [15] in April, but this festival was not included in the regular round of state ceremonies. The fact that it is one of the oldest rites of Rome would indicate that, in early days, the sacred meal may have had greater importance. The practically complete disappearance of this sacred meal profoundly influenced Roman religion, and passed its influence to Christianity in the West where Rome ruled. [16]

Another marked difference of Roman religion was the almost complete disappearance of blood rites as forming a part of worship.[17] These were not wholly forgotten; vestiges of them were retained in three of the oldest festivals of the Roman calendar. At the annual horse sacrifice in October,[18] after a two-horse chariot race, the near horse of the winning pair was slain with a spear. His tail was cut off and carried to the Regia, the "castle of Numa" on the Via Sacra devoted to the use of the priests. There the warm blood was dripped on the hearth and the ashes preserved. The head, after a battle for its possession by men of the two neighbouring quarters, was carried off by the winners and fixed to a prominent place; its blood also was preserved.

At the annual *Fordicidia* in April,[19] one of the oldest Roman festivals, pregnant cows were slaughtered; the unborn calves were torn from the wombs of the mothers and burned; the ashes were preserved by the Vestals for a week.

The *Parilia* festival,[20] six days later in April, another of the oldest festivals, was a series of genuine purification rites. In the country places shepherds purified the flocks by sprinkling and sweeping the fold, and by driving the sheep through fires of straw and olive and laurel branches. Millet cakes, baskets of millet, pails of milk, and other food were offered to Pales, a vague, impersonal vegetation power, for aversion of all harm that might come from unwitting sacrilege, such as trespass on sacred ground, disturbing sacred springs, or misuse of boughs of sacred trees. Then milk and heated wine were mixed in a bowl and drunk until the drinkers were intoxicated enough to leap over burning heaps of branches. At the same festival in the city the preserved blood of the October horse and the ashes of the calves burnt at the Fordicidia were mixed and thrown upon heaps of burning straw. Over the smoke and flames men and women leaped for purposes of purification.[21]

At the innumerable other regular Roman sacrifices wine was poured on the sacrificial fire. This may have been a substitute for blood; wine is regarded as "the blood of the grape."[22] Genuine blood rites never left enough impression to be noticed or given attempted explanation by Roman writers.

The use of hepatoscopy seems to have been introduced by the Etruscans. This is not surprising, since these strange people probably, or at least possibly, came into Italy after a long sojourn in Babylon, if they were not native Semites.[23] Before Etruscan influence the *exta,* as the vital organs were called, were always examined for lack of defect; any kind of defect, external or internal, in the victim would render it unfit for sacrificial use.

The important feature of Roman religious rites was the precision of ceremonial prescribed and required by the *ius divinum,* which carefully protected and regulated all rites. To make a single mistake in word or act would necessitate repeating the whole rite from the very beginning.

The chief element of all these rites was the ceremonial preparation and the slaughter of the victim, the examination of the exta, and the burning of these exta upon the altar, the whole rite being conducted in strict silence, except for the strains of pipers whose business was to drown any unlucky sound which might mar the sacrifice. Until the burning of the exta the victims were wholly sacra or taboo. After the ceremony had been completed they seem to have lost their holiness; they became the property of the priests.

The purpose of all Roman rites was the propitiation, that is, retaining the favour, of friendly powers and the aversion of hostile powers. The lugubrious precision and silence with which they were conducted preserved their quasi-magical character and gave a peculiar turn to the development of Roman religious ideas.

Chapter VII. VOTIVE OFFERINGS, *DEVOTIO* AND DEDICATION

Roman history has a strange story of Publius Decius Mus at the battle of Vesuvius in the war between the Romans and the Latins (340 B.C.).[1] The Romans were commanded by Decius and Titus Manlius as consuls. It had been determined before the battle that the consul, on whose flank appeared any weakening, should "devote himself for the Roman people." (*Se consul devoveret pro populo Romano.*) Manlius had just ordered his son slain for breach of army discipline. Omens from sacrifices indicated a favourable issue for this act. When the flank commanded by Decius began to weaken he called to Marcus Valerius, the *pontifex publicus,* "There is need for the help of the gods. Come, dictate the words with which I may devote myself for the legions" (*verba quibus me pro legionibus devoveam*). Valerius attired him in a purple toga, bade him stand upon a spear, and recited a long formula which he repeated verbatim. Calling upon the gods of both the Romans and the Latins to prosper might and victory for the Romans and to strike fear and death to the foe, he declared that, in behalf of the Roman people and their army, he devoted the legions and auxiliaries of the enemy, together with himself, to the shades and to the earth. (*Legiones auxiliaque hostium mecum deis Manibus Tellurique devoveo.*) Thus saying, he donned the *cinctus Gabinus,* a priestly vestment, vaulted his horse and rode headlong into the forces of the Latins to be slain "as if sent from heaven as a piaculum of all the wrath of the gods" (*sicut caelo missus piaculum omnis deorum irae*). The mad plunge into the thick of the line of the enemy struck the Latins with consternation; the Romans, "their spirits set free from religion" (*exsolutis religione animis*), that is, "free from fears prompted by the religious fear that the gods were against them," rallied to the attack and won the battle. The body of Decius was not found until the next day, when it was given a burial befitting his death (*par morti*). A similar story is told of the son and grandson of Decius.

To this account Livy appends an interesting note. Writing almost four hundred years later, when extravagant efforts had been made to restore the almost forgotten religion of ancient Rome, he thus voices his disapproval of the modernism which had supplanted the pristine faith.

> It ought to be added here that, when a consul, dictator or praetor devoted the legions of an enemy, it was permissible for him not to devote himself; he might devote a citizen whom he chose from an enlisted Roman legion. If he who was devoted should die, the deed was opportune. If he did not die, a symbol of him, seven feet or more in length, was buried in the earth. It was blasphemous (*non fas*) for a Roman magistrate to ascend to the site of the buried symbol. If one wished to devote himself, as Decius did, and did not die, he was disqualified from performing any private or public sacred act (*neque privatum neque publicum divinum pure faciet*), either with victims (*hostia*) or with anything else. For him who devoted himself it was permissible to vow his arms to Vulcan or to any other god he chose. It was blasphemous for the spear, upon which the consul stood while praying, to fall into the power of the enemy. If it did, a piaculum must be made with a *suove-taurilia* (pig, sheep and ox). I have thought it was not extraneous to refer to these details in the very words in which they were pronounced and given to me, although every memory of sacred and secular custom (*mos*) has been obliterated because people prefer all novel and foreign things to those which are ancient and native.

Devotio is described as an apparently well-known institution in ancient Rome, long in abeyance by the beginning of the Christian era. It must not be understood as an instance of human sacrifice. After the Sibylline tradition supplanted the old *ius divinum* (i.e., after 200 B.C.) human sacrifice became known among Romans;[2] under the old "divine law" there is no evidence for the custom.[3] However, *devotio* was a quasi-sacrificial act, definitely religious, possibly expected in time of battle. Livy's account indicates that, in this instance, it was certainly expected and prepared for as a religious rite.

(1) The act was determined after examination of sacrificial omens had confirmed a predictive dream which each of the consuls had had the previous night.

(2) The pontifex publicus was ready and at hand with the instructions, the garments and the formula for the devoted person.

(3) The consul was the proper official for *devotio*; the function of the priest was to protect the precision with which all Roman rites must be carried out. The consul might devote himself or any soldier whom he selected.

(4) While the gods were specifically called upon to give the blessings designed to attend the desperate act, *devotio* was not to them but to the chthonic powers, Tellus and the Manes, the earth power and the shades of the ghosts departed.

(5) If the person devoted met his death, all was well; but adequate provisions were made in the event of his returning unscathed from the act. Added provisions concerning the consul who devoted himself, and returned unscathed, give further precautions.

Devotio, which is left untranslated because the English language has no suitable word for the purpose, is plainly an extreme form of the *votum* or vow. Vows were common in Roman, Greek and Hebrew religions and usually consisted of pledges to do so-and-so for a god, or to give so-and-so to a god if such-and-such a plan had a favourable issue.[4]

2. GREEK VOWS AND VOTIVE OFFERINGS

Vows were common in Greece both in the premigration days described by Homer and in the historical, strictly Greek days. The vow to sacrifice twelve heifers to Athene, if she would grant victory, is well known.[5] Agamemnon vowed to present Teucer with a tripod, or two horses, or a concubine, if Zeus and Athene would allow him to conquer Ilium.[6] Before the battle of Marathon the Athenians made a vow to Artemis pledging, if they won, to sacrifice to her she-goats equal in number to the number of corpses of the slain enemy. They slew so many that the vow could not be discharged immediately; they accordingly divided their pledge into installments of five hundred per year, and seem to have continued the payment for many decades.[7] Vows to perform acts for the gods abound throughout Greek legend and history. The pledge and performance of such vows must be regarded in the light of purchase price, voluntarily offered by the worshiper, for the coveted blessing. This transaction is familiarly known as *do ut des* (I am giving in order that you may give), or *dabo ut des* (I shall give in order that you may give). It will appear later in interpretations of sacrifice.

Greek religions teem with sacred gifts formally vowed or dedicated to the gods.[8] To these is applied the general Latin word *vota* (vowed, or dedicated things). Some were in payment of pledges; others were totally unpledged, but spontaneously expressed appreciation of blessings conferred. They consist of gifts for the exclusive use of a god and therefore banned from all secular use. Articles of all sorts, from a temple to a simple utensil or garment or wreath, were offered to the gods, largely as thank offerings for victory in battle, for restoration from illness, for the safe return from a voyage, for the safe birth of a child, for success of an undertaking and for innumerable minor blessings. The temples were filled with these offerings which were usually carefully listed.[9] The name applied to any offering of this sort was *anathema*. Such an offering might be made by a private person or it might be publicly voted by a city. The important element in these gifts is not their devotion or dedication, but the fact that they were spontaneous acts of thanksgiving from happy devotees who gladly gave the richest offerings in their power to express their joy and thanksgiving. Spontaneous thanksgiving is seen in the application of the words *charistērion* or *eucharistērion*, both meaning thanksgiving, to describe these gifts.[10]

3. ROMAN *Vota*

Roman vows and votive offerings have not been as exhaustively collated as those of the Greeks, but we have enough informa-

tion to know much of their character.[11] Many instances are
known of private vows similar to those of the Greeks, such as
the vow of Aeneas to Venus, promising to offer sacrifices if he
were delivered from shipwreck.[12] Some of the oldest vase inscriptions indicate private votive offerings, apparently as acts of
thanksgiving.

Rome was a state which grew both by expansion and by
accretion, while Greece was never more than an aggregation of
states which were unable to effect practical political unity.
Therefore in Rome, from the beginning of its existence as a
state, religion assumed an official character. Thus were made
possible the many public vows in the form of a contract between the state and a deity. The conditions of the contract were
formally made public; the exact form of words was prescribed
by a priest; the officer representing the state was responsible for
carrying out the provisions of the vow. State emergencies, such
as war or pestilence or famine, became occasions of such vows.
Consuls, at the beginning of their office, marched to the Capi-
toline temple and there fulfilled the vows of sacrifices made by
their predecessors of a year previous, and made new vows for
their successors of a year later. A common vow was the institution of special games.

The basic principle of the votive offering was that the thing
devoted, whether man or beast or building or utensil or garment or ornament, was henceforth *sacer,* that is, untouchable
for any kind of secular use. The idea probably arose from taboo;
the creation or institution of a taboo upon an object is certainly
a part of magical rites. As soon as the powers in the universe
were understood as beings marked by volitional functioning,
long before they assumed personal or individual character (as
was always the case in ancient Rome), the thing vowed to them
became their possession, and that possession must be defended
at any cost. For temples and utensils and ornaments it would be
sufficient to protect them from secular use; this could be done
by the priests and other sacred ministers. When a living thing
was devoted the very act of feeding it might violate or even

transfer the taboo; to let it run at large would be for the whole group to incur perpetual danger. Therefore it must be killed for the safety of the community. In the event of military *devotio,* such as that of Decius, there is no record of the return of a devoted person alive. Barring him from participation in any religious act (this penalty was sufficient in itself), official burying of an image of him, and the taboo of the spot where the image was buried, show the attitude of horror of coming into contact with such an one. It were better for him if he had died.

An illustration of *devotio* is seen in the ancient Roman method of dealing with a condemned criminal.[13] One who was guilty of a crime which was sufficiently heinous was solemnly made *sacer* to the deity principally offended. Any person was then at liberty to kill him on sight and was even supposed to do it. The customary reasoning which finds in this a vicarious sacrifice offered for the people seems to be in reverse. The killing of the victim might be for the purpose of vengeance; the shedder of blood must shed his own blood to break the taboo. On the other hand, the killing might easily have been for the protection of the community. The shedder of blood was taboo; the taboo was solemnly and officially declared; the group must be protected against it, for this taboo could not be broken.[14] A devoted thing can have no secular contact.

4. HEBREW VOWS

Among the Hebrews, both from legendary days and in historical days, simple vows were familiar. The best known is possibly that of Jacob, who "vowed a vow," saying:

> If God will be with me, and will keep me in this way that I go, and will give me bread to eat, and raiment to put on, so that I come again to my father's house in peace; then shall the LORD be my God: and this stone which I have set for a pillar, shall be God's house: and of all that thou shalt give me I will surely give the tenth unto thee.[15]

Samuel was vowed by his mother to the work of Yahweh [16] and is described as giving his life to that work. Absalom reported that he had made a sacrificial vow.[17] Careful provisions were worked out in the levitical law for reception and payment of vows.[18] St. Paul had his head shorn to fulfil a vow,[19] and forty men made a vow to kill St. Paul.[20] Vows were well enough known to be referred to in hymns,[21] to form illustrations in Wisdom sayings,[22] and to be the subject of prophetic exhortation and commendation.[23]

In the post-exilic legislation was a provision called the "law of the Nazir" [24] for which we know the details but of which we know no concrete instance. The Nazir placed himself under temporary taboo. He was pledged, during this time, to drink no wine or liquor, not to shave and not to come into contact with a corpse. The expiration of the period was to be marked by appropriate sacrifices. More stringent than the law of the Nazir was the vow of the Rechabites [25] who apparently were pledged for life not to touch wine or liquor or any product of viniculture and to live in tents rather than in houses. For their fidelity in observing the provisions of the vow they received the hearty commendation of Jeremiah.

Three striking instances of *devotio* occur in the Old Testament, that of the city of Jericho,[26] that of the daughter of Jephthah,[27] and that of Saul and Agag.[28] In all of them a highly personal deity is represented as the recipient of the vow which went to the extent of *devotio*.

In the story of the taking of Jericho, Yahweh required that everything in the city be devoted to him.[29] Because of this *devotio* the inhabitants were to be slain (with the exception of the traitor Rahab the harlot), all valuables to be collected for the "treasury of Yahweh," and all other things to be burned. A certain Achan filched some of the valuables and thereby had the *devotio* communicated to him. He and all his family must be slain and their goods and chattels burned.

When the Hebrew hosts were hard pressed by the Ammonites, their leader Jephthah vowed that, if victory were given

him, he would devote whatever came forth first to meet him
when he returned home. He won the victory and, when he
arrived home, his daughter was the first to greet him. With
great grief he fulfilled his pledge and burned his daughter.[30]

The prophet Samuel announced that Yahweh had ordered
him to devote the Amalekites, slaying all their people and
animals. Saul obeyed the order but spared the Amalekite king,
Agag. Samuel was wroth at the violation and himself slew
Agag and sentenced Saul to lose the kingdom for violating
devotio.

People and things described as being devoted in the Old
Testament were usually prisoners of war and booty from
battle.[31] When Yahweh gave victory to his people, the profits
of the victory were to be devoted to him. It is not to be supposed
that a religious ceremony was always carried out; the frenzy of
victory would probably drown much religious sentiment.

The late legislation of the last chapter of Leviticus recognized
that one might vow a member of his family to Yahweh. Human
sacrifice had long been outgrown, and temple service, like that
of Samuel, had become restricted to levites. Provision was
accordingly made to commute the vow into money to be paid
to the priests. The commutation values were as follows:

Age	For a male	For a female
1 month to 5 years	5 shekels	3 shekels
5 to 20 years	20	10
20 to 60 years	50	30
over 60 years	15	10

Even these figures might be more than one could afford; under
this circumstance the vower and the priest could make a satisfactory arrangement.

One could make a votive offering of an animal or a house or
a field, and such an offering could not be revoked; it was the
property of Yahweh. An animal so vowed, if eligible for sacrificial purpose, could not be redeemed. An "unclean" or defec-
tive animal could be redeemed at a value fixed by the priest,

plus one-fifth that price. A house or a field could likewise be redeemed at a value fixed by the priest, plus one-fifth that price.[32]

5. ANATHEMA IN THE NEW TESTAMENT

The six uses of the substantive *anathema,* and the four uses of the verb *anathematizein* in the New Testament illustrate all the varieties of the meaning of the term. Once it has the old flavour of *devoted;* [33] once it refers to the ornaments of the temple; [34] four times it refers to taking an oath; [35] once it may mean *accursed* or have the old flavour of *devotio;* [36] three times it is used in the old votive offering formula, "Let him be anathema." [37]

Whether St. Paul was seriously abandoning the persons to *devotio* or whether he was just using strong language in the heat of temper without too strong an implication, we cannot say. He did not always restrain his temper and he was not famous for the use of mild and euphemistic language. The majority of people who say, "Go to the devil," today do not suppose that the person so addressed will go anywhere; they do not even believe there is a devil to whom one can go. By the first century of our era *anathema* may have become a simple expletive to express hearty disapproval. The same phrase was probably used with greater seriousness by Church councils which were in the habit of listing heretics and solemnly saying of each, "Let him be anathema." From all we hear of these holy worthies, they were quite capable of the *devotio* which was performed by Joshua or Jephthah or Samuel.

Chapter VIII. RITES IN WHICH AN ANIMAL WAS WHOLLY EATEN

In the majority of instances the common meal, when transformed into a religious rite, assumed a form resembling the Greek thusia. Choice portions of the victim were burned on an altar for a deity before the commencement of the meal. Among many peoples, however, is found in historical times a feast in which none of the victim is burnt on an altar or in any way offered to a god. The meat was eaten by the devotees; sometimes it was eaten raw. In the accounts of these feasts one can frequently find later features which have been added after men had developed a concept of deity.

All of these feasts are strictly annual; many occur at the beginning of a year. Some are described as memorializing an historical event of some kind. To some accounts the name of a deity has been awkwardly added; the feast is described as eaten to or for the god. All of these additions are plainly later interpretations by way of explaining why such a feast was continued.

From these feasts the following examples will be chosen:

1. The Athenian Bouphonia.
2. The Magnesian Bull festival.
3. A primitive Arabic rite which continued into historic times.
4. A Mohammedan rite in Algiers.
5. The Jewish "passover," best known of all.

1. THE BOUPHONIA

One of the oldest and strangest of Athenian rites was the Bouphonia, which occurred at the Diipoleia (variously spelled Diipoleia and Dipolieia), the annual festival of Zeus Polieus held on the Acropolis on the fourteenth day of Skirophorion, the day of the full moon of the last month of the Athenian year. By the time of Aristophanes, at the end of the fifth century B.C., the height of the classical period, the feast was already so antiquated that its meaning had been forgotten; the word had become a common noun denoting things which were so outmoded that they were "full of grasshoppers." The five extant accounts [1] differ greatly in details; from them, however, a picture may be reconstructed for the peculiar feast.

1. Androtion, quoted in a scholion to Aristophanes, *Clouds,* 984-985.

> Bouphonia was an ancient feast when they thueined an ox as reminiscent (*eis hypomnēsin*) of the first ox murdered in the Acropolis, after he had taken the pelanos at the feast of the Diipoleia, also a very old feast of Athens. For at the Diipoleia they say an ox ate the cake prepared for the thusia. Because of this they thuein an ox at the Diipoleia because the ox ate the cake and was thueined. (They say) that a certain Thaulon, as he was, killed the ox with the axe.

2. Theophrastus, quoted by Porphyry in *De abstinentia* ii, 29 *ff.*

> It is said that, during a public thusia in Athens, when pelanos and sacrificial things were lying visibly on a table to be thueined to the gods, and one of the oxen, entering from work, ate some and trampled the rest, a certain (Diomos or) Sopatros, not a native but a farmer in Attica, became angered at the ox because of what had happened. Seizing an axe which was being whetted nearby, he struck the ox. When the ox died and he recovered from his anger, he considered what sort of act had been committed, buried the ox and voluntarily fled to Crete as one who had become taboo.
>
> When drought struck them and there came dearth of fruit, they inquired publicly of the god. The Pythia answered that the fugitive in Crete could break this spell; when they had punished the murderer and raised up the dead in the thusia in which he had died, it would be better for them to taste of the dead and not to hold back. Search was made and Sopatros was found. Thinking the disaffection toward him, because he was under a curse, might be changed if all did the same thing, he said to those who had visited him that an ox must be slain by the city and, since they were at a loss who the smiter should be, he would provide this if they would make him a citizen and thus share in the murder. When these things were agreed upon, they went up to the city and so ordered the ceremony as it continues today.
>
> They chose virgins to carry the water. These prepared the water to whet the axe and the knife. When they had finished whetting,

one gave tne axe, one struck the ox, and another killed him. After this, when they had flayed him, all tasted the ox. When this had been done they stitched the hide of the ox after stuffing it with grass, stood him up in the same form he had when alive and yoked a plough to him for working.

Then, holding a trial for murder, they summoned to defense all who had had part in the ceremony. The water carriers accused those who had whetted. The whetters accused the one who had handed the axe; he accused the one who had killed the ox; the one who had done this accused the knife. From the fact that the knife was speechless, they discovered the murderer and threw it into the water.

3. Pausanias i, 24, 4.

There is an image of Zeus which is the work of Leochares, and one called Polieus. While I shall describe the customary thusia to him, I do not interpret it. Some barley mixed with wheat is placed on the altar of Zeus Polieus and left with no guard. The ox which they have prepared and are keeping for the thusia goes to the altar and takes the seeds. They call one of the officiants a Bouphonos. Throwing the axe down there (so is the custom) he runs away in flight. As if they did not know the man who had performed the deed, they bring the axe to trial.

4. Pausanias i, 28, 11.

The [place] in the Prytaneum, where they hold court for iron and all inanimate things, started, I think, in this way. When Erechtheus was king of Athens the Bouphonos killed the first ox at the altar of Zeus Polieus. Leaving the axe there, he went away from the country in flight. The axe was immediately judged and acquitted. In this way the trial is performed each year.

5. Porphyry, *De abstinentia* ii, 10.

Diomos, who was a priest of Zeus Polieus, first killed an ox because, during the Dipoleia, when fruits had been brought and prepared, the ox had tasted of the sacred pelanos. Taking all present as associates, he killed him.

By conflation of the five accounts, four scenes can be reconstructed: (1) the selection of the ox, (2) the killing and eating of the ox, (3) the mimetic resuscitation of the ox, and (4) the trial for the murder of the ox. Taken together these form a ritual pattern totally different from that of the historic thusia.

(1) The selection of the ox is not mentioned by the two oldest accounts, those of Androtion and Theophrastus, although both state that the rite harks back to an incident in which pelanos (a mixture of meal and honey) was left lying on a table, or altar, for sacrificial use and was stolen by an ox which was killed by a certain Thaulon or Sopatros. Neither of these accounts mentions Zeus Polieus as figuring in any way in the rite; Androtion, however, observes that the feast occurred in connection with the Diipoleia, and records the original ox as eating not pelanos but a cake. Pausanias suggests that a mixture of barley and wheat was placed on the altar of Zeus Polieus and left unguarded. An ox which had already been selected for the purpose was apparently brought to the altar and allowed to eat of the seeds.

Dr. A. B. Cook gives two pictures of two Attic black figured vases on each of which is portrayed a scene of four oxen apparently walking around an altar.[2] He interprets these scenes as depicting the selection of the ox for the Bouphonia and, by conflation of sources, describes the scene thus:

> (Barley and wheat), made up into semi-solid porridge and solid cakes, was placed on the bronze table (or altar of Zeus Polieus). Oxen assigned for the purpose were then driven round, and the ox that drew near the altar and tasted of the meal was slain.

(2) Killing and eating the ox.

All accounts agree that an official, called by Pausanias a *Bouphonos,* seized a freshly whetted axe, struck the ox, threw down the axe and fled. According to Theophrastus the Bouphonos was followed by another officiant who took a freshly whetted knife and killed the ox. Immediately after the slaughter the ox was flayed and those present tasted or ate him, apparently raw. This is the only scene which is recorded by all accounts.

(3) The mimetic resuscitation of the ox is recorded by Theophrastus alone. The ceremony of stuffing the hide with grass is usually linked with the annual renewal of life in vegetation, thus leaving wholly unexplained the yoking of a plough

to the hide.[3] If, as is probable, the victim in earliest days had been a wild bull, the yoking of the plough might indicate desire or endeavour to effect domestication. It is no wilder than many rationalizing conjectures to suppose that primitive farmers were practical enough to try to find some way to make the powerful bull work for the tilling of the soil. Any suggested interpretation of this curious ceremony is, at best, but a conjecture.

(4) The trial for the murder of the ox, according to Pausanias, involved only the axe, which was acquitted. Theophrastus alone mentions the rest of the trial in which the blame was shifted along the line to the knife which was convicted and punished.

Killing the ox, although a necessary prelude to eating his flesh, was nevertheless somehow regarded as reprehensible, and required both explanation and punishment. The explanation was that the ox had brought the fate upon himself; he ate the cereals set out for sacrificial purposes. Accounts are uncertain whether a stray ox came in from work and, finding the grain unguarded, ate it, or whether a number of oxen were led toward the grain and left to eat it or discard it as they chose. In either event the ox was not brought to his fate by violence; he went to it of his own accord.

The word *murder* originally signified not merely taking life, even that of a human being, but killing one who was a member of the same clan or of a friendly clan. The persistence of the name *Bouphonia* (meaning *ox murder*) suggests that the origin of the rite is to be traced to totemistic or semi-totemistic days. Among totemistic peoples who killed and ate the totem upon special occasions, profuse apologies were made to the animal before slaying; he who killed a totem animal without such an apology was punished by death or by being driven from the clan.[4] This would account also for the trial of the murderer which, in the course of centuries, degenerated into a mock trial of the instrument with which the ox had been killed.

Thus the reprehensible murder was satisfactorily rationalized by the prelude which stressed the ox's voluntary action, and was satisfactorily punished by the trial and ejection of the knife. Moreover, the officiant who had wielded the instrument had satisfied traditional taboo principles by ceremonial flight.

Thusia and *thuein* are used by Pausanias and later writers in description of the feast. This is of no significance; both words had lost their technical meaning before the beginnings of our era and had come to designate any religious rite in which an animal was killed, or even any kind of killing as preparation for a meal.[5]

The Bouphonia differs entirely from the ritual pattern of the classical thusia. Save for the fact that the ox was chosen (by later accounts) at the altar of Zeus Polieus, no god is mentioned in connection with the ceremony. No prayer is made; no libations are offered; no part of the animal is burnt upon an altar; no fire is mentioned. The flesh was apparently eaten raw. The feast evidently antedated any concept of a god. When the cult of Zeus Polieus became established in Attica, its altar was located at the scene of the ancient Bouphonia, but the god had no part in the feast.

The feast has been variously interpreted as a vestigial survival of rain-making magic, as a sacramental feeding upon the corn-spirit, as a vegetation fertility rite and as an initiation ceremony. The scholiast to Aristophanes knew it only as "an antiquated feast when they killed an ox as reminiscent of the first ox murder on the Acropolis," thus bearing testimony to the early origin of the tendency to interpret religious rites as linked with and symbolizing historic events.

The two central scenes of the feast plainly form the important elements. The first and fourth scenes arise from the desire to rationalize or mitigate the killing. In the second and third scenes the patent purpose is to apprehend and utilize the power of the bull. The tasting or eating of the raw flesh indicates the endeavour to appropriate this power by the eaters for themselves and thus to compensate the finiteness of which all men are conscious. Yoking the plough to the hide, however interpreted, has something to do with linking this power with human activity and thus again points to compensation of finiteness.

Every historical religious rite commences with a simple and familiar physical act. To this act a symbolic interpretation becomes attached. In the course of time the act itself becomes symbolic instead of simple and physical. Thus the common meal of raw flesh became a symbolic meal for appropriation of *mana* or "spiritual" power. The meal itself finally became symbolic; conditions were satisfied by tasting the flesh instead of making a meal of it. The Bouphonia presents as close a preservation of primitive religious customs and ideas as is possible in sophisticated civilization. Its continuance was regularized when the cult of the god which Athenian life had adopted was attached to it.

2. THE MAGNESIAN FEAST

In the year 196 B.C. a truce was declared between Magnesia, near the mouth of the Meander River, and Miletus, not many miles southwest. The chief deity of Magnesia was Artemis Leukophryene, whose fabulously grand temple had been restored shortly after the time of Alexander the Great. The chief deity of Miletus was Apollo Didymus whose temple, almost equally grand, had been restored about the same time. The truce between the two cities was solemnized by sacrificial oaths taken in the name of the two deities.

Coincident with the adoption of the truce a decree was passed by the city council of Magnesia ordering the details of a composite festival quite different from the Bouphonia but with enough similarities to warrant comparison.[6] Instead of being so antiquated that its pattern had to be reconstructed from widely varying traditions, the pattern of the Magnesian festival was definitely fixed more than two centuries later than Aristophanes. Three thanksgiving thusias, one to Artemis, one to Apollo, and one to Zeus Sosipolis, the mythical founder of the city, were curiously attached to an old rite which reached back to primitive days.

The title of the decree is

For exhibiting annually to Zeus a bull at the beginning of seedtime, for prayer, procession and thusia, for erecting a *tholos* in the agora and for making the beds.

It is decreed by the council and the deme that

The stewards in office are to purchase the best bull [obtainable] in the month of Heraion at the annual fair. They are to exhibit it to Zeus at the beginning of seedtime on the first of the month Kronion, with the priest and priestess of Artemis Leukophryene, the stephanephorus, the sacred herald and the public sacrificer in the city. The officers of the boys are to send nine boys, each with both parents living. The officers of the girls are to send nine girls, each with both parents living.

At the exhibition of the bull the sacred herald is to pray, with the priest and the priestess, the stephanephorus, the boys and the girls, the military officers, the cavalry officers, the stewards, the secretary of the council, the auditor and the general, for the safety of the city and the land, the citizens, the women and children and all the inhabitants of the city and the land, for peace and wealth and bearing of corn and all other fruits and possessions.

It is decreed by the council and the deme that

The permanent stephanephorus, with the priest and priestess of Artemis Leukophryene, lead the procession on the twelfth of the month Artemision and thuein the exhibited bull.

In the procession with them are to be the senate, the priests, the appointed and lot-chosen rulers, the young men, the youths, the boys, those who have won contests in the Leukophryene, and all others who have won crown contests.

The stephanephorus, leading the procession, is to bring the wooden images of all the twelve gods in their finest attire. He is to erect a tholos in the agora at the altar of the twelve gods. He is to prepare three beds, as fine as possible. He is to furnish players, a flutist, a piper and a harpist.

On the twelfth of the month Artemision the stewards are to furnish three victims which they are to thuein to Zeus Sosipolis, to Artemis Leukophryene and to Apollo Pythios; for Zeus a ram, the finest obtainable, for Artemis a goat, and for Apollo a he-goat, "thuing" to Zeus on the altar of Zeus Sosipolis, to Artemis and to Apollo on the altar of Artemis. The priests of these gods are to have the customary perquisites.

When they thuein the bull they are to distribute to all the participants in the procession.

The ram, the she-goat and the he-goat they are to distribute to the stephanephorus, the priestess, the military officers, the presiding officers, the temple stewards, the magistrates and those who have given public service. The stewards are to distribute this.

When the bull is exhibited the stewards are to farm him out that he may be supported by the contractor. The contractor is to lead the bull to the agora; he is to collect from the corn merchants and the other merchants what is fitting for his nourishment. It is better for those who give.

The stewards are to record this vote at the temple of Zeus.

This composite rite which, to say the least, must have made the twelfth of Artemision a very busy day, may be outlined as follows:

1. Preparation of the bull

      (1) Purchase at the annual fair in Heraion
      (2) Exhibition on the first of Kronion
          a. Procession
          b. Prayer
      (3) Support of the bull

2. Procession on the twelfth of Artemision
3. The three thusias

      (1) To Zeus Sosipolis
      (2) To Artemis Leukophryene
      (3) To Apollo Pythios

4. Killing and eating the bull

      (1) The killing
      (2) Distribution of the flesh

A. Selection of the bull
(1) Purchase

The month of Heraion, in which the original purchase was made, was probably the month immediately preceding Kronion, which is described as the "beginning of seedtime." This locates the first transaction at the middle of the summer. At this time the secular stewards of the city (*oikonomoi*) were directed to purchase the finest bull obtainable. No reference is made to the temple of Zeus or its officials or any other city.

(2) Exhibition to Zeus

On the first of the month Kronion the stewards exhibited this bull (*anadeiknunai*). The exhibition is described as "to Zeus" but the officials of Zeus had nothing to do with the act. Neither does the temple of Zeus figure in any way. One cannot avoid the supposition that the phrase "to Zeus" was a later reflection and not part of the oldest tradition. The exhibition seems to have been really to the whole populace.

a. The Procession

The exhibition took the natural form of a long procession in which the city stewards were accompanied by almost everybody except any official of Zeus. The priest and priestess of Artemis were there, along with the *stephanēphorus,* a crowned official of some sort, whether secular or religious is not certain. The sacred herald was there, and a sort of general religious official not belonging to any deity in particular. His title, the *leitourgōn thutēs,* forms a combination of secular and religious functions. The verb *leitourgein* described any public activity for the benefit of the state, that is, any service rendered to the people as a group. *Thutēs* is a late word, appearing only after the verb *thuein* was beginning to lose its technical significance.[5] The word would denote "public slayer for religious rites." Nine lads and lasses, with the city stewards and the secretary of the council, completed the long list of participants in the procession. The complete omission of any reference to Zeus or his officials strengthens the supposition that, at least originally, the god had nothing to do with the feast.

b. Prayer

The sacred herald was directed to make the prayer *with* the other members of the procession. Whether this indicated that he was to make it in their name, or whether all were to make the prayer together, we do not know. The prayer seems not to have been addressed to any deity; its content is significant. One is not surprised at a prayer made at seedtime for abundant harvests. The thanksgiving for peace and safety may have been suggested by the treaty just made, as Kern thinks.

(3) The support of the bull for the next nine months is provided by an appendix at the end of the decree. The officer in charge was to lead the beast to the public market during the period, and there to solicit his food from the grain merchants, with the quaint observation that it would be "better for those who contribute."

From the particular mention of grain merchants Frazer concludes a necessary identification of the bull with the "corn spirit." As a matter of fact, grain merchants would be the most likely persons to have provisions for support of a bull. No recondite vestiges of totemism are necessary to explain this most natural appeal.

The significant note that it would be better for those who contributed has a familiar ring. Supporting a bull for nine months of every year would be an expensive luxury in a small town and might well need more than mere moral encouragement. The support of large physical activities whose spiritual significance must be rationalized has always been a problem for religious organizations.

B. Procession of the twelfth of Artemision

The month Artemision corresponded roughly with our March–April. This procession, therefore, must have coincided with the vernal equinox. It was formed by senate, priests, all elected and appointed officers, youths, lads, boys, all who had won contest prizes and all who had won crowns. The stephanephorus again led. This time he provided appropriate music by a flutist, a piper and a zither player.

A strange and unassimilated feature is introduced into this

procession by carrying the images of the twelve gods all decked in best attire, erecting a temporary shelter called *tholos,* and preparing three beds, probably for the images of the gods. The function of these gods is apparently to be witnesses of the ceremony, which is performed quite independently of them and is in no way addressed to them.

C. The three thusias form another intrusion into the ceremony to which they seem wholly irrelevant. They serve no part of a ritual pattern and their omission would have had no effect upon the rite as a whole. Whether they were offered consecutively or simultaneously is not said. These thusias were very official; the only participants were civil, military and temple officers.

D. Killing and eating the bull

Despite the fact that *thuein* is used to describe the disposition of the bull, no prescription of an altar is given. No priest has his customary fees as was specified with the thusias. No temple officers are mentioned. The flesh of the bull is to be distributed to the large crowd which formed the procession.

We are apparently dealing with another record of a communal meal in which no part was burnt to a god and which has the indications of coming from a day which preceded worship of divinities. The parade of the divine images and the performance of the three thusias may well have been introduced as thanksgiving acts for the treaty of peace, as Kern thinks.[6]

3. SUGGESTED INTERPRETATIONS

The Bouphonia and the Magnesian bull feast are both instances of an annual ceremony in which the flesh of the whole animal was eaten immediately after the slaying. This slaying had been simply for the purpose of the meal and had no significance in itself. At least in early days the flesh was probably eaten without cooking. The Magnesian feast occurred near the spring equinox.

Both feasts antedated the concept of personal gods and, when that concept arose, a preliminary gesture to Zeus was added to both at the selection of the animal. Both feasts hark back to the same culture period and may be two local versions of the same ceremony. Miss Harrison [6] must be correct in interpreting them as survivals of the old pre-deistic communal meal in which men tried to share the life power long before they reasoned about its nature, and certainly long before they thought of it as personal.

If we could project ourselves back to the days of primitive farmers we might appreciate their yearning, at the end of the old agricultural year and the beginning of the new year, to understand and link themselves with the earth life power. We might understand their vague identification of this power with that of the bull, the symbol *par excellence* of invincible might which could well compensate the feeble efforts of finite man. Upon the vigour of this unseen power men's whole life depended. We might understand how the annual recurrence of the feast stimulated the reasoning processes of the leaders who would explain it, as best they could, to questioning youths. In two generations these youths would have become the old leaders and rehearsed the tradition to their children and grandchildren. With the dawning of new concepts, new ceremonies would be added to the rite. When men began to think of the gods as personal, they gave proper attention to these beings at the time of the feast. When they migrated to new homes they continued the traditional rite, enriching it with local ceremonies which they learned.

Customs changed; life became more complex; farming and hunting ceased to be man's sole occupations. Increase of knowledge and the culture of material things gave rise to more concrete, albeit less enduring purposes than the quest of the life power. Nevertheless, the traditional bull feast served to keep alive in men's minds the conviction that the ultimate source of compensation of human finiteness is found in the things which are unseen and are eternal.

4. AN ARABIC PARALLEL

In the last years of the fourth century of our era a certain Neilos, a former pupil of St. John Chrysostom, went with his son Theodolos to Mount Sinai to embrace the monastic life. There they lived, surrounded by Saracens, bedouin Arabs, who finally raided the monastery, captured Theodolos and sold him as a slave. Father and son were finally reunited in Palestine and both were ordained priests. Among the many writings left by Neilos was a treatise on "The Slaughter of the Monks on Mount Sinai," in which he recorded many observations on the life and habits of the Saracens.[7]

Neilos was particularly impressed by the fact that the Arabs, having no agriculture, were carnivorous, sometimes eating their own burden camels when they were unable to secure meat by hunting or plunder. He was nonplussed that they seemed to have no concept of a god and used no idols. Plainly he had been observing men in a very low stage of civilization, barely removed from savagery. Particularly valuable is his description of a sacrifice which he says was "offered to the Morning Star." The rite seems not to have been offered to the morning star or any other recipient of worship. Rather it seems to have been performed at the time of the shining of the morning star— therefore only at certain seasons of the year.

> The camel chosen as the victim is bound upon a rude altar of stones piled together, and when the leader of the band has thrice led the worshippers round the altar in a solemn procession accompanied with chants, he inflicts the first wound while the last words of the hymn are still on the lips of the congregation, and in all haste drinks of the blood that gushes forth. Forthwith the whole company fall upon the victim with their swords, hacking off pieces of the quivering flesh and devouring them raw with such haste, that in the short interval between the rise of the day star which marked the hour for the service to begin, and the disappearance of its rays before the rising sun, the entire camel, body and bones, skin, blood and entrails, is wholly devoured.[8]

The religious character of the ceremony is indicated by the solemn procession about the bound camel, accompanied by the singing. These features of the rite are significant:

1. The time of the performance was at night; all must be completed by daybreak.

2. No part of the camel was offered in any way to a deity. Even if the Morning Star had already been deified, its function was only as a witness to the rite.

3. The solemn drinking of the blood at the commencement of the feast indicates that the primary purpose was to apprehend or appropriate the life, or the life power, of the camel.

4. The flesh was eaten raw.

5. Absolutely nothing remained when the feast was over.

The sacred meal in which no part was offered to a deity, and at which, in more civilized days, a deity might be imagined as present, was plainly not confined to the Greeks and their predecessors. Its presence on Semitic soil as late as the fifth century of our era, and in the presence of a Christian of higher culture who could not understand or interpret its significance, marks at least one point of similarity between Arabs and Greeks and indicates the rude communal meal as the earliest known religious rite.

5. A MOSLEM PARALLEL

It is well known that, despite the violent objection of Mohammed to all sacrificial rites, many of his followers clung tenaciously to crude and primitive practices and habits. An illustration of this is seen in a rite of the Aisawa, a Mohammedan confraternity of Algeria, referred to by Nöldeke.[9] A regular ceremony of this group is the devouring of the raw flesh of a he-goat, together with skin, hair and all, thus affording an instance of a primitive rite, whose significance has long since been forgotten, attaching itself as part of a higher religion which is fundamentally opposed to it in theory.

6. THE JEWISH PESACH

The best known rite in which an animal is wholly eaten in the name of a deity is the Hebrew *pesach*,[10] which is one of the oldest religious festivals in the world and which is popularly translated as "passover." Because of the uncertainty with which any meaning can be assigned to the word, it will be transliterated as pesach and treated as an English word.[11]

Directions for this feast are found in three places in the Old Testament. The age of the accounts is not unanimously assigned.

DIRECTIONS FOR THE PESACH IN THE OLD TESTAMENT

Ex. 12:3–10	Deut. 16:1–8	Num. 9:2–14	Lev. 23:5	Num. 28:16	Ezk. 45:21
		1. Selection of the victim			
10th day of first month.					
Perfect male, of first year.	From flock or herd, i.e., calf, lamb or kid.				
Lamb or kid.					
		2. Killing the victim			
Evening of 14th day of 1st month.	Month of Abib.	14th of 1st mo. or of 2nd.	Even. of 14th of 1st mo.	14th of 1st mo.	14th of 1st mo.
At house of eaters.	At Jerusalem.				
		3. The blood rite			
Blood smeared with hyssop on door posts and lintel of house.					
		4. Eating the victim			
1. Roasted not raw not boiled.	1. Roasted.	No bones broken.			
2. With unleavened bread and bitter herbs.	2. Unleavened bread.	2. Unleavened bread.			Unleavened bread.
3. None remains till morning.	3. None remains till morning.				
Any that remains to be burnt.					
4. Eaten in haste. Loins girded, feet shod, staff in hand.					

The stories from Exodus and Numbers may both be post-exilic, or one of them may contain traces of the southern prophetic interpretation of early Hebrew history which was possibly commenced in the eighth century B.C. and is known as J. The account from Deuteronomy may have been composed shortly before the exile.[12] The pesach, therefore, has at least twenty-five hundred years of unbroken history, and probably had many centuries of use before any written account was made.

No reason is assigned for selection of the animal several days before the feast. Both the Bouphonia and the Magnesian bull festival had the same requirement. The simplest reason for an interval between selection and use would be to give opportunity for examination of and conditioning the animal.

Naturally the animal had to be killed and dressed in order to be eaten. No significance was ever attached to the fact that the animal had died or that he was killed. The fact of the death of the victim had no significance in any sacrifice.

All accounts agree that the date of the pesach should be the fourteenth day of the first month of the year. This would be the first full moon of the year. The account in Numbers 9 recognizes the possibility that one might be travelling or be taboo, ceremonially or morally, at the time of pesach; such a one was directed to postpone his performance until the fourteenth day of the second month. The late account of 2 Chronicles 30 describes Hezekiah as taking advantage of this provision because the priests were ceremonially unclean.

The older accounts assume that the pesach will be eaten at the home of the eaters. Several small households might well unite for the feast. Deuteronomy, in its sanctioning of the movement for centralization of all worship at Jerusalem with the consequent destruction of all "high places," includes the pesach in its provision and prescribes the feast to be performed at "the place which Yahweh shall choose," i.e., the capital. The pesachs ordered by Hezekiah and Josiah were described as conforming to this provision. Inasmuch as the northern kingdom had been destroyed and little Judah represented "all Israel" at these times, no one would have to journey more than fifty miles to reach Jerusalem. The desire to eat pesach in Jerusalem was in perfect keeping with the natural religious tendency to make a periodic pilgrimage to a holy place. Modern Christians are thrilled if they can keep Easter in Jerusalem or have their children baptized in water from the Jordan River.

The proper officiant for the pesach was the head of the household. Stories in 2 Chronicles connect the pesach with temple cult and describe priests and levites as functioning; the feast ordered by Hezekiah had to be postponed a month because of the inability of the priests to act. This must not be construed as making the pesach a "sacredotal" act. It has always been understood that a number of families might unite for the pesach. Today, in many Jewish communities, many families keep the feast at the synagogue; at such an occasion the natural officiant would be the rabbi. If any large number of families in the days of Hezekiah or of Josiah had wanted to do this, the only possible place of assembling would have been a temple building; upon such an occasion the natural functionaries would be the temple officers.

The blood rite was always of utmost importance among Hebrews. A very old prohibition against eating blood has always been taken literally; rare meat of any kind is taboo. Before every sacrificial rite particular directions were given for disposal of the blood of the victim. It must neither be eaten by the devotee nor be burnt on the altar for Yahweh. We shall see that, in the majority of instances, the blood was poured around the altar to purify it. The pesach was the one rite which needed no priest, no temple, no altar. The head of the family was the officiant in his own home. The most natural disposition of the blood was the purification of the house where the pesach was to be eaten. Frazer gives several instances among primitive peoples of application of blood to door posts for purpose of purification.[13]

The specified prohibition against eating the raw flesh of the animal implies that this had once been the custom and that there were known instances in which this earlier custom had been continued. The omophagy, or banquet of raw flesh, was strictly taboo among Hebrews, possibly as a result of the strict prohibition of eating blood. The simple reference to the earlier custom makes one more point of contact between the pesach and other similar rites.

The use of unleavened bread would naturally require less time for preparation and would therefore be in keeping with the attitude of haste which was prescribed for eating the pesach.

The requirement that all the flesh must have been consumed before morning reminds one of the other two Semitic wholly eaten sacrifices which have been noted.

Eating "on the run" and removal of every trace of a meal suggest early nomadic or agricultural days when proximity of enemies frequently gave little opportunity for eating and necessitated removal of all traces of the performance in order to make pursuit more difficult.

The religious value of the pesach is indicated by its auxiliary words. In one account which is probably pre-exilic is found a specific injunction to "preserve this act of worship," [14] which is described as "a sacrifice to Yahweh." [15] In another account of almost equal age are three verses containing directions to "sacrifice the pesach." [16] The killing of the pesach is mentioned three times; [17] eating the pesach is mentioned twice.[18] The common expression is "to perform the pesach." [19] At the beginning or at the end of a number of accounts is found a phrase describing the act as "Yahweh's pesach" or a "pesach for Yahweh." [20]

The feast itself, like other feasts of its kind, probably antedated any concept of personal deity. Its continuation, long after the invisible Power had been thought of as an intelligent, volitional Being, necessitated definite reference to the Being when the feast was kept. In the Bouphonia this reference had been satisfied by having the ox selected by placing grain on the altar of Zeus Polieus. In the Magnesian bull feast the animal was "indicated"—exhibited—to Zeus Sosipolis. The pesach was dedicated to Yahweh. After the reference was made no part of the rite was addressed to the god.

To this day, when the annual pesach is performed by devout Jews, the youngest person at the table asks the four great questions which are all variants of the simple question, Why is this night different from all other nights? The four variants are:

Why do we eat only unleavened bread?
Why do we eat bitter herbs?
Why do we dip the vegetables twice?
Why do we preserve a certain posture?

The officiant addresses himself to the answer of those questions and tells the story of the liberation from Egypt. This is all reminiscent of the direction in Exodus 12:25-27.

> And it shall happen, when ye are come to the land which Yahweh will give you as he has promised, that ye shall perform this act of worship. And it shall happen, when your children say, What mean ye by this service?, that ye shall say, It is the sacrifice of Yahweh's pesach because he passed over the houses of the Hebrews in Egypt when he smote the Egyptians and delivered our houses.

The origin of the pesach, like the origin of many religious rites and ceremonies, will never be known. For more than twenty-five centuries it has been continued in memory of the simple fact that the Jewish people owe their very existence not to their own power and virtue, but to the power of Yahweh upon which they will continue to depend, convinced that if they neglect Yahweh they will pass into the oblivion which has swallowed all other ancient peoples of western culture.

Chapter IX. THE GREEK THUSIA

From the island of Crete, in the third millennium before the Christian era, a highly developed culture spread through the islands of the Aegean Sea and to the flanking mainlands now known as Greece and Asia Minor. This culture left no literary remains; therefore our knowledge of it is fragmentary. The vicissitudes of immigration and invasion attacked it many times; the Troy sacked by the homeric heroes was the sixth city built upon that site.

By the beginning of the millennium immediately preceding our era, two very different peoples were struggling for adjustment. One group was composed of several tribes which had come down from northern lands; these we may call the Northmen. The other group, also composed of many tribes, had been living in the Aegean world long before the Northmen arrived. Whence they had come does not concern us.

Nearly five centuries were required for the fusion of these tribes into a group of peoples who spoke more or less the same language, who worshiped more or less the same gods with more or less the same ceremonial, who were able to unite temporarily for purpose of resistance to enemies but never succeeded in effecting a real union. During the short period commencing with resistance to Persia about 500 B.C., and ending with the death of Alexander the Great, Demosthenes and Aristotle in 323 B.C., literary and cultural activity of every kind reached its height. To this classical period the word Greek is frequently limited.

The next few centuries are called the Hellenistic period. Although Greece would never bother the world politically, she set upon a conquest far more penetrating and more nearly permanent, by literally hellenising the Mediterranean world. The hub of Greek thought and letters moved from Athens to Alexandria, from which radiated influence reaching to Palestine and Asia Minor, to Rome and to distant Gaul.

Thus flowed from the Aegean world for forty centuries a constant cultural force which always left permanent impress upon the whole spiritual life of the peoples which it touched. Its influence on Rome was known and felt from the earliest days of that city's life. Its influence on Palestine may have commenced with the Philistines from whom that country received its name. Within two centuries after Greek culture was introduced by Alexander the Great, it threatened the very existence of Palestinian Judaism.[1] In the Jewish dispersion the influence was so strong that the Hebrew Scriptures had to be translated into Greek in order to become accessible to Jewish readers, while most, if not all of the so-called Apocryphal books were composed in Greek. By the beginning of our era an Alexandrian Jew, Philo by name, tried to harmonize Moses and Plato.

All early Christian literature has been preserved only in Greek. Christian theology owes its rise to the endeavours of Greek-speaking converts to justify and defend their faith, and to express it in terms understood by Greek philosophers. The oldest liturgical fragments, sole survivors of early Christian worship, are all in Greek. Any history of Greek thought would start with the pre-hellenic age of Homer and culminate in Christian theology and worship.

2. GREEK CULTS AND GREEK RELIGION

An official cult of any kind obtains only in the territory controlled by the people who guarantee it. Because Greece remained an aggregation of independent city-states never achieving political unity, no official Greek religion appeared such as was known in Babylonia, in Egypt, in Rome and among the Hebrews. Cults remained local; their influence depended upon the size and culture and influence of their sites. Occasionally the fame of a local cult spread and attracted visitors from great distances. Cults were sometimes transported by devotees to new sites or spread by missionary efforts. Other cults gained fame for effectiveness and were copied by new communities. New cults were practised side by side with older established cults; sometimes they were fused with the older cults into a single new rite which might be addressed to two or more gods at once, or to one divinity bearing two names; one of these names would probably become an epithet.

However innumerable the recipients of worship may have been, however diverse may have been the purpose of the cults, however the rites may have differed in detail, and however hostile the devotees may have been to one another, the basic content of all Greek worship was so similar that we can rightly speak of sacrifice in Greek cults, or of Greek religion and its sacrifices.

The relative importance of an idea or a thing or an act among any people may be inferred from the variety of words used to describe it, and from the extent and the latitude of the use of those words. The vocabulary of any kind of activity indicates the importance and the extent of the activity; if that vocabulary is used by all kinds of speakers and writers, it probably describes an activity with which all kinds of hearers and readers are familiar.

The Greek cultic vocabulary is probably larger than that of any other language, both in variety of roots and in number of derivatives. Hardly a Greek writer fails to employ these words as of common occurrence; secular inscriptions abound in their use. Cultic development reached so high a mark among the Greeks that we are not surprised at the legacy which these people left to the generations which succeeded them and to the religions with which they came into contact.

Three hundred compound words contain the element *theos* (god). The fact that nearly half of these words were coined in hellenistic and Christian days indicates that the habit, which was well established in homeric days and continued through classic times, was continued by those who thought and wrote in Greek. Another hundred and fifty words stem from the single adjective *hieros* (holy) which is applied to gods, to persons, to rites, to places, to times, to buildings, and to things concerned with them. Many other roots contribute to the Greek cultic vocabulary.

Greeks thought of their gods as directly interested in every imaginable human activity and determined to aid or thwart it in accord with their friendship or enmity toward those engaged therein. Some dwelt in the upper air and had their homes for a while on the uncharted peak of Mount Olympus, whence they journeyed to aid or punish mortals. Some dwelt beneath the earth—chthonic deities they are called—there they ruled the powers of vegetation and cared for the souls of the departed. Some dwelt in the waters—the rivers or the salt sea—and controlled the destinies of mariners and passengers.

The well-known gods were definitely anthropomorphic from homeric days and, like the men and women with whom they were concerned, they hungered and thirsted and wearied and loved and hated and fought and played. Nectar and ambrosia constituted their divine diet but they loved vegetables and wine and tidbits of meat; they would journey far to enjoy a banquet prepared for them by devotees.[2] So insistent were they upon this attention that failure to receive it incited them to anger against the negligent ones; and the anger was immediately calmed when the dereliction was repaired.

Side by side with these sophisticated, anthropomorphic deities were other forms, vague and with neither personality nor myth; they were but powers with capitalized names. From the negligence of some and the malignity of others unwary men could receive much harm. To some was shown tendance that they would not neglect their devotees; to others were applied all known means of averting or counteracting their evil.

In addition to these divine and quasi-divine powers, the shades of the departed were regarded as meriting religious attention. They who had been part of the community, for example, ancestors and local heroes, might conceivably continue their friendship after death. Enemies of the group and those who had suffered at its hands might well be expected to prolong their hostility or their desire for vengeance. To hosts of these were addressed such rites of tendance or aversion as were proper.

Four entirely different kinds of cult were known through all the historic days of Greece. They differ in content, in ceremonial, in purpose, in interpretation, in patronage and in the vocabularies which described them. Their differences were marked through all their history, although they were sometimes mingled. In later years, when surveyed in retrospect as forgotten rites, they easily became confused, and the confusion increased with the march of time. These cults were:

1. Public and official, or quasi-official worship addressed to ouranian deities.

2. Pre-deistic rites which have been fused with rites addressed to ouranian deities.

3. Private rites addressed to chthonic deities and lesser powers and to shades of the departed.

4. The secret worship of what are known as the mysteries, at first private and local, but later more extensive and official.

3. DEVELOPMENT OF THE THUSIA

The commonest rite in Greek religions was the *thusia,* which culminated in a common meal after a portion of the flesh had been solemnly and ceremonially burnt on an altar. In modern languages no adequate translation exists for the word which, in English dictionaries, is translated *sacrifice*; the verb *thuein,* which meant "to perform a *thusia,*" is uniformly translated "to sacrifice." In the present study, because these translations are inadequate, the words will be transliterated as English words.

The root *thu* had a long and interesting history and has always presented a problem to lexicographers who, as a rule, have not been historians of religion. A common root in Indo-Germanic languages, it has been credited with three divergent forms of development, (1) violent, excited motion, (2) smoke and (3) sacrifice. The problem has been to find a greatest common denominator which would satisfactorily explain all three forms. This seemed impossible upon the old gift theory or propitiatory theory of sacrifice.

All three forms of the root are found only in Greek.[3] Sanskrit and old High German preserve the first two forms. Gothic, Slavic and Lithuanian preserve only the second form. English preserves the first two forms.[4] It is not difficult to find the connection between the second and third forms when we remember that the thusia was that act in which a portion of the meat literally became smoke, and that this was the important feature of the act. There are, therefore, only two forms of development of the root, and the relation between these two is not difficult to picture.

A root which persisted in so many languages for over three thousand accountable years, and for many centuries before that accounting begins, may well be supposed to stem from primitive days, long before sub-species languages were distinguished. If we picture primitive man terrified by a raging forest fire accompanied by wind and storm, we can see how such a phenomenon would be described by the onomatopoeic syllable *too-oo-oo.* The same root persisted after the ideas of smoke and raging violence had separated. With the gradual development of sub-species languages came the long and varied history of the root, whose primary meaning would therefore be *what raging fire does.*

It has frequently been observed that man's civilization spells his mastery of natural powers. As a matter of fact, man has never mastered these powers. He cannot prevent the rain from falling or the lightning from flashing or the wind from blowing or the sea from surging. Man's civilization is more accurately described as spelling his understanding of and co-operation with the powers of nature. The first force to be approached was that of fire.

Consuming forest fires and burning volcanic lava were familiar sights to man and beast which both fled in terror at the approach of these destructive forces. The fear of fire has never

left man or beast but, ages ago, man commenced the rudimentary thinking which marked him off forever from the
beasts, by the discovery that the power which he thought was
his deadliest enemy could become the greatest contributor to
his material progress and a mighty aid to spiritual progress. It
would keep him warm, make his food more palatable and
digestible, speed his travels, make industry possible and thus
begin the transformation of his life.

Greek myth and tragedy proclaimed that fire had been stolen
from Zeus himself by Prometheus and given to man at the dawn
of human thinking. Literatures of later peoples have never
ceased to dwell upon the theme. A Hebrew story told of
Yahweh first making himself known to his people in a burning
bush and in the mountain lightnings.[5] When Isaiah saw the
Lord the house was filled with smoke.[6] Christian tradition told
of the Holy Spirit coming down upon the first believers in
tongues of fire.[7] Among all peoples fire is a sort of link between
earth and heaven. Lightning, the obvious source of much fire,
came just as obviously from heaven to which it returned, laden
with the things of earth. As soon as gods were pictured as individuals with human forms and emotions and dwellings, the
king of the gods became the lord of fire. We do not know
when this came about, but it was centuries before the time of
Homer. Thereafter a bolt from heaven was a signal from Zeus
—either of his wrath or of his favourable answer to prayer.

With recognition of the gods as voluntary wielders of the
forces ruling earth and heaven and the lives of men, it became
fitting and necessary that their gift of fire should not return to
them empty. No time was more appropriate for this attention
than that of the common meal which had been prepared by the
mysterious fire. The gods became guests at this meal; choice
parts of the victim were consigned to the sacred fire to be sublimated into smoke and thus ascend to the powerful beings who
ruled and cared for men.

This must not be confused with the gift theory of sacrifice.
To invite a person to a meal is not construed as a gift to the

person; to serve one with a choice cut of meat is not interpreted as servile tribute. So much a part of life had the gods become that their presence at any important meal was taken for granted. Men did not forget the unseen powers upon which they depended for everything in life.

The rite may well have arisen from contemplation of the mystery of fire. When it became definitely and consciously religious, it was called the *fire rite* or the *smoke rite,* the *thusia.* To perform this rite was *thuein.* Thus started on their centuries of history, these words began to suffer many changes of connotation, after the manner of words.

Thusias had become a fixed element of Achaean life long before the time of Homer. They were occasional rather than regular; that is, they were performed when circumstances called for them, but we know of no fixed calendar which provided regular times for them. Meat had not become the staple diet of man.[8] Expense and lack of refrigeration would limit its use to special occasions. Men were convinced that to kill and eat without due recognition of the gods would be to stir their anger and bring misfortune. Present although unseen, they would not tolerate rudeness.

Thusias of many animals at a time were so well known in pre-homeric days that a special word had come to designate these feasts. A hundred animals might be thueined at once; such an act was a *hekatombē,* meaning a hundred oxen.[9] By the time of Homer this word had become strictly technical and had lost its numerical connotation. On one occasion the hekatomb consisted of eighty-one oxen.[10] Fifty rams are mentioned at another time.[11] Again we read of a hekatomb of twelve oxen.[12] Often the number is undefined.[13] Distant Ethiopia seems to have been a country famed for this rite; it is described as "the land where they *rezein* [14] hekatombs for the immortals." [15]

The basic meaning of a word is frequently illuminated by study of the verbs with which it is described. In modern English two groups of verbs are related to worship. A person may be described as (1) saying or reading or singing, or (2) performing or conducting or celebrating a religious service. In both instances the verb describes the action of a single person, or of a very small group of persons. Others who may be present are spectators or auditors who attend and watch or hear the service, which may be perfectly transmitted by radio or television. When a Protestant goes to church he is apt to speak of going "to hear Mr. So-and-so"; a western Catholic is apt to say he is going "to hear mass."

We have become so accustomed to this method of thinking that we do not always realize the radically different concept of worship which obtained among ancient Greeks. Verbs of saying and performing and hearing and seeing were proper for pageantry and play; they had no place in description of a thusia, for which the only adequate verbs were those of group action in which every member had a part; none was a mere spectator or auditor.[14] Too much stress cannot be placed upon this fundamental concept of ancient Greeks who thought of a thusia as an action to be performed and not as a scene to be witnessed.

We can reconstruct fair pictures of the homeric period of Greek life and of the classical period of Greek history but, for the intervening centuries, our knowledge is marked by so many lacunas that it becomes exceedingly difficult to note the sequence of events or the changes in the way of living. In homeric days thusias were spontaneous and occasional; there was no thought of a calendar or of regular and regulated times of worship. By classic days thusias, while still continued spontaneously on appropriate occasions, had become stated acts for the express purpose of honouring the gods; an elaborate calendar regulated the times of their performance and careful provision was made for ceremonial detail.

The development of civilization always issues in increasing attention to material things and in corresponding forgetfulness of the unseen powers which were so real to primitive man. With the widening of the limits of time and space and might, we are prone to lose sight of those limits and to imagine ourselves self-sufficient to reach the infinity for which we yearn. We become so busied with the manipulation of things that attention to the supernatural is crowded out. In times of stress and danger we realize our helplessness and we cry for aid to the gods of whom we have heard but whom we have ignored. Regular worship, at times and places set apart for the purpose, is the sole act which can keep in mind the realization that, after all, the unseen powers are the only ultimates and that to forget them is to become the slave of things.

No one knows how the idea of fixed times and places of worship arose, but it has constituted the basis of every religion the world has known. Thus only can men give the gods the honour due them. Thus only can they maintain friendly or co-operative relation with the gods whom to ignore is folly. The idea may well have resulted from the inspiration and exhortation of gifted leaders; all constructive ideas have so arisen and this was probably no exception. By classic days in Greece the thusia had become the regular means of addressing human attention to the powers upon whom men depended, and of co-operating with those powers. It was the one means which men knew; many centuries had to roll by before a better means could be learned. The words of historians, philosophers, poets, orators, and dramatists, and even routine records of proceedings of councils and legislatures preserved in hundreds of inscriptions, all make constant reference to thusias as constituting a normal feature of the life of Greek peoples on both sides of the Aegean Sea.

4. THE RITUAL PATTERN OF THE THUSIA

Several descriptions of thusias occur in Homer. Every account shows the same ritual pattern already developed; in four of these accounts many lines are identical.[16] This verbal repetition of lines forms one of the problems of textual criticism in the study of Homer; whatever may be the ultimate solution of this problem, it may be assumed that, by the time of the final redaction of the epics these lines had taken traditional importance.

The account from the first book of the *Iliad* (lines 447-473) described the thanksgiving thusia presided over by Chryses, priest of Apollo, who had finally secured the return of his daughter who had been captured by Agememnon. With the Greeks who returned the girl he joined in glad thanksgiving.

> The sacred hekatomb they
> Quickly arranged in order about the well built altar.
> First they washed their hands and took up the grains of barley.
> Chryses then made the prayer, holding his hands to heaven.
>
> .   .   .   .   .   .
>
> When they had finished the prayer and scattered the grains of barley,
> First they drew up the neck of the victims, then slew and flayed them.
> Then cut out the thigh pieces; with fat they covered them over,
> Making a double fold, and placed raw pieces upon them.
> These the old man burnt on the wood, while pouring upon them
> Sparkling wine; the youths held the five-pronged fork beside them.
>
> When the thigh pieces were burnt and all had tasted the *splanchna,*
> Then they cut up the victims and pierced the spits through the pieces;
> Carefully roasted the whole, preserving every fragment.
> When they had ceased from labour, they made them ready the banquet;
> No lack of spirit was there, for each had his equal portion.
> When they had gratified their thirst and hunger, the young men
> Straightway turned their hands to the bowls prepared for libations.
> Deftly they poured the wine, a few drops first in each goblet.
> All the day long they gave to lauding the god with singing,
> Chanting glad paeans of praise, these striplings from far Achaea.

The ritual pattern, already well established long before the days of Homer, and therefore before the migration of the Northmen, was preserved through many centuries. New accessories and more elaborate ceremonial were added from time to time. Magnificently built and adorned temples replaced improvised open-air altars. The worship became officially adopted by different city-states which provided for whole hierarchies of sacred ministers and for glorious processions with orchestras and choirs, but the simple pattern of homeric days remained the base for every thusia. The rite falls easily into three parts; in each part are a number of fixed or constant features. The outline is as follows:

I. The preparation
  1. Lustration
  2. Barley grains ceremonial
  3. Prayer
  4. Casting the hair of the animal into the fire
  5. Slaying and flaying of the victim
  6. Processions

II. The thusia proper
  1. Burning thigh pieces and fat: libations
  2. Eating the splanchna

III. The feast
  1. Roasting the victim
  2. The banquet
  3. Libations
  4. Music: song and dancing

The historic and religious values attaching to each of these features explain the long continuance of the thusia and its facile sublimation when it was baptized and made the basis of Christian worship. At the beginning it was the act of a group in which every individual had a part. A few officials were needed to superintend and direct the people in carrying out the action but never to perform it for or instead of the people. It became naturally impossible for everybody to have a literal part in the act in classical days when worship had become located in temples, groups had greatly increased in size and temple officers had multiplied.

This kind of religious act is somewhat difficult of understanding by modern westerners who are conditioned by the concept of Christianity which, in its catholic form, makes "hearing mass" the supreme act of worship and, in its protestant form, interprets worship as "hearing the Scriptures and a sermon." In the ancient Greek thusia worshipers were not passive listeners but active participants in the whole event.

Lustration of the hands was well known long before the time of Homer as an indispensable prelude to every formal meal.[17] It was natural that it should be retained before a thusia [18] or even before prayer unaccompanied by a thusia.[19] The importance of running water for the rite is mentioned by Sophocles.[20] Originally necessary when men turned from working to eating, it naturally became symbolic of the innocence and purity which

Hesiod mentions as requisite qualities for making a thusia.[21]
The purity may refer to normal or accidental uncleanness
acquired in performance of daily tasks; it might refer to acts
which constituted barriers to worship, such as engaging in
funeral rites, visiting a tomb, criminal acts and, in the cult of
Athene, sex acts. This fundamental necessity for ceremonial
purity for acts of worship, thus appearing in the early days of
man's culture, has obtained through the centuries and still continues in traditional Christian rites, although post-Reformation
churches have excised all such ideas.

The invisible powers of the universe are not obvious but
implicit; conscious attention is required to apprehend them, as
it is required for development of every human activity. Part of
this attention is deliberate, temporary elimination of routine
interests which are obvious and necessary in daily life. Lustration symbolized this direction of attention. It may well be
descended from efforts to remove taboo; all lofty spiritual concepts have arisen from rude beginnings. Life's valuable things
must be refined from ores whose importance is undiscernible
by the untrained eye.

Ceremonial manipulation of grains of barley is likewise
familiar as a prelude to a thusia or to prayer when unaccompanied by a thusia. The grains might be placed in a basket near
the devotee [22] or they might be scattered or cast about.[23] Oak
leaves might be substituted if barley grains were unobtainable.[24]
The origin of the rite is obscure; its continuance is due to religious conservatism, strengthened by the idea that "doing something with something" is a necessary accompaniment of prayer.
In fact, the spoken words are the accompaniment; the scattering
of barley grains constitutes the act of prayer. The deeply sacred
character of this idea is not always realized by many modern
people whose concept of prayer is limited to speaking words. It
is quite possible that the barley grain ceremony was a vestigial
survivor of days when the first fruits of harvest were returned
to the earth whence they came, in order that the life cycle might
not be broken. Later, when the givers of life had become deities,

the first fruits continued to be offered; they thus became offerings to the deities.

The eating of the flesh of large animals, such as constituted thusias, was an exceptional event; grain and vegetable products were the staples of life. Thus the older ceremony of manipulation of grains of barley continued, whether a thusia was offered or not.

A constant element of preparation was the prayer which set forth the purpose of the particular thusia to be offered. The regularly repeated phrase describing the officiant as "holding up his hands to heaven" indicates the formal and official character of the prayer. The spiritual value attaching to prayer from early days is illustrated by a striking and not well enough known passage from the *Iliad* (ix, lines 502–513).

> Prayers are the daughters of Zeus, of Zeus the great and mighty.
> Halting and shrivelled they are, and making the eyes cast downward;
> Trailing the woes of Sin; for Sin is fleeter and stronger,
> Wandering abroad on the earth and gaining the start upon them,
> Tripping men's steps; then Prayers will follow the sins to heal them.
> Him who honours these maidens and welcomes their timely approaches,
> Him they cover with blessings and free him while he is praying.
> If men stiffen the neck and bid these maidens to leave them,
> Leave them they will, and hasten to pray to the Son of Kronos,
> "Let Sin follow these rascals and trip them with full requital."

The primary idea of the word for prayer, *euche* (verb, *euchesthai*) was not petition but vow. He who prayed was frequently, but not always, making a petition; the purpose of the prayer was to vow or to offer something to the deity, or to express proper recognition of his unfailing care. For the average man today prayer has ceased to be an active factor of his normal life and has become either a periodic aggregation of petitions prefaced by an accumulation of complimentary superlatives, or else an emergency gesture in which the deity is summarily called to rescue him or his friends from inconvenience or danger beyond human control. It is therefore difficult for many today to appreciate the natural and intimate place which prayer occupied in the minds of ancient Greeks. They who smile at some of the petitions might well envy some of the spiritual heights to which these "pagans" attained.

An interesting phrase is found in two old inscriptions [25] describing men as *thuontes kai euchomenoi*—thuing and praying. The two words belonged together; prayer was the preparation for a thusia; a thusia was the most desirable form of prayer. Sometimes they prayed for rain,[26] or to avert impending or threatening danger or harm.[27] It was assumed that they would pray before starting on a journey,[28] or before going into battle.[29] They must pray for omens before any serious undertaking,[30] or for oracles[31] or for guidance in casting lots.[32] Prayer was a frequent accompaniment of oaths[33] although we shall see another rite than the thusia used for many such instances. A dedication of a temple was a normal occasion of prayer and thanks. In the inscriptions we often read of prayers "for the safety and health of the council" or "of the people." [34] Such rites were called by the name *sotēria*,[35] a name we shall see appearing again under Jewish sacrifices. Thusia and prayer were sometimes offered at a marriage.[36]

Frequent occasions of thusias and prayer were after success in an undertaking or achievement of purpose, when prayer took the form of thanksgiving and the ceremonial of the thusia was most elaborate. It was inconceivable that one could ask a god for any kind of aid and not express profound appreciation after receiving it. Our concept of thanksgiving is briefly to say, "Much obliged," when we do not forget it; the Greek concept was to offer a thusia.

If men naturally pray before going on a journey, especially by water, they should give glad thanksgivings for a safe journey or for deliverance from dangers.[37] Thusias were offered for victory in battle.[38] Physicians offered thusias to Hygeia for those whom they had healed.[39] A thusia was ordered by Smyrna because Seleucis of Antioch had freed the city from tribute.[40] A well-known phrase for thanksgiving offerings was *thuein eucharisteria.*[41] One method of showing great honour to prominent men and benefactors and to slain warriors was to offer thusias for them.[42] They had not developed their thinking so far as to reason or argue upon just what was accomplished by such offerings. They were happy and thankful; a thusia expressed that attitude.

The importance of formal acts of thanksgiving, as expressions of appreciation for benefactions, increased with the growth of city-state government. By the third century B.C. they had become quite conventional in Asia Minor and the Aegean Islands. The technical term *eucharistia,* which occurs in many inscriptions,[43] denotes a formal group act of thanksgiving and appreciation. These expressions of *eucharistia* were marked by enthusiastic secular activity, such as adoption of verbose resolutions by the council of a city, or colourful processions or erection of commemorative tablets in a temple. The verb *eucharistein* [44] was used to denote these acts, and the council which decreed the honours described itself as *eucharistos,*[45] meaning appreciative or thankful, and at least once by the additional adjective *mnēmoneusa,*[46] meaning mindful. Formal thanksgivings to god and man, as proper appreciation of blessings, always had important consideration among the ancient Achaeans and their successors, the Greeks. They occupied a prominent place in the religious and secular life which were so interwoven as to be well-nigh indistinguishable. The thusia was the most adequate expression of thanksgiving.

Another group of expressions from these secular inscriptions illustrates the importance of thanksgiving in ancient Greek life. The standard phrase for "to return thanks" is *charin* (or *charitas*) *apodidonai.* That this is considered a normal attitude is seen in an inscription from Megalopolis, earlier than 200 B.C., where public expressions of appreciation to a benefactor are described as *dikaian apodidontes charin* [47] (returning right, or due, thanks). That the gratitude should be somehow commensurate with the benefaction is seen in such phrases as *charin axian,*[48] *charitas . . . kat' axian,*[49] *charitas axias* [50] and *charitas kataxias*[51] (worthy thanks, or meet thanks). The influence of these phrases upon Greek thought led to their incorporation in early Christian liturgies.

During the prayer the officiant cut some hair from the neck of the victim and cast it into the fire. While this act is not specifically mentioned at every thusia in Homer, its mention in conventional language is frequent enough to warrant the assumption that it was a regular part of the rite.[52] The customary word to describe it is *aparchomai,* which is the technical word for offering first fruits and also for commencing libations. The noun *aparchē* is used by Euripides to indicate the beginning of a thusia.[53]

Reference has already been made (p. 100) to the custom of returning the first bit of harvested grain to the earth to continue the life cycle. The harvest was not touched until this ceremony had been performed.[54] The use of the same substantive to denote the first few grains of a harvest, the first few drops of wine for a libation, and the first few hairs of the animal to be thueined, would suggest that definite kinship was recognized between these ceremonies which lend themselves readily to interpretation as acts of dedication.[55]

Before slaying the victim, it was frequently customary to adorn it with wreaths and garlands and, especially in thusias to Athene, to tip or overlay the horns with gold.[56] This was particularly appropriate for festive occasions and times of thanksgiving. Naturally the use could have arisen only after the knowledge of precious metals had become well known. The rationale might be for sake of mere adornment.

The slaying, flaying and dissecting of the victims required the longest time for performance and the fewest words for description. The operations were necessary for every flesh meal and, of course, for every thusia, but they were never given any sort of religious significance or interpretation. "They drew up the necks of the victims and slew them and flayed them; then cut out the thigh pieces."

The absence of mention of any sort of blood rite in connection with the thusia is important. The blood of the victim was apparently allowed to drain upon the ground. Apollodorus tells a story of Aeson who, at a thusia, drank freely of the bull's blood and instantly died.[57]

Between the time of Homer and that of Pindar the custom of elaborate processions at elaborate thusias had been established. Pindar's mention of "processions redolent with fat"[58] suggests that the place of the procession was after the slaying and dissection of the animal. The reference may well be to triumphal carrying about of the pieces which were shortly to be burnt upon the altar. Thucydides connects processions with the Panathenaean festival.[59] They are referred to in the inscriptions as definitely connected with thusias,[60] as well as with festivals of heroes.[61] If the procession occurred immediately after the slaying of the victim, as has been suggested, it would serve both as a means of covering the time necessarily occupied by the long process of preparing the animal, and as an appropriate introduction to the thusia proper.

The central action of the thusia—that which gave the rite its name—was the solemn burning, over the altar fire, of pieces of thigh (we should call them steaks) wrapped in fat and overlaid with other bits of meat. The long-handled, five-pronged fork used for the purpose is frequently portrayed in vase paintings and other works of art. The officiant superintended the action; the fork was held by young attendants. "Curling about the smoke, the savour went up to heaven."[62]

Gums and fragrant wood of various kinds were thrown upon the burning pieces and into the fire, possibly for the original purpose of neutralizing the odour of burning flesh. The spiritual rationalization of the practice was that the gods enjoyed the fragrance. With the progress of civilization and the consequent importation of luxuries from distant lands, arose the use of fragrant gums for this purpose. In the inscriptions are mentioned incense, myrrh, cassia and cinnamon.[63] Incense was naturally used upon other occasions than thusias.

The *splanchna*[64] were those organs below the diaphragm—

the liver, kidneys, etc.—and are to be distinguished from the *entera* or entrails. Because there is no English word with this exact connotation, the word will be simply transliterated.

In the homeric thusia the splanchna were tasted or eaten. The ritual importance of the act may be inferred from the specific mention of it in so many thusias. Whether the verb *pateomai* means "eat" or "taste" is hard to determine. A little light is shed upon the problem by a passage in the *Odyssey* [65] reading, "When they had roasted the splanchna, they apportioned them." Since at least a quarter of them belonged to the priests,[66] if everyone present at the thusia had a portion, the share of each would be little more than a taste. In later days the priests sometimes burnt their portions within the sanctuary and sometimes ate them or sold them. The frequent mention of liver as a favourite Greek dish would indicate that the splanchna were sold as were the skin and legs which were perquisites of the priests as part of their fee.

In post-homeric days the technical name for the splanchna was the *hiera* (usually rendered "sacred parts"). The general name for the officiant at the thusia, and later at all kinds of rites, was the *hiereus*; the functioning of this individual was described by the word *hiereuein*. Jane E. Harrison [67] made a significant distinction between the two verbs *hiereuein* and *thuein*. "*Thuein* is strictly applicable only to the portion of a sacrifice that was actually burnt with a view to sublimation; whilst *hiereuein* applies rather to the portion unburnt, which was sacred indeed, as its name implies, to the gods, but was actually eaten in communion by the worshipper." It is possible that a much older history than Miss Harrison suggested was implied in the word *hiereuein*.

At the beginning of the *Iliad* the Achaeans are pictured as holding council to determine the reason for their continued failure to take Troy. The reason was plainly beyond human understanding, and Achilles suggested inquiring of three different kinds of diviners to learn why the gods were against them. These three were a seer, a dream interpreter and a *hiereus*.

The business of the seer was the explanation of accidental
omens as, for instance, the flight of birds. The business of the
dream interpreter is evident from his name. "Dreams," says
Achilles, "come from Zeus." [68] The business of the *hiereus* had
plainly to do with interpretation of some kind of omen different
from those obtained from birds or from dreams.

While the *hiereus* might well offer a thusia, he was in no way
a necessary officer for the rite, which could be performed by the
head of a family or by the leader of an army.[69] The *hiereus* was
here regarded as a professional interpreter of omens of some
kind. The simple mention of the name indicates that the office
was well recognized. It is not unreasonable to suppose that the
omens which he interpreted were those presented by the *hiera*,
the well-known post-homeric name for the splanchna. [70]

While hepatoscopic references in Greek are rarer than those
in Babylonia and Assyria, they are sufficient to warrant the
assumption that hepatoscopy was practised in connection with
some Greek sacrifices.[71] The connection between *hiera* as the
splanchna and as the rites, *hiereus* as the practitioner, and
hiereuein as the performance of the rites, cannot be accidental.
All are related to the adjective *hieros* which is conventionally
translated "divine." [72] The *hiera* must have been the divining
objects, *hiereus* the diviner, and *hiereuein* to divine. In Diodorus
the *hiereus* was the custodian of a sacred image, from the nod-
ding of which he practised divination.[73] In the course of time
the *hiereus* became the ordinary, but never the exclusive per-
former of thusias.

The climax of the thusia was the banquet, described in detail
many times. Reminiscent of the technical name *dais*, by which
this feast was called, are the pregnant words of Homer, "each
had his equal portion." [74] Only in imagination can we try to
reconstruct the primitive flesh meal. By historic times it had
already become a religious feast. It was therefore not merely a
meal, but a rite in which provision was made for equal distribution. An Attic inscription of about 330 B.C.[75] preserves a roster
of this distribution as follows:

> Five pieces each to the presidents
> Five pieces each to the nine archons
> One piece each to the treasurers of the goddess
> One piece each to the managers of the feast
> The customary portions to others.

In classical days part of the regular furniture of a temple was the table on which meats were set out for distribution to the feasters. As early as 300 B.C. this was called *the table of the god* [76] in an inscription from Cos.

In an inscription listing regulations for the Andanian mysteries about 100 B.C. [77] is an interesting direction. "When, from the sacrifices carried in the procession, the priests have taken those parts belonging to the gods, they shall use the rest for *the holy supper (to hieron deipnon)*. The reference is plainly to the feast which was the climax of the thusia before the mysteries, but the older term *dais* has been replaced by the less formal *deipnon* to which is prefixed the adjective holy.

Libations were of common occurrence throughout the history of Greek religions. Wine, blood and wine, oil and honey were used for various purposes; if these were lacking, water could be used as a surrogate. They are found in all sacrifices, before the mysteries, at visits to tombs, before a journey, before and after meals, before retiring at night, at marriages, for purposes of purification, and as accompaniment to simple, private and family devotions. In general it may be observed that the pouring of libations was the natural expression of prayer and of thanksgiving. They occur twice in the thusia: once at the actual burning of the parts for the god, when a cupful of wine was poured over the burning flesh and into the fire; again after the meal, when a few drops were ceremonially poured into each cup, and thence upon the ground, before the cups were filled for drinking.

Music and dancing formed a fitting conclusion to the glad thusia. Apollonius of Rhodes described the worshipers as standing around the altar, as they had done before the rite, and thus proceeding to the dancing which brought the ceremony to a close.[78] Whether this custom dates from homeric times or later, the music and dancing formed an action in which all participated. In post-classical days is reference to singing of a hymn by the free children standing around the altar after the prayers and libations.[79] In the *Odyssey*, after a heifer sacrifice to Athene, the women stand around and sing or wail.[80] Singing might be in order even without a thusia. Penelope sang to Athene after her prayer and scattering of barley grains.[81]

Hymns, paeans and odes are all mentioned from early times. By classical days professional choirs were trained to lead the singing, but never to perform it as a substitute for the worshipers. At first the singing and dancing were probably unaccompanied but, from classical days onward, flute players, harpists and sacred trumpeters were among the regular officers of a well-equipped temple.

5. OFFICERS OF THE THUSIA

In the thusia of homeric times few special officers were needed. Rites were performed in the open air, at suitable places usually chosen at the time, although many permanent altars had been erected. The groups performing the action were relatively small; each member of the group had his part and performed it naturally. "The old man" presided; younger men assisted.

In classical days we find worship by large groups at places marked by glorious and expensive temples set apart, adorned and maintained for the sole purpose of regular cult. This transition to a more sophisticated way of life necessitated organization to guarantee continuance. In literary sources and in inscriptions we find many evidences of the extensive organization required for maintenance and continuance of thusias.

The general charge of cult seems at first to have been under the secular officers of the city-states. The president, the vice-presidents and secretary of council, the public herald and the state treasurer included religious duties in their ordinary responsibilities. Large temples with frequent and elaborate thusias needed special officers. We are not surprised, therefore, to read of temple presidents and vice-presidents, of temple recorders, temple heralds and temple treasurers. These administrative officers developed naturally from necessity. In addition to these, were needed special officers for actual performance of rites.

At many temples were officers who had peculiarly local names and whose functions are hard to identify. These may be dismissed from consideration in the present study. In all the well-known temples were officers with recognized conventional names and clearly defined duties. The majority of these names were naturally formed by addition of common verbal or substantival endings to the roots *hier, thu, the* and *na* (temple). The more important of these may be classified as follows:

1. General officers

> The *theokoloi* [82] were general cult officers.
>
> *Ho leiturgōn thutēs* [83] was the public sacrificer.
>
> The *naōpoioi* [84] had general charge of a temple. So important was their office that lists of these officers over long periods of years were preserved.
>
> The *hierourgos* [85] was a sort of master of ceremonies who arranged the details of rites.
>
> The *hieropoioi* [86] were responsible for seeing that sacrifices were offered and that the victims met requirements. Frequent references are made to them both in literary works and in the inscriptions.
>
> The *hierotamias* [87] or treasurer of sacred things was also a commonly mentioned official.
>
> The *grammateus tou theou* [88] was "secretary of the god," the official recorder of sacrifices and resolutions referring to them.

2. Subordinate officers

> The *zakoros* [89] occurs many times in the inscriptions. He seems to have started as a temple sweeper and cleaner,

but his office increased in dignity during the Roman period. At least once, his name was *diakonos*.[90]

The *neoi*,[91] or young men, held the five-pronged fork for the thusia in homeric times. In classical days they became an "order" or younger group subordinate to the *hiereus*.

The *neōkoroi*[92] had the responsibility of the care of utensils, and sometimes of exclusion of foreigners from worship.

3. Officers of the thusia proper

The *hiereus* was the officer *par excellence*. Originally he was possibly a diviner. In classical days he had to do with the offering of the thusia. In post-classical days many of his detailed duties were taken over by minor officers such as the *zakoroi*.

The *hierothutēs*,[93] as his name indicates, was a general sacrificial officer, possibly the same as the *hiereus*.

The *xuleus*[94] had to do with cutting the wood for the fire.

4. Officers for the banquet

The cook, the flutist, the harper, the sacred trumpeter, the chief wine pourer and the libation bearers were all necessary for the banquet, the libations and the music.

5. Officers in oracular temples, in addition to thusia officers

The *mantis*,[95] or seer, was the normal interpreter of accidental omens in homeric days. In classical days the Pythian priestess of Apollo was called a *mantis*.

The *prophētēs*[96] was originally the man who "spoke in front of the cave," and translated into understandable Greek the inspired babblings of the Pythia. Later, when a temple housed the oracle, the prophet was the interpreter of the will of the god as revealed by the oracle.

The *exēgētēs*[97] originally seems to have been a leader in the mysteries. However, the same name was also applied to the interpreter.

Some of these officers were elected by the state council. Some were appointed by benefactors. Some of the offices were hereditary; some were frankly for sale. Some incumbencies were for a term; some were for life.

The common word for appointment to any of these offices was *cheirotonein,* which literally means "stretching of hands." The regular method of polling a vote in the council was by stretching of hands. Not only religious officers, but generals, and all state officers elected by the council were so chosen. From this fact the meaning of the word was extended to any sort of formal appointment to an office, whether by public election or otherwise.

Many of the officers were inducted into their duties by taking a formal oath of faithful and responsible performance of work. Some of these oaths were preserved. An illustrative oath was that taken by officers of the mysteries:

> I swear by the gods for whom the mysteries are performed, that I will have care that the details of the initiation will be carried out as is fitting to the gods and to all that is right. And I myself shall do nothing irregular or wrong at the performance of the mysteries or suffer another to do so, but shall follow out the things which are written.[98]

6. INTERPRETATION OF THE THUSIA

Examination of the ritual pattern of the thusia reveals the integral development of a rite which incorporated three primitive ideas. (1) The base of the rite was the common meal which was originally necessitated by physical circumstances attending the slaying, cooking and eating of a large animal. (2) Early reflection convinced men that to eat an animal was to appropriate or apprehend his power, both his life principle and whatever peculiar properties he had possessed. (3) The desire to know the future, and thus to have definite aid in making decisions, expressed itself in examination of the splanchna, the supposed seat of the life power.

These three ideas were integrated by the later conviction that the life power was not an automatic, mechanical process, but the gift of personal beings who, by this very fact, were superior to men. "The immortals" they were called from early days, because the life force which they controlled was completely superior to the individuals whom it seized for a short time, only to loose the hold which it had upon them. By their very gift of life power, the immortals were sharing their prized possession with men. It is not surprising that men thought of the choice bits of meat which they sublimated into smoke as perquisites of the immortals.

A rite in which gods and men shared common food would eventually easily lend itself to cultic expression of voluntary co-operation of men with the god. This was also the logical development of the rite by which men sought to gain knowledge of the future. Such knowledge was plainly sharing the knowledge of the god; it might be expressed as ascertaining the will of the gods. Men sought to learn this will that they might do it; this also was co-operation with the immortals. Complete co-operation with divinity may be said to be the spiritual ideal to which the thusia pointed. This is still the remote goal of all religion, although few religions have expressed it simply as their ultimate purpose.

It is easy for men to forget the gods for the reason that retention of implicit concepts requires constant and directed attention. The opposite of forgetting the god is remembering him or thinking of him. This idea has been preserved in English by a group of cognate words which spring from the same root. The Old English *thancen,* from the same root as the German *danken,* has developed in two directions from a single starting point. The meaning of the root was "to keep in mind," "to be mindful of." Like many words, it took one set of forms for intellectual activity, and another for moral activity.

On the intellectual side *thancen* became think, which denotes both "to form a concept" and "to keep in memory." The old verb had two pasts, *thought* and *thank*; the second disappeared with Middle English.

On the moral or volitional side *thancen* became *thank*. The idea thus pictured might be expressed in words or in action. If expressed in words it easily became praise, which might be sincerely fulsome. If expressed in action it involved shaping of one's behaviour in accord with the will of him to whom one was thankful. We are reminded of the General Thanksgiving in Anglican prayer books—"That we show forth thy praise, not only with our lips, but in our lives." Thus worship and thanksgiving, starting from a common point, must needs meet again when both become perfect.

Thus is explained why the thusia was increasingly employed by ancient Greeks to express the thanks which they had to the gods who gave and directed and ordered their lives.

Chapter X. JEWISH SACRIFICES: THE 'OLAH AND ZEVACH

Set well inland from the eastern coast of the Mediterranean Sea is a country about the size of the American State of Vermont. Bounded on the north by the Lebanon mountain range, on the east and south by deserts, and on the west by a strip of land which separated it from the sea, this little country lay on the only roads which led from ancient Babylon and equally ancient Egypt. It has been united and independent for seventy-three years of the four thousand it has been known.

The name Palestine comes from early inhabitants known as Philistines, an Indo-European people who had probably come from Crete in the days of Minoan-Mycenaean culture. Another Indo-European people whose influence was strongly felt in the latter part of the second millennium B.C. were the Hittites, whose empire reached from Asia Minor down into Palestine, and whose people were still known in the country in the time of David.[1]

In addition to these two Indo-European peoples, a number of Semitic tribes were in the country, probably migrants from the Arabian peninsula. Best known are the Phoenicians, who were well established by the middle of the second millennium B.C., and who set the pattern for much of the culture of the land. Moabites, Edomites, Ammonites and Amorites also need no introduction to biblical readers. Walled cities and iron weapons and furniture testify to the progress which the culture had made by 1200 B.C.

2. HEBREW AND JEWISH TRADITION

Into this motley group of peoples came another tide of Semites, apparently the last northern migration from the Arabian peninsula. They seem to have entered the country in two waves,

one from the south and one from the land east of the Jordan
River, about the thirteenth century before our era. From the
beginning they recognized themselves as somehow different
from the Canaanites. Within two centuries they had not only
gained a foothold but had become the dominant people of the
land. The country was organized into a united little kingdom
under David, a descendant of one of the southern immigrants,
whose great grandmother had been a Moabitess and who himself married the widow of a Hittite and established a dynasty
which has become proverbial. Thus the traditional dynasty of
the Hebrew kingdom represented that strange blending of
Semitic and Indo-European blood which produced what has
always been recognized as a peculiar people. Four centuries
later, when the little kingdom had been destroyed forever,
Ezekiel said of Jerusalem, "Thy birth and thy nativity is of the
land of Canaan; thy father was an Amorite and thy mother
was a Hittite." [2]

At the death of Solomon, David's son, the little kingdom
split. The southern immigrants, while dominating the country
for seventy years, had never really united it. The northern tribes
continued a checkered existence for two hundred and fifty
more years. They finally fell victims to Assyrian attacks and the
best of their people were scattered so successfully that their
identity has been lost forever except as romantic heroes of pious
sentimentality.

The davidic remnant managed to maintain its independence
for another hundred and fifty years, when it succumbed to the
attack of Babylon, whither the best of its people were transported, although a few managed to escape southward to Alexandria in Egypt. In Mesopotamia the Judaites had opportunity
to collect and expand and copy the stories and poems and religious reflections which had already become traditional. After
fifty years some of the third generation began to straggle back
to their ancestral land, while many remained in and about
Babylon to establish another tradition. The straggling process
continued another seventy-five years. By the middle of the fifth

century B.C. the Jews succeeded in building another temple and starting the strictly endogamous existence which marked them for twenty-five centuries.

The Old Testament, which contains all that has been preserved of Hebrew literature, was over a thousand years in the making. A few parts of it seem to come from men of the northern tribes; most of it was written in the south, and all of it was edited after traces of the northerners had disappeared and Jewish ethical, sacrificial monotheism had been firmly established. This literature was collected and copied with no regard for time or place or agent of composition. Hebrew ceased to be a spoken language. In Palestine its place was taken by Aramaic, in which rabbis composed much by way of explanation of ancient writings. In Alexandria, long before the beginning of our era, Hebrew literature was translated into Greek, and was arranged and supplemented with additional Greek writings.

The thousand years which included the period of composition of the Old Testament also marked much development in the religion of Israel, in the concept of sacrifices, and in the attitude to them. When the literature was finally edited, the general assumption was that the sacrificial worship of Yahweh at a central shrine had been part of the original tradition of the people. Some of the oldest literature shows Hebrew religion to have been akin to that of all primitive peoples. Some of the latest literature preserves spiritual interpretations loftier than any the world has known. The historical study of Hebrew and Jewish religion throws much light upon the origin, the direction and the goal of spiritual culture.

One of the chief problems of this study is the unraveling of three elements, (1) a Canaanite element, itself a blend of early Semitic and Indo-European culture, (2) a later Semitic element brought in by Hebrew immigrants, and (3) the element contributed by the fusion of the peoples. In the third element the southern Judaites or Jews were dominant and finally gave the name Judaism to the remnant of the culture, producing one of the loftiest religions the world has known. This is naturally the easiest to trace; the separation of the other two has not been completed.[3]

The period from the entrance of the Hebrew immigrants to the destruction of Jerusalem by Babylon, a total of some seven centuries, was marked, according to all traditions, by controversy in religion. Clarification of the details of this controversy forms one of the problems of Old Testament scholarship upon which the last word has not been spoken. The northern Hebrews are pictured as having strong inclination to the religion of the Canaanites; the south is pictured as preserving the religion brought in at the last immigration. Neither of these pictures is wholly correct. Each affected the other and the cleavage remained until the north disappeared. The controversy was about three subjects—the recipients, the place and the method of worship.

Many traditions deal with the question of the proper recipients of cult, and pitch the controversy as between Yahweh, whose cult had been brought in by the latest immigrants, and the deities whose cult was well established when the Hebrews entered. The north was portrayed as the chief offender by adoption of or by defection to Canaanite cults. There the controversy reached its climax in the days of Ahab, who was possibly the greatest of the northern rulers. He married the daughter of a Phoenician king and erected in Samaria a temple to the Baal of Sidon,[4] although his primary devotion to Yahweh was indicated by the names of his children. His opponent was a picturesque prophet named "Yahweh (is) my god" (Elijah) who, after a successful test of divine efficiency, slew the priests of the Phoenician god.[5] After this event the north seems to have proceeded uneventfully with its mingled cults.

The south, however, was far from free of this mixture of cults. Even David, the best of kings, began his reign by establishing Phoenician influence in the country,[6] and Solomon, his glorious son, not only strengthened that influence, but increased it by having a Phoenician temple erected by Phoenician workmen as his royal chapel.[7] He also established the cult of Moabite and Ammonite deities,[8] which is described as continuing until the time of Manasseh, four centuries later.[9]

In many traditions the controversy is concerned with places of cult. In the south arose an early tendency to confine the cult to Jerusalem, which David had made his capital. The north always resisted the centralizing efforts of the davidic dynasty; even in the south, Jerusalem became the centre of cult only just before its destruction.[10] Nor was this achievement taken very seriously. In the latter part of the fifth century b.c., well after the completion of the second temple, a Jewish community at Assuan in Egypt, nearly a thousand miles up the Nile River, had a temple of Yahweh, with its complement of animal sacrifices.[11] The members of this community may well have been descended from the Jewish refugees who had fled nearly two centuries earlier. Whoever they were, it seems never to have occurred to them that Assuan was not quite as good a place as Jerusalem to erect a permanent cult place.

A serious form of the controversy was concerned with the method of worship. Prophetic tradition is confused upon this subject. One strain preserves a positive tradition that sacrifices were no part of genuine Hebrew religion; they must have been adopted from the Canaanites whom the Hebrews displaced.[12] Another strain pictures the prophets themselves as performing sacrifices as a normal function of their office.[13] By another tradition sacrifices might be tolerated but they were always to be regarded as secondary to moral requirements and might even have to be repudiated.[14] After the return from the exile they were assumed as proper to Jerusalem only. This meant that their influence was limited to those Jews who dwelt in or visited the Holy City. By the time of our Lord the vast majority of Jews had probably never seen a sacrifice as part of their own religion. After the destruction of Jerusalem, rabbinic Judaism had comparatively little difficulty in making the transition from sacrifices to study of the Torah and almsgiving as adequate surrogates for them.

In view of the persistent prophetic tradition that Hebrew religion borrowed its sacrificial elements from the peoples whom they found in the land, it becomes necessary to examine Canaanite religion as far as possible. Only an imperfect reconstruction can be made of this religion. The Old Testament records are all radically antagonistic, since they come from prophetic and priestly sources which were written long after Hebrews had gained mastery of the land and since they were designed to justify any violence which Hebrew immigration entailed.[15] A discussion of the details of this religion is manifestly out of place here, but we must note those features which may have influenced the sacrificial cult of Israel.

Our present interest in the Canaanite pantheon is only in the extent to which it has influenced Hebrew thought forms. It will not be necessary even to present by title the long list of deities whose cult was known to Palestinian soil. Best known of all the deities were the local baals or "cult lords," as, for instance, the Baal of Tyre (whose proper name was Melqart), the Baal of Sidon, the Baal of Lebanon, etc. The plural *baalim* is translated in AV as if it were a singular proper name Baal. In DV the plural form is transliterated *Baalim*. RV and JV both use the same transliteration with the definite article, *the baalim*. It would probably be closer to the original thought if the term were translated local gods.

A common Phoenician title for a deity was *adon* or *adoni* (lord, my lord). Thus we read of Adoni Shalman,[16] Adoni Reshef,[17] Adon Melqart,[18] Adon Eshmun,[19] Adoni Baal Lebanon,[20] Adon Baal Shamem[21] and Adon Baal Hamman.[22] The Hebrews rejected the title *baal* but almost immediately appropriated the title *adon* or *adoni* as proper to *Yahweh*.[23] In the course of time the title was improved by calling Yahweh the *adon* of all the earth.[24] It required only one more step to complete the process, viz., the omission of any proper name or place. Yahweh became known by the simple title *adonai*. Pious rationalization soon concluded that the reason for omission of the word Yahweh was that proper reverence might be shown to the sacred name of Israel's deity. Like all such rationalizing, this gave a satisfactory explanation not for adopting the custom, but for continuing it.

The commonest word for a place of worship in the Old Testament is *house of God* or house of Yahweh, who was thought of as actually dwelling in the place as a man dwells in a house. The same word is used of the temples of other gods than Yahweh, as of Baal,[25] of Dagon in Philistia,[26] of Rimmon in Syria [27] and of Nisroch in Assyria.[28] The same word was used by the Canaanites. Thus we read of the house of Ashtart,[29] the house of Eshmun,[30] the house of the Baal of Sidon,[31] and, in the plural, of the houses of the gods.[32]

The word *miqdash* to describe a sanctuary or holy place is very frequent in the Old Testament. The same word was used in Phoenician inscriptions with the same denotation.[33]

In most of the Canaanite inscriptions the word for altar is *mizbeach* the same as in Hebrew.[34] In the second line of the Moabite inscription,[35] however, is a statement that the king built "this bamath" to Chemosh the god of Moab. In all the translations of the text of the stone [36] *bamath* is rendered "high place" which has long been the technical term for Canaanite cult places, as a translation of the Hebrew *bamah*. This is the uniform rendering of AV, RV and JV. DV sometimes uses it but also uses the word "temple," as a proper rendering of the Latin *fanum*.

The translators of LXX were not sure of the meaning of *bamah*. They varied between "altar" and "height" and a simple transliteration of the word as *bama*, thus indicating that the term had become strictly technical [37] and had lost its etymological significance. It is linguistically akin to the Greek *bōmos*, the best-known word for "altar."

It is possible that *bamah*, like the Moabite *bamath*, connoted not the lofty location of the "high place" as much as the building erected thereon. The one Greek word by which it might have been adequately translated was *naos*, but this was reserved, by the translators of LXX, for the cult places of Yahweh, much the same as the word *church* in English is reserved for Christian places and the word *synagogue* for Jewish places. *Bamah* was originally applied to spots where Yahweh was worshiped[38] but soon became limited to cult places of Canaanite deities. There is no word in English which applies equally to all places of worship and therefore no single word which will adequately render *bamah* or *bamath*.

The best-known word for cult officer in all Canaanite worship was *kohen,* a common root in west Semitic languages and dialects. The basic concept of the word seems to be related to oracular activity of some kind. The root does not appear in verbal form in north Semitic inscriptions, but is known in · Arabic, where *kahana* means "to divine." The diviner or seer was normally connected with some sanctuary where he "inquired the will of the god" either by the simple method of interpreting chance signs and of casting lots, or by the more elaborate method of hepatoscopy which was developed to its height in Babylonia, whence the Etruscans may have carried it to Italy. It was also known in west Semitic cult where, as we shall see, it was definitely practised or just as definitely opposed.

The translation of *kohen* by *hiereus* in Greek was more accurate than the translators may have supposed. The *hiereus* was probably a diviner in the first instance.[39] Although his activities multiplied and became more complicated, he never completely abandoned his original forte of divination. The Canaanite *kohen* likewise multiplied his activities and never abandoned divination. The Hebrews apparently took the word from the Canaanites to describe their cult officers, but their radical opposition to divination robbed *kohen* of all its original significance. *Hiereus* had already been well established as a synonym and had developed its connotations similarly; it was therefore the best translation and was so continued by LXX writers.

Scattered through north Semitic inscriptions are the names of nine rites. Preservation of five of these in the Old Testament suggests that they may have been appropriated by the Hebrews and continued in the name of Yahweh, much the same as pagan

Yuletide rites attached themselves to the Christian Christmas, and pagan spring rites to the Christian Easter. The rites are as follows:

1. *'olath* is mentioned only once, in a neo-Punic inscription of the second century B.C. Its similarity to the Hebrew *'olah* is evident, but the simple mention of the name is accompanied by no further description which would identify it.

2. *kalil* is much more frequent, both by itself and as an adjective describing other rites. Despite its meaning of "perfect" or "whole," it was not wholly burnt on an altar; certain parts were specified as belonging to the worshipers.

3. *shelem* likewise is continued by Hebrew rites. It was used both along with and modified by *kalil*. This raises the question whether there were two kinds of *shelem* among the Canaanites.

4. *zevach* in the Canaanite inscriptions, as in Hebrew literature, is the best-known rite. Many writers think of it as approximating a generic word for "sacrifice," i.e., including all rites. Its use, however, is strictly limited to those rites in which only a part of the victim was burnt.

5. *minchath* was likewise taken over by the Hebrews. It denotes a rite in which the subject was not an animal, but a cereal, raw or cooked.

6. *balal* was apparently a variety of *minchath*.

7. *chazath* may come from the root of *chazah* which has to do with divination. The Hebrew *chozeh,* usually translated "seer," comes from the same root. This may have been a rite similar to, and possibly borrowed from, Babylonian hepatoscopic rites.

8. *so'ath* may have been some sort of prayer rite.

9. *shasaf* is a rite of which we know nothing.

The sacrificial pattern of the Canaanites seems to have been similar to that of the Hebrews, although not so highly developed. Some of the Hebrew prophets contended that this pattern was not brought into Canaan by the Hebrews but that it was assimilated from the peoples whom they found in the land.

The well-substantiated tradition that much of Hebrew culture came from Phoenicia makes it quite possible that the Phoenicians furnished not only the temple for Solomon, but also much of the pattern of the rites connected with that temple and its successors.

After a process of development of about six centuries, Jewish rites were finally codified about 450 B.C., after which they remained in operation for about five more centuries, or until the destruction of the temple in 70 A.D. This codification, found in the books of Leviticus and Numbers, represents the best ancient endeavour to collect, analyze and generalize religious rites. In its final form the codification contains versions of different periods; these are not conflated but are preserved separately. As a result, the same rite may be described two or three times and in two or three different ways.

The principal rites are grouped together in the first seven chapters of Leviticus, in which two sources can be distinguished. To the final redaction of these chapters is given the title "The Law of the Qorban." Qorban[40] seems to be an approach to a genuine term for a religious gift. It is limited to certain rites and refers chiefly to the subjects used in these rites. Its meaning is extended to include such votive offerings as the silver utensils used in worship.[41] The theory underlying a qorban was that, once an article had been presented for Yahweh's work, whether it was animal or vegetable or utensil, it could never be used for any other purpose. Some proper disposition must be made of it.

All religious rites are primarily doing something with something. A later addition was the saying of something, either to a deity or to the worshipers, or to both, by way of accompaniment or explanation of what was done. The "something" with which something was done was the qorban, the subject of the rite. The "something" which was done with it was the operation, or the rite proper. In the "Law of the Qorban" both animal and vegetable subjects were described, as well as the rites which constituted the disposition of them.

The rites may be classified upon the basis of the content and purpose of the operation performed. The Hebrew words describing the rites have no exact equivalents in English. Confusion in understanding these terms arises from inadequate and inconsistent translations. It will be more accurate to transliterate the terms and use them as common English words. In addition to the rites in "The Law of the Qorban" will be included those in other parts of Leviticus and in Exodus and Numbers.

The Jewish rites may be classified as follows:

I. RITES OF WORSHIP

   A. Animal rites
      1. Animal wholly eaten by devotees: *Pesach*
      2. Animal wholly burned on altar: *'olah*
      3. Animal partly burned on altar, partly eaten by worshipers: *zevach*
        (1) *Shelem* (2) *Todhah* (3) *Nedher* (4) *N'dhavah*
   B. Vegetable rites
      1. Cereal: *Minchah*
        (1) Alone
          a. Wholly burned
          b. Partly burned and partly eaten
        (2) As accompaniment of other rites
        (3) As substitute for other rites
      2. Libations, as accompaniment of other rites: *Nesek*

II. RITES OF PURIFICATION: blood rites

   A. Regular: Purification of altar by blood rite before rites of I,A.
   B. Special
      1. Elaborate blood rite: animal partly burned on altar; remainder solemnly eaten by priest in sanctuary
        (1) *Chattath* of layman
        (2) *Asham*

2. More elaborate blood rite: animal partly burned on altar; remainder burned "outside the camp"
    (1) *Chattath* of priest and of whole congregation
    (2) *Millu* bullock
3. Blood rite: animal wholly burned not on altar
    (1) *Red cow rite:* animal burned "in sight of priest"
    (2) *Yom kippurim rites:* animal burned "outside of camp"

3. THE 'OLAH

The most solemn form of worship in the Jewish cult was the 'olah, which is usually rendered "burnt offering" in AV, RV and JV, and "holocaust" in DV. The distinguishing feature of the rite was that an animal was wholly burned on an altar; no part was eaten. The animal might be an ox or a sheep or a goat or a fowl. The description of this definitely post-exilic ceremony, preserved in Lev. 1, 6:1–6 [42] and 7:8, is as follows:

The law of the 'olah. Lev. 1

2. If any of you bring a qorban to Yahweh, ye shall bring your qorban from the cattle, i.e., from the herd and from the flock.

3. If his qorban be a 'olah	10. If his qorban be	14. If the 'olah for his qorban to Yahweh be
of the herd,	of the flocks, of the sheep or of the goats for a 'olah	of the fowls,
he shall bring a male without blemish.	he shall bring a male without blemish.	he shall bring his
		qorban of turtle doves or of young pigeons.
He shall bring it for acceptance to the door of the tent of meeting before Yahweh.		
4. And he shall put his hand upon the head of the 'olah. It shall be accepted of him to make purification for him.		

5. And he shall kill the
bullock

before Yahweh.
And the priests,
Aaron's
sons, shall
bring the blood and
dash (pour) the blood
around the altar
that is by the door of
the tent of meeting.

6. And he shall
flay the 'olah and
cut it into pieces.

7. And the sons of Aaron,
the priests, shall put fire
upon the altar
and lay the wood in
order on the fire.

8. And the priests, Aaron's
sons, shall lay the parts,
head and fat,
in order on the wood.

9. Its entrails and its legs

he shall wash in water
And the priest shall
burn all on the altar

to be a 'olah
an ishsheh
a reach nichoach
to Yahweh.

11. And he shall kill it
on the side of the altar
northward
before Yahweh.
And the priests,
Aaron's
sons, shall

dash (pour) the blood
around the altar.

12. And he shall

cut it into pieces
with its head and fat

And the priest
shall lay them

in order on the wood.

13. The entrails and the
legs
he shall wash in water
And the priest shall
bring and
burn all on the altar.
It is a 'olah
an ishsheh
a reach nichoach
to Yahweh.

15. And the priest shall
bring it to the altar
and wring off its
head and
burn it on the altar.

16. And he shall pluck
away
its crop with its
feathers
and cast it
beside the altar
on the east side by the
place of the ashes.

17. And he shall
cleave it with its
wings but
shall not divide it
asunder.

And the priest
shall burn it
on the altar on the
wood.

It is a 'olah
an ishsheh
a reach nichoach
to Yahweh.

Lev. 6:1–6

This is the law of the 'olah, for the burning upon the altar
all night till the morning;
and the fire of the altar shall be burning on it.
And the priest shall don his garment of linen.
He shall cover his flesh with breeches of linen.
And he shall take up the ashes which the fire has consumed
with the 'olah on the altar.

And he shall doff the garments and don other garments.
And he shall take the ashes outside the camp to a clean place.
And the fire on the altar shall be burning; it shall not go out.
And the priest shall put wood upon it morning by morning.
And he shall arrange the 'olah on it,
and burn the fat of the shelems on it.
The fire shall burn always on the altar. It shall never go out.

Lev. 7:8

The skin of the 'olah which anybody brings shall belong to the priest.

Etymologically *'olah* means "that which goes up"; it apparently refers to the ascending smoke into which the victim was sublimated and which went up to Yahweh. Nothing in the word indicates whether the victim was wholly or only partly burned; nor does the word occur in cognate languages except in the late neo-Punic inscription to which reference was made (p. 123).

Rendition of *'olah* into Greek was one of the problems of the translators of the LXX. Any Greek rite in which an animal was completely burned was an act not of worship and adoration but of aversion and placation.[43] The Greek *karpoun* occurs twice to describe such a rite.[44] The noun *kautos* likewise occurs twice to describe the animal so burned.[45] The verb *holokautein* or *holokautoun* occurs twice.[46] The translators of LXX carefully avoided all these words to render *'olah,* but used other words from the same roots, most of them apparently invented for the purpose, thus leaving no doubt that *'olah* connoted a victim completely burned.[47]

Kalil, meaning "wholly" or "perfectly," occurs fourteen times in the Old Testament; only five of these have sacrificial reference, and each is translated by a different Greek word.[48] Once it stands by itself as an apparent equivalent of *'olah.*[49] Once it is used adjectivally to modify *'olah.*[50] Once it is a substantive linked with *'olah,* possibly as a synonym.[51] Twice it is used in connection with *minchah* in such a way as to leave no doubt of its meaning.[52] "The minchah shall be burned *kalil*; no part shall be eaten." *Kalil* stresses not how much of the animal was burned (the skin belonged to the priest); it stresses the fact that none of the sacrifice was to be eaten, whether animal or cereal.

No difficulty seems to attach to explanation of *ishsheh* as a technical term. The derivation is, to all appearances, from *ēsh*, meaning "fire"; the term would therefore designate all rites in which fire was used for sublimation of all or part of a victim into smoke which ascended to Yahweh. An apparent exception to this had been noted in Lev. 24:7-9, in which an ishsheh is said to designate the "sacred bread and frankincense which was placed on the table as a memorial and finally went to the priest." [53] If this were true, one might be tempted to accept the derivation of Lagarde,[54] that *ishsheh* stems from the root *anash*, meaning "to be friendly, social," and therefore refers to rites by which association or union with God was effected. This homiletic etymology is as unnecessary as it is strained. Josephus [55] makes plain that, in the Leviticus passage, *ishsheh* refers only to the frankincense, which was placed in a pot beside the bread of presence, and was burned on the altar when that bread was eaten by the priests in the sanctuary.

Reach (pronounced ray-ach) *nichoach* literally means "odour of rest." In Greek it is always translated *osmē euōdias*; in Latin it is always *odor suavitatis*. All the English versions render the phrase "a sweet savour." The term is used of every fire rite; the basic meaning is evidently that Yahweh is pleased with the odour of the rising smoke. The only pre-exilic use of the phrase is in Genesis,[56] where it is applied to the 'olahs which Noah offered to Yahweh after he came from the ark. When Yahweh smelled the sweet savour he immediately decided never to send another flood.

It may be seriously questioned how many people, in the days of the final compilation of the Torah, really thought of Yahweh as gratified by aromatic thrills. Physical phrases continue in use long after their meanings cease to be literal.

The only records available for study of the ceremonies of

'olahs are those in the post-exilic book Leviticus, which may have been commenced in Babylon and which was not completed until about 450 B.C. None of the compilers had ever seen a 'olah performed; for their information they were wholly dependent upon a tradition which had continued for the century and a quarter that had elapsed since the destruction of the first temple. The motif of this tradition was expressed in Psalm 137, "How shall we sing Yahweh's song in a strange land?" The worship of Yahweh could be validly performed only in the land which really belonged to him, at the place which he selected, by the people whom he had appointed, and with the meticulous ceremony which he directed.

The compilers of the Torah were plainly unacquainted with the prophetic tradition that 'olahs had not been known by Hebrews in nomadic days but had been adopted from the Canaanites. They naturally assumed that Yahweh's cult had been appointed and directed by Yahweh when he chose their ancestors as his people, and that the place of that cult had likewise been selected from the beginning.

It is characteristic of all historic religions that they either "have their day and cease to be," or that their originally simple ceremonies become symbolically interpreted. Despite the proverbial conservatism of all religion, cult gradually acquired new elements. This is more easily accomplished when the principle of symbolic interpretation is established. The cultic act becomes a unit; few of the devotees are able to address themselves to consideration of the stages of its development. They invariably rationalize it as definitely linked with the earliest form of the religion.

Western Christianity furnished abundant illustrations of this principle. The Roman Church insists that its peculiar doctrine, the papacy, must necessarily be linked with Peter. Baptists insist that immersion was definitely the primitive method of baptism and that it has always remained the only valid method of administration of the sacrament. Anglican devotees are at pains to link their system with the little known Celtic Christianity and to insist that Rome never had quite as much authority in England as people think it had. Eighteenth-century revival meetings are defended as having been linked with earliest Christianity. Any doctrine, such as that of the Trinity or the Eucharist or predestination or justification, must, if possible, be traced to St. Paul as the best-known representative of first generation Christianity.

Devout Jews of the fifth century B.C., in enduring the hardships necessary for the restoration of 'olahs in Jerusalem, were not pursuing any whim or fancy; they were seeking to establish what they considered as necessary to the very existence of their religion. Nobody knew when 'olahs were first performed, and nobody knew of a time when they were not performed. These devotees are not to be blamed for assuming that, in establishing the ceremonies of the second temple, they were restoring rites which they were sure Moses himself must have given them. Their work may well have been the first written record of ceremonies which were orally communicated for centuries, and which had continued only as parts of an unpractised tradition for nearly a century and a half. Nor are they to be blamed for supposing that some equivalent of the "tent of meeting"[57] must have existed from the beginning of Israel's conscious life as a peculiar people.

The ritual pattern of the 'olah is as follows:

I. Presentation, by the layman
  1. Selection of the animal
  2. Bringing to entrance of sanctuary
  3. Laying on of hand
  4. Killing of animal

II. Preparation, by the priest
  1. Preparation of the altar— pouring of the blood
  2. Preparation of the animal
    (1) Flaying of the animal
    (2) Dissection of the animal
  3. Preparation of fire

III. Burning of animal
  1. Laying of dissected parts on wood of fire
  2. Washing of entrails
  3. Burning of entrails

IV. Removal of ashes
  1. Donning of linen garments by priest
  2. Taking up of ashes
  3. Change of garments
  4. Carrying ashes to clean place

Upon festival occasions silver trumpets were to be blown "over the 'olah."[58] Upon certain occasions tradition recorded that "the people sang and worshipped till the end of the 'olah."[59]

The Hebrews apparently never gave attention to the method of selection of sacrificial animals. It is always specified, however, that the victim must be physically perfect. In the majority of instances a male victim was prescribed, although a female was required for some rites. Selection was limited to domestic animals.

For the 'olah the animal might be an ox or a ram or a buck. An old tradition related that the king of Moab had given his own son as a 'olah,[60] thus indicating that human victims were not unknown. The story of Abraham, preparing, with no misgivings, to offer his son Isaac as a 'olah, and being directed by Yahweh to substitute a ram,[61] seems to confirm a tradition that the idea of human sacrifice had not been shocking. The poor man who could not afford a large animal might present a fowl.

For the animal to be brought to a central sanctuary, equipped with priests and attendants and costly accessories of worship, it was assumed that there was such a place. In the post-exilic writings called "priestly" and abbreviated as P, this place is described as the portable tent of meeting which served as such a sanctuary from nomadic days until the erection of the temple by Phoenicians for Solomon.

The legendarily grand temple of Solomon had been erected between two and three centuries after the immigration of the Hebrews into Palestine. With many vicissitudes and a few repairs, it stood for four centuries, after which it was destroyed by the Babylonians. Less than fifty years before it was destroyed, a book was found in it which advocated its being the sole sanctuary of Judah and called for the destruction of all other altars in the little land. Before this drastic reform had been successfully completed, the temple was destroyed and its ministers deported. Nearly another hundred and fifty years passed before the second temple was finished and the P writings were incorporated with certain other writings to form the Torah, the first completed piece of Palestinian literature. Thus nearly eight centuries passed between the immigration of the Hebrews and the completion of the first elaborate sacrificial document. This was a period nearly twice as long as America has been known to the white man, and corresponds to the time intervening between the crusades and our own age.

In our well-documented and accurately recorded history are innumerable traditions of uncertain age and origin, which are invariably extended farther back than can be justified by any known facts. This tendency is not to be explained by wishful thinking or by deliberate falsification. It frequently comes from an honest opinion of history, however erroneous that opinion may be. It always articulates a sincere conviction that "this is older than people think it is," and that its long history warrants its permanent continuance and possibly assures its divine authorship.

The great symbol of the davidic dynasty was the Phoenician temple which was planned by the founder and built under the aegis of his son, and which became the chief cult place in the country. By the time the second temple was built, the tradition of the importance of such a place had been projected back to the earliest days of Judah as a conscious people. Yahweh must certainly have prepared the pattern and specifications of the only place where 'olahs could be offered. To the door of the tent where they met Yahweh the animals were to be brought to be burned for him. This "tent of meeting." which was pictured as having been carried about during the desert wanderings and erected every time they made camp, must have been elaborately equipped with gold, silver, and other valuable cult accessories, and must have been cared for and administered by properly constituted officers to whom an animal must be formally presented for sacrifice.

At the door of the sanctuary the worshiper was directed to place his hand upon the head of the animal to be burned. The significance of this act has been variously interpreted. It occurs here and in three other instances of the 'olah.[62] Four times it occurs with the zevach of shelems, or shelem.[63] Nine times it occurs with the chattath.[64] Once it occurs with the "ram of consecration." [65] Both hands of Aaron were to be placed upon the goat to be devoted to Azazel.[66] Moses laid his hand or hands upon Joshua to set him apart as his successor.[67] The people were directed to lay their hands upon the levites to set them apart for their office.[68] Preparatory to the stoning of a curser, the witnesses were directed to lay their hands upon his head.[69]

In the instance of the goat to be devoted to Azazel on the day of kippurim, the specific explanation of the imposition of hands is that the sins of priest and people are thereby transferred to the goat which is to be driven away into the wilderness. This is the only instance of explanation of meaning of the act and is not in connection with a sacrifice, but refers to an animal which is *not* to be sacrificed. Manifestly this explanation will not obtain in the instances of official setting apart for special service or in that of stoning the curser. It is equally inapplicable in connection with any sacrifices. He who is "in sin" cannot sacrifice; he is taboo until he is properly purified, usually by a blood rite of some kind, which removes his sins; therefore there are no sins to be transferred at the time of sacrifice.

About the only explanation which will obtain in all the instances is that, by this means, some sort of identification of subject and object was ceremonially expressed.[70] The details of the relationship of identification would depend upon specific instances. In the 'olah, which was completely burned to Yahweh, the layman who brought the animal imposed his hands as he delivered it to the priest. The ceremony of imposition of hands probably arose after men ceased offering their own 'olahs.

Despite the fact that the layman would not see the animal again, or be near it, he enacted the solemn statement, "This is my animal, I am really performing this rite."

The translation, "And it shall be accepted of him to make purification for him," differs from all the standard translations.

AV, RV, and JV render the Hebrew phrase, "And it shall be accepted for him to make atonement for him." DV translates, "And it shall be acceptable and help to its expiation." The whole problem of the basic meaning of the Hebrew word *kipper* will be discussed in Chapter XI. For reasons there presented, "purification" seems to be the nearest to the root idea; that translation is therefore followed.

If the 'olah was of an ox or a sheep or a goat, the animal was killed by the worshiper who presented it. In the more elaborate ceremonies of Ezekiel the levites were appointed to slay the victim.[71] Thus the killing was not part of the sacrifice proper; it was the last act of the preparation.

A 'olah of a fowl was much less formal. The living bird was handed to the priest, who took it to the altar, wrung its neck, plucked the feathers and removed the crop, cut the bird, but not clear through, and placed it on the fire. This was apparently a substitute for a regular 'olah.

Three different phrases are used to describe the place of killing for the three different animals. The ox was to be killed "before Yahweh." The sheep and the goat were to be killed "on the north side of the altar." The neck of the fowl was to be wrung by the priest, apparently at the altar. There seems nothing mysterious or symbolic about the place of killing. At the east side of the altar was "the place of the ashes," the repository for sacrificial offal, such as the feathers (or filth) of the fowls, etc.[72] On the south side was the gradual acclivity of unhewn stone leading toward the top of the altar.[73] On the west side was the huge laver, "between the altar and the congregation." [74] The only remaining position for slaughtering animals was on the north side.[75]

By the post-exilic sacrificial ceremonial it was assumed that, while the layman performed the preliminary part of selection, presentation and killing of the animal, the important part of the rite could be performed only by the properly appointed priest. In pre-exilic traditions no such distinction existed. 'Olahs could be offered almost anywhere, and by almost anybody.

Noah offered them when he came from the ark.[76] Abraham went, at the command of Yahweh, to offer Isaac and concluded by offering the ram provided for the purpose.[77] 'Olahs were offered by Jethro,[78] by young men sent by Moses for the purpose,[79] by Balak and Balaam,[80] by Joshua,[81] by Gideon,[82] by Manoah,[83] by Samuel,[84] by David,[85] by Solomon at the beginning of his reign [86] and at the dedication of the temple,[87] and by Elijah.[88] Naaman, after his cure from leprosy, promised to offer 'olahs to Yahweh when he returned to Syria.[89]

When the Hebrews entered Canaan they found regularly established bamoth (p. 121) provided with kohens. It is quite possible that, while almost anybody could offer a sacrifice, only the professional kohen was able to give oracles; he could be found only at his sanctuary. The prerogatives of the kohen were twofold: he only could give oracles, and he only could officiate at the sanctuary of which he was guardian. The prerogatives increased with the importance of the sanctuary. With the movement toward centralization of worship came the exclusiveness of the Jerusalem priesthood. By the time of the erection of the second temple the old bamoth, or "high places," had ceased to exist for sacrificing Jews. With the projection of the idea of the central sanctuary back into nomadic days, the exclusive priesthood was also projected; only "the tribe of Levi" could qualify.

With the rigid Hebrew opposition to hepatoscopy, the giving of oracles had passed to the prophets.[90] The kohen, or priest, was left with but one prerogative—the inherent right to minister at the sanctuary. This meant that he alone could perform sacrifices and adjudge the right of others to present them.[91] This gave rise to a gradually increasing chasm between clergy and laity. When sacrifices came to an abrupt end at the final destruction of the temple in 70 A.D., the study of the Torah, with prayer, fasting and almsgiving, were already being interpreted as surrogates. Rabbis, the chief interpreters of the Torah, inherited the sacrosanctity formerly attaching to the priests.

Immediately after the animal had been killed, the priest performed the rest of the rite. The first element was the purification of the altar. AV and RV both read "he (or they) shall sprinkle the blood round about upon the altar." JV reads "dash" instead of "sprinkle." DV reads "pour," as a translation of the Vulgate *fundere*. The Hebrew word *zaraq*, thus variously translated, occurs thirty-two times. Twenty-six of these are in connection with the cultic use of blood. In twenty-one of these instances the Greek equivalent is *proschein*, which means "pour at"[92] and therefore is properly rendered *fundere* in Latin. DV therefore seems nearest to the meaning of the original.

The blood, which was caught in a basin by the priest as it spurted from the severed arteries of the animal, was poured around the base of the altar. The altar might have incurred some taboo since the preceding 'olah. The only alteration of this ceremonial was in the story of the ratification of the b'rith (covenant?) after the proclamation of the commandments, when half of the blood of the 'olahs was poured around the altar and the other half about the people.[93] The meaning of this ceremony was apparently the cleansing of the people from taboo that they might be dedicated to Yahweh and to the keeping of his commandments.

The obvious reason for flaying the animal was for proper disposition of the skin. In Greek sacrifices the perquisite of the priest was normally the skin, usually the legs, and a fee.[94] For north Semitic customs two Punic inscriptions are preserved, one from Carthage dating near the turn of the fourth and third centuries B.C.,[95] and the other from Marseilles but apparently sent from Carthage, and dating slightly earlier.[96] In the earlier inscription the skin belonged to the person bringing the sacrifice; the priest was assigned a definite fee. In the later inscription the skin went to the priest and another part to the person bringing the sacrifice. By the levitical rule the skin, except in rites in which it was to be burnt,[97] belonged to the priest.

The skin had not only a commercial value as an article of clothing; in many early rites worshipers were clad in the skins of the animals sacrificed.[98] The development of special cultic officers doubtless gave rise to the question, "Who wears the skin?" After the hide lost its cultic significance and had become commercially important, the question took the form, "Who shall have the skin?"

The remainder of the preparation needs but passing reference. The dissection of the animal is obviously necessary to make the burning possible. The preparation of the fire was likewise an obvious process. The necessity of some sort of perpetual fire can readily be seen when we reflect upon the difficulty attending commencement of a new fire, especially in wet weather, before the days of matches.[99] It became natural that the constant burning or smouldering of the fire should be symbolically explained.

In the burning of the flesh no instruments were used such as the five-pronged fork of the Greek thusia.[100] The pieces of flesh were "laid in order" upon the wood. After this the entrails and legs were washed and placed on the fire.

The separate treatment of the entrails was not peculiar to Hebrews. In an inscription from Cos dating about 300 B.C.[101] are directions for sacrificial ceremonies, including one of the rare instances of a *kautos,* a "wholly burnt" victim. After the pig had been placed on the altar for burning, the "kings" in charge of the rite were directed: "when they have washed the entrails beside the altar, they shall burn them," or, "when they have washed the entrails, they shall burn them beside the altar."

The reason for this separate treatment of the entrails is not given. In both the Greek and Hebrew instances the reference is not to the splanchna [102] but to the *entera* or *enkoilia,* which had no oracular significance. They were plainly the most "unclean" part of the animal, actually as well as technically. Both instances refer to disposition of entrails in a wholly burnt sacrifice. In all other rites this disposition might be guided by common sense or desire; only certain portions of the animal were to be burnt on the altar. In the 'olah, in which the whole animal was to be burnt, it was well to specify that, before the entrails were burnt, they must be thoroughly washed. It is difficult to understand why the same direction applied also to the legs in the 'olah. The suggestion of both Baentsch and Bertholet, in their commentaries *in loco,* is that the feet were taboo from contact with the ground.

It was assumed that the fire would burn all night before the 'olah was completely consumed, and that it would be tended throughout the night. The ashes were to be ceremonially removed the next morning.

Directions for particular rites do not specify special garments for the officiants. It may be assumed, however, that in postexilic days the semi-regal vestments described for the consecration of Aaron [103] were expected to be worn for many, if not all, of the rites. The first part of the 'olah was apparently performed in the grand vestments. The next morning the priest was to vest in linen, especially in linen breeches, and in this attire he was to take up the ashes and put them beside the altar. Again he was to change into his "other clothing" and carry the ashes "out to a clean place."

The only other occasion upon which linen vestments were prescribed in the levitical ritual was the day of kippurim, when the high priest was directed to wear them during the chattath and the Azazel rite, after which he was to change to regular vestments.[104] Ezekiel, on the other hand, prescribed that the priests should wear flaxen vestments every time they entered the "inner court." Inasmuch as the altar of the 'olah was located in this inner court of Ezekiel's temple, this would be equivalent to a requirement to wear linen vestments throughout the rite.[105] They were to change their vestments "when they go forth into the outer court to the people." The reason assigned was that "they shall not sanctify the people with their garments." The taboo attaching to the sacrifice could be communicated by the clothing which came into contact with it.

References to specific 'olahs in pre-exilic times were all occasional. By the time of the promulgation of P they were still proper to occasions, but they had also come to constitute the climax of the regular worship of the second temple. This was probably the crystallization of a tradition connected with the first temple; the erection of any place of worship, in any religion, is invariably associated with fixed and regular cultic acts.

The study of occasions upon which a rite is performed throws much light upon the purpose of the rite. Inasmuch as fixing and promulgation of all Hebrew records were definitely post-exilic, it must always be remembered that the traditional 'olahs of early days were evaluated from the point of view of priestly recorders who were primarily not historians but religious enthusiasts.[106] We must not expect the viewpoint of the modern historian, which is less than two centuries [107] old, to have been known twenty-five centuries ago.

As the chief cultic act, a 'olah marks almost every imaginable occasion in which a friendly and happy relation between a devotee and Yahweh is present. As a preliminary to an oracle it expresses the request that Yahweh will reveal his will that the worshiper may perform it.[108] It is a natural accompaniment of a petition for Yahweh's help.[109] It is frequently the expression of a great act of thanksgiving.[110] It forms a test and proof of devotion.[111] It is a fitting climax to a solemn vow.[112] It is a natural ratification of the b'rith (covenant?) between Yahweh and Israel.[113] It is the expected method of dedication of the temple [114] and the natural climax of the consecration of a priest.[115] Inasmuch as one who is morally or ceremonially taboo is automatically disqualified for worship, a 'olah naturally follows a specific act of purification, as, e.g., from childbirth,[116] from leprosy [117] and from sex taboo.[118]

When the 'olah had become established as a regular cultic act, it was prescribed daily,[119] every morning [120] and evening,[121] with two additional each sabbath.[122] These were never to be omitted and were therefore called "the continual 'olah." [123] In addition, large 'olahs were prescribed for the great feast days, i.e., every new moon,[124] the seven-day feast of unleavened bread immediately after pesach, the feast of first fruits, the feast of trumpets and the eight-day feast of booths.

In Hebrew no technical term corresponds to *heḳatomb* in Greek, but it was generally recognized in later post-exilic days that greater value resided in 'olahs which were larger than ordinary. This was especially true of 'olahs which were associated with petition or thanksgiving. The normal 'olah was a single bullock or lamb.

Balaam's 'olah before his oracle was of seven bullocks and seven rams,[125] as was Job's 'olah.[126] The feast of trumpets called for a 'olah of one bullock, one ram and seven lambs.[127] The new moon feast and the feast of first fruits called for two bullocks, one ram and seven lambs.[128] The feast of unleavened bread called for the same large 'olah upon each of the seven days.[129] For each of the first seven days of the feast of booths a 'olah consisted of two rams, fourteen lambs and a diminishing number of bullocks, commencing with thirteen the first day, twelve the second day, and so on, down to seven the seventh day. On the eighth day the 'olah was of one bullock, one ram and seven lambs. The total of 'olah slaughters for eight days was 191.[130] Solomon was said to have inaugurated his reign with a thousand 'olahs.[131] Tradition made Hezekiah's 'olahs consist of seventy bullocks, a hundred rams and two hundred lambs.[132]

The following calendar indicates the 'olahs for each of the days of the year. The biblical references are only to those sections which specify 'olahs.

1. Daily: morning and evening. Num. 28:3–4.
   Two lambs: one in morning; one in evening.
2. Sabbath. Num. 28:10.
   Two lambs in addition to daily 'olah.
3. New moon. Num. 28:1–15.
   Two bullocks, one ram, seven lambs.
4. Unleavened bread (Nisan 15–21). Lev. 23:4–8; Num. 28:17–25.

On each of the seven days
    An ishsheh. Lev.
    Two bullocks, one ram, seven lambs. Num.

5. First fruits (feast of weeks). Lev. 23:15-20; Num. 28: 26-31.
    Fifty days after (putting sickle to corn)
    One bullock, two rams, seven lambs. Lev.
    Two bullocks, one ram, seven lambs. Num.

6. Trumpets (Tishri 1). Lev. 23:24-25. Num. 29:1-6.
    An ishsheh. Lev.
    One bullock, one ram, seven lambs. Num.

7. *Yom kippurim* (Tishri 10). Lev. 23:26-32, 16:3, 5; Num. 29:7-11.
    An ishsheh. Lev. 23.
    Two rams. Lev. 16.
    One bullock, one ram, seven lambs. Num.

8. Feast of booths (Tishri 15-22). Lev. 23:34-36, 39-44; Num. 29:12-40.
    A feast of eight days.
      An ishsheh each day. Lev.
    On the first day (Num.)
    Thirteen bullocks, two rams, fourteen lambs.
    On each succeeding day
    One less bullock, e.g., twelve on second, eleven on third, etc., down to seven on the seventh day.
    On the eighth day
    One bullock, one ram, seven lambs.
    A total of 191 'olah slaughters in eight days!

Careful distinction must be made between the historical origin of a rite or custom, and the social or other reason for continuing it. Wearing of clothes may well be traced to desire for decoration, or to sense of modesty or to need for protection. Any or all of these may have given rise to the custom; without question, all are factors in its continuance.

The same principle obtains in religious uses. The origin of

the use of the cross as a religious symbol will probably never be known. It was an accessory in early Minoan-Mycenaean cult and was well known in early Judaism.[133] Minoan-Mycenaean cult has disappeared and Judaism has forgotten its use of the sign of the cross. Nascent Christianity adopted the familiar symbol because of its connection with the death of Jesus. The original reason for the use of the cross is purely archaeological and has probably been lost forever. Of far more significance is the deeply religious reason for its continuance and elaborate development.

The same principle appears in the history of the 'olah. No data substantiate the time and manner of its origin. The "gift theory" of sacrifice is based upon the uncritical assumption that the concept of deities antedated rites addressed to them. No distinction is made between rites; all are explained as reasoned processes designed to produce certain results.[134] Advocates of the communal meal theory of the origin of all rites find difficulty in explaining the 'olah, of which worshipers ate nothing. Robertson Smith[135] classified it with the holocaust of all religions and developed an ingenious theory to explain them. Finding human victims in the early days of all religions, he concluded that all such rites must be what is called piacular. Aversion to cannibalism dictated that the victim be burned "because it was too sacred to be eaten and yet must not be left undisposed of." The bullock or ram or buck he regarded as a later substitute for the original human victim.

In attempting to speculate what *may* have been the origin of the 'olah, five facts must be remembered.

(1) The only resemblance between this Jewish rite and the Greek holocausts was that, in both instances, an animal was burned. The 'olah contrasted in every way with the dismal, eerie, gruesome, silent, aversive night rites which persisted in popular Greek religious practices and never earned the title of worship. So striking was this contrast that the LXX translators rejected any word as a translation of 'olah if it were already descriptive of a Greek holocaust.[136]

(2) Similarity to other Semitic rites is problematical. Both 'olah and kalil had their counterparts in Punic sacrifices, but differed in nature from the Jewish rite. Part of the kalil in the Punic rites belonged to the priest and part to the worshiper; [137] the victim was *not* wholly burned.

(3) While the elaborately developed ceremonial of the 'olah was post-exilic, the definitely pre-exilic tradition that Noah performed a 'olah when he came from the ark seems to voice the conviction that burning an animal completely for Yahweh as an act of thanksgiving and worship was older than anybody knew. In that tradition was the further conviction that the aroma of the burning animal was physically acceptable to Yahweh.

(4) While the 'olah was logically the most important of Jewish rites and received first mention in the levitical roster, it was chronologically probably the last rite to appear. The communal meal and the thusia seem both to have antedated the concept of deities; their origin, therefore, cannot be attributed to any form of gift theory. The 'olah seems not to have arisen until long after men took for granted that in the upper air lived intelligent, volitional powers which exercised authority over the world and over human actions.

(5) The 'olah did not reach the height of its development until after the exile, when the earlier monolatry of Israel had given place to the uncompromising monotheism of the Second Isaiah and his successors.

The origin of the 'olah may possibly be found in a Canaanite rite appropriated by immigrant Hebrews. The impetus given by Phoenician culture undoubtedly increased the importance of the rite. By the time of the destruction of Jerusalem in 587 B.C. the deuteronomic reform had already given to Jewish sacrificial thought and practice the direction to the ideal of the worship of one God in one place.

For a hundred and fifty years Jewish priestly leaders in Babylon were deprived of the opportunity of performing their sacrificial duties. At the same time they had abundant opportunity for observation of Babylonian hepatoscopic rites in which, after the liver of an animal had been carefully examined, the carcase was solemnly burnt. Hebrew religious thought had early developed radical opposition to hepatoscopy; Babylonian Jews might well be expected to continue the opposition. Some carried it to the extreme of aversion to all animal sacrifice; others tried to differentiate between objectionable and unobjectionable elements in a rite.

After Babylon fell to Persia a thin stream of Jews began to trickle back to Palestine, thus articulating the new Zionism which found expression in the 137th Psalm. Their kinsmen who remained in Babylon represented the influence of the Diaspora which led Judaism away from animal sacrifice. The returning immigrants who had never seen Hebrew sacrifices, and whose ideas of such rites were based wholly upon nostalgic contemplation of golden days of the past, finally succeeded in building another temple and making possible the restoration of the worship which seemed to be the embodiment of the glory of the davidic dynasty. Thus was set in operation the deuteronomic idea which by this time had become an inspiring ideal: the worship of one God in one place.

When the second temple was built, the accepted interpretation of every sacrificial rite was that of a qorban or gift to the deity. Hebrew tradition was well acquainted with acts of devotion in which an object was made over entirely to a deity and wholly removed from human use and touch (Chapter VII). Living devotion of this kind had become the natural obverse of the uncompromising monotheism which was now the fanatical glory of Judaism. It required little imagination to symbolize all this by giving to Yahweh the whole of a sacrificed victim and keeping none for oneself. Thus was laid the foundation of the cultic expression of complete surrender or giving of oneself to the deity.

The 'olah symbolized the loftiest in Jewish religious ideas and, in doing this, paved the way for its own disappearance. Even if Vespasian and Titus had not beleaguered Jerusalem, strong religious influences were making it increasingly probable that the 'olah would not have dribbled along as did the Greek sacrifices. 'Olahs limited to the shrine at Jerusalem became but vestigial, academic ideals to the constantly increasing Jewish population of the Diaspora. When they were finally discontinued at the destruction of the Holy City, the majority of Jews in the world had never seen one.

'Olahs had been outgrown long before they were officially discontinued. Their extravagant, clumsy, stinking character made them increasingly inappropriate as acts of worship. Fasting, prayer, almsgiving and study of the Torah had long been accepted first as adequate surrogates for them and finally as far superior to them for spiritual development. When they were discontinued they had made their permanent religious contribution of the intensification of the necessity of man's giving himself completely to the God from whom he received his being and upon whom his life depended. The rejuvenated Zionism of today does not even contemplate restoration of 'olahs as it tried to do two thousand years ago.

4. THE ZEVACH

Study of the comparative table of Hebrew and Greek sacrificial terms in the Old Testament will show references to the zevach to be little more than half as many as those to the 'olah. Despite this fact the Hebrew word *zevach* is frequently regarded as a general term for sacrifice and is invariably so translated, like the Greek *thusia*. Careful examination reveals that, also like *thusia*, the word was limited to those sacrifices in which part of a victim was burnt on an altar for a deity and the remainder eaten either by the worshipers who presented the animal or by the priests. The identity of the two rites was recognized by the Septuagint translators who rendered *zevach* by *thusia* 138 times and by one of the immediate cognates like *thuma* or *thusiasma* 24 times. Only once is the word rendered otherwise—in Amos 5:25, where *sphagion* is used.

The root of the word is found in practically every semitic language; it expressed not the simple idea of killing or slaying, but the idea of preparing an animal for eating. The word for "to kill" was *shachat*. *Zevach* probably harks back to days when meat diet was rare; if one killed an animal for food, one must have a rite of some kind with the act. Earliest rites may have been totemistic, but this supposition cannot be argued. Lowliness of early ancestry leaves no stigma of shame if later generations continue the process of spiritualization. Deliberate selection and killing of an animal for food presuppose flocks and herds from which selection may be made; one does not select a wild animal but takes whatever prey appears.

An interesting law is preserved in Leviticus 17:2–5, which must contain an early tradition despite its late form. Whoever killed an ox or a lamb or a goat (all domestic animals) in the field without offering a qorban would be guilty of bloodshed and must be "cut off from the people." [138] The use of the word *qorban* plainly comes from later days when all sacrificial rites were interpreted as gifts to Yahweh. The import of the old tradition is that eating the flesh of a domestic animal must be accompanied by a rite.

Two stories from Judah assume a supposedly well-known tradition that, in the early days of the Hebrews in Palestine, the zevach as a communal meal was already a regular religious festival. When young David wanted a good excuse to absent himself from the new moon feast of Saul, it was sufficient for him to suggest that he wished to attend the annual family zevach at his native town of Bethlehem. [139] A similar town zevach marked the occasion when Samuel anointed Saul king. [140]

Like all sacrificial rites, the zevach was much older than any special group of officials. The head of the family was the proper official in early days and, even after some sort of priesthood had arisen, prophets or kings or prominent men were considered competent to perform zevachs, or zevachs might be offered without reference to any kind of presiding officer. Jacob offered them; [141] Samuel presided over them; [142] David performed his own zevachs; [143] Solomon offered them at the dedication of the temple.[144] Jeroboam inaugurated his new sanctuaries by offering zevachs at them.[145] After his restoration from leprosy, Naaman of Syria promised to perform zevachs only for Yahweh; he had apparently performed them for other deities.[146] The Philistines offered zevachs to Dagon; [147] one tradition tells of an occasion when Hebrews joined with the Moabites in offering zevachs to the local deity of Peor.[148]

Eventually the proper minister of a zevach, as of a 'olah, was a *kohen,* which is translated *priest.*[149] A vestige of the earlier function of this individual as a minister of divination appears from a study of the shelem, which is the only form of zevach whose ritual pattern has been preserved, and which probably differed from other zevachs only in purpose or intention and not in ceremony.

The fee of the kohen is mentioned in four places.[150] In the deuteronomic code it was "the shoulder, the two cheeks and the maw." In the post-exilic codes it was "the breast and the shoulder." At first the fee was probably simply removed and kept by the priest. After the return from Babylon this process was accompanied by a ceremony called *t'rumah* when used with the shoulder and *t'nufah* when used with the breast. The former has been translated "heave offering"; the second is translated "wave offering." [151]

In both these ceremonies the portion of the animal was apparently solemnly elevated but not placed upon the altar, since it was designed not for Yahweh but for the kohen. The t'nufah may have included a motion to and fro while the part was elevated. A modern vestigial reflection of this ceremony is preserved in some Anglican churches at the taking of the collection which is not only sometimes held aloft and even waved while a choir sings an anthem, but which is placed upon the altar and homiletically construed as a gift to God when everybody knows it is to pay expenses.

The kohen seems to have been as subject to human frailty as many of his successors in other religions. The sons of Eli were remembered in the tradition as men who had their servant insert a "three-pronged fork" into the sacrificial pot and who kept for themselves all that adhered to the fork.[152]

The word *zevach* was analogous to the word *mass* as used in Catholic Christendom today to designate a certain kind of service. Different masses may be distinguished by special names, such as a *low mass* or a *solemn mass* or a *requiem mass* or a *nuptial mass,* etc. In the same way we read of a *zevach of shelems* or of a *shelem*; we read of a *zevach of todhah* or of a *todhah;* we find the expression *zevach of todhah of shelems.* Any ishsheh, a zevach or a 'olah, could be offered as a vow or a gift. A zevach so offered was a shelem, sometimes called zevach of shelem for a vow (or gift) or simply vow or gift. We might translate this as a "votive zevach" or "votive 'olah," or as a "gift zevach" (or 'olah).[153] In all these zevachs the ritual pattern was the same. Differences were only in the place or time allowed for eating the part belonging to the worshiper.

Even the pesach is twice called a zevach.[154] This would be surprising to those who expect the writers of the Old Testament to hew closely to logical and etymological and philological rules; none of the pesach was burned on an altar.

A late post-exilic tradition [155] gives a curious and illuminating note upon a pesach kept by Josiah who is described as having given the people 30,000 lambs and kids for the feast and 2,600 oxen to the priests for the same purpose. This feast was kept not at the homes but at the central sanctuary in Jerusalem and seems to have been a sort of "solemn high pesach." The levites killed the animals, "removed the 'olahs" and gave the remainder to the people who roasted the pesach while the priests offered the 'olahs and the fat. Apparently the chronicler is trying to note that, in keeping the pesach, the people observed the dietary prohibition of eating fat and that therefore the fat was offered with the 'olahs. This marks an unusual exception to both 'olah and pesach and makes of them both a zevach. None of a 'olah animal was eaten; none of a pesach animal was burnt upon an altar.

A tradition like this is never carved out of the whole cloth; it must have developed from some event recognized as unusual. Such a tradition may well have been known to the writer of the account in Exodus; he may well have applied the word *zevach* to describe a pesach. Irregularity in ritual and ceremonial performance and in diction should not be surprising, especially in days of the distant past when compulsory uniformity had not been devised. Even after a few centuries of attempted compulsory regularity, ritual and literary oddities are to be found almost anywhere and at any time.

The root of the Hebrew word *shelem* means "peace." "Peace be to thee," was the usual form of greeting between Semitic friends and is the equivalent of our "good evening," or, "It is good to see you." [156] The origin of the greeting can easily be imagined. To man in the morning of civilization, as to the animals to which he was so akin, the appearance of a stranger was the sign of a potential enemy. The exchange of the *shalom,* as of *chaire* among Greeks or *ave* among Latins, was plainly equivalent to "You can trust me; I shall not harm you." It was an easy step to conventionalization of these phrases into standard friendly greetings. The very pronouncement of the phrase indicated that the persons were friendly. It is not surprising, therefore, that one of the normal acts of Canaanite worship was called a *shelem* or a *shelem kalil.*[157] The primary supposition of such an act was that the worshiper was on friendly terms with the deity. The shelem did not create the terms; it assumed them as already existent.

The same word appears in Hebrew to describe a zevach offered as a simple act of worship not as formal or as solemn as a 'olah but, like the 'olah, implying friendly relations between the devotee and Yahweh. The usual phrase is "zevach of shelems."

As the meaning of *zevach* was so clear that the LXX translators had no difficulty in rendering it into Greek, so the meaning of *shelem,* as a particular kind of zevach, was equally clear. We are already familiar with *sōtērion* as a particular kind of thusia in Greek.[158] Sixty-four times this word, either alone or in combination with other words, renders the Hebrew word *shelem* or its plural *shelamim*.[159] Twelve times the Hebrew is translated as literally as possible by *eirenikon,* the neuter of the Greek adjective for *peaceful.*[160] Twice it is rendered by the plural of *teleion,* which means "a sumptuous banquet." [161]

The significance of the todhah as a kind of zevach is not always realized. The word occurs only thirty-one times [162] in the Old Testament and invariably describes something which must be given to Yahweh and which may be given to him only. As Israel passed from the feeble monolatry of early days to rigid Jewish monotheism, the connotation of *todhah* undoubtedly extended to include a spiritual attitude as well as physical acts. The difficulty of translating the word arose from the fact that, by the time translations were necessary, Judaism had not only become rigidly monotheistic, but it was averse to the notion that it had ever been anything else. Wherever monotheism has been accepted, at least in the western world, it has been the gift of Judaism or of her equally exclusive daughter Christianity. The languages of other peoples had no equivalent for the *todhah* of Judaism. It is not surprising that eight Greek words and phrases, thirteen Latin words and phrases and fifteen English words and phrases have been utilized to render the idea denoted by *todhah.*

The todhah was definitely an act of worship.[163] In every instance it expressed an act or attitude addressed solely to Yahweh and always marked by gladness and song.[164] As an act of worship it was clearly a form of zevach.[165] The chief difference between it and other zevachs seems to have been that the flesh of the todhah must be eaten the same day that Yahweh's portion was offered. None might remain until the next day.[166]

The word *todhah* means "thanksgiving," which played an increasingly important role in the worship of Judaism [167] and in the achaean, the hellenic and the hellenistic cults on both the eastern and western coasts of the Aegean Sea.[168] It is scarcely known in any other semitic religion or in the native religion of the Latins. It is significant that, in the two religions which gave form to the worship, thinking and living of early Christianity, the very phrase *sacrifice of thanksgiving* should have been so prominent. It is significant also that, in all three religions, the same phrase describes both a cultic act and a spiritual attitude.

The ritual pattern for zevachs is found in Lev. 3 and 7:11–21, with a note in Num. 10:10. The texts are as follows:

Lev. 3:1–5	Lev. 3:6–11	Lev. 3:12–16
If his qorban be a zevach of shelem	If his qorban be for a zevach of shelem unto Yahweh	If his qorban be
if he offer of the herd he shall offer it without blemish before Yahweh.	of the flock he shall offer it without blemish.	a goat he shall offer it before Yahweh.
And he shall lay his hand upon the head of his qorban and kill it at the door of	And he shall lay his hand upon the head of his qorban and kill it in front of	And he shall lay his hand upon the head of it and kill it in front of
the tent of meeting.	the tent of meeting.	the tent of meeting.
And Aaron's sons, the priests, shall smear the blood around upon the altar.	And Aaron's sons shall smear the blood around upon the altar.	And Aaron's sons shall smear the blood around upon the altar.
And he shall offer of the zevach of shelem an ishsheh to Yahweh;	And he shall offer of the zevach of shelem an ishsheh to Yahweh; its fat and the whole rump he shall remove close to the backbone;	And he shall offer of it an ishsheh to Yahweh;
the fat covering the entrails and all the fat which is on the entrails and the two kidneys and the fat on them which is by the flanks and the yothereth hakkavedh with the kidneys he shall remove.	the fat covering the entrails and all the fat which is on the entrails and the two kidneys and the fat on them which is by the flanks and the yothereth hakkavedh with the kidneys he shall remove.	the fat covering the entrails and all the fat which is on the entrails and the two kidneys and the fat on them which is by the flanks and the yothereth hakkavedh with the kidneys he shall remove.

Lev. 3:1−5	Lev. 3:6−11	Lev. 3:12−16
And the sons of Aaron shall burn it on the altar upon the 'olah which is on the wood on the fire	And the priest shall burn it on the altar	And the priest shall burn it on the altar
	food	food
an ishsheh a reach nichoach	an ishsheh a reach nichoach	an ishsheh a reach nichoach all the fat
for Yahweh.	for Yahweh.	for Yahweh.

An eternal statute for your generations in all your dwellings: ye shall eat no fat or blood.

Lev. 7:11−21

This is the law of the zevach of shelems which he shall offer to Yahweh.

If he offer it for todhah, he shall offer, with the zevach of todhah, unleavened cakes mixed with oil, and unleavened wafers smeared with oil, and cakes of soleth mixed with oil, fried.

Besides the cakes he shall offer for his qorban leavened bread with the zevach of todhah of shelems.

And the flesh of the zevach of shelems for todhah shall be eaten the same day that it is offered; he shall not leave any of it until morning.

If the zevach of his qorban be a nedher or a n'dhavah it shall be eaten the same day that he offers the zevach; and on the morrow also the remainder of it shall be eaten; but the remainder of the flesh of the zevach on the third day shall be burnt with fire.

If any of the flesh of the zevach of shelems be eaten at all on the third day, it shall not be accepted; neither shall it be credited to him that offered it; it shall be an abomination and the one who eats of it shall bear his taint. Flesh that touches any unclean thing shall not be eaten; it shall be burnt with fire.

All that be clean shall eat of the flesh. But the one who, when he is unclean, eats of the flesh of the zevach of shelems that have to do with Yahweh, that one shall be cut off from his people. The one who shall touch any unclean thing of man or of unclean beast and eat of the flesh of the zevach of shelems that have to do with Yahweh, that one shall be cut off from his people.

Numbers 10:10

On a day of gladness, on solemn days and at beginnings of months, ye shall blow with trumpets over your 'olahs and over the zevachs of your shelems, that they may be to you for a memorial before your God.

Analysis of this pattern shows a rite resembling the Greek thusia.

I. Preparation
  1. Of worshipers: remote: sanctification
  2. Of the victim: by the worshiper
    (1) Selection
    (2) Presentation
    (3) Laying on of hand
    (4) Killing
  3. Of the altar: by the priest Smearing with blood of victim
II. The zevach proper
  1. Dissection of sacrificial parts
  2. Burning on an altar with minchah of unleavened bread
III. The Banquet

The additional note of Numbers, directing trumpets to be blown over the zevach on "days of gladness," is evidently by way of differentiating between what today would be called "low masses" and "high masses."

In all ancient religions and in many modern ones, any rite demanded preparation. This may have descended from primitive notions of taboo: lowliness of ancestry leaves no stigma of shame if later generations continue the process of spiritualization. The place, the victim and the agents of the rite must be "proper" for the occasion. Directions for preparation of participants in a zevach are prescribed in Lev. 7:19–21 and are specified in a much older verse of 1 Samuel.[169] All who proposed to take part must be clean, both from transmitted taboo, and from contact with an "unclean thing" or with flesh which had touched a tainted thing. One who dared to participate in worship after touching an "unclean thing" was to be "cut off from the people." It is not easy for modern protestants to appreciate the grave importance attaching to the requirement of ceremonial purity as indispensable to worship.

Failure to understand this importance has given rise to much homiletical misinterpretation of the parable of the "good Samaritan." The priest and the levite, as professional conductors of worship, must be meticulous in maintenance of ceremonial purity. To all appearance the unconscious victim of the highwayman was dead; contact with a corpse would render one taboo for a week.[170] The Samaritan had no need to observe such precautions. To a Jew he was unclean by nature; he could therefore receive no further taint from touching a corpse. Moreover, he would transmit his taint to anyone whom he touched.[171]

Holiness or sanctification was a natural quality of Yahweh. His worshipers, before they could approach him, must therefore be certain that they had no taint or taboo, whether moral or ceremonial.[172] A number of places in the Old Testament prescribe specific purifications as necessary preliminaries to worship.[173] The reference in Samuel implies a general or conventional requirement for purification before worship. The ceremonial described in Leviticus is for the actual offering of the zevach; the sanctification was, by its very nature, not immediate but remote.

Normally the victim was a ram or a bullock or an ox, male or female, depending upon the purpose of the shelem. As with the 'olah (p. 131), the animal must be physically sound. This soundness would naturally include freedom from taboo or ceremonial uncleanness. References to extra large shelems indicate that, as with the 'olah, the sacrifice was always as large as possible. At the setting up of the tent of meeting each of the princes was said to have brought two oxen, five rams, five he-goats and five yearling lambs.[174] At the dedication of Solomon's temple the shelem was said to consist of 22,000 oxen and 120,000 sheep.[175]

The presentation, laying on of the hand and killing of the victim and the ritual preparation of the altar were the same as with the 'olah.

Because the major part of the animal was to be eaten at the banquet, the dissection of the parts to be burned on the altar was carefully carried out. Four parts were especially to be burned for Yahweh: the rump, the fat, the kidneys and the little upper lobe of the liver called the *yothereth hakkavedh*, and translated usually as "the caul above the liver." The burning of the rump and the fat is reminiscent of burning pieces of the thigh wrapped in fat at the Greek thusia (p. 105). So similar are the two ceremonies that one cannot help suggesting that both may be descended from a common ancestor. The common ceremony might well have been part of the later Minoan-Mycenaean religion. Its development into the thusia on the soil of Greece and Asia Minor is natural. It might have been brought to Palestine by the little known Philistines who left no written records but who undoubtedly made permanent impression upon Canaanite civilization. They are remembered in Hebrew tradition as offering zevachs or thusias to their deity Dagon.[176]

Rabbinic discussion upon the reason for selection of the yothereth hakkavedh as particularly to be burnt have been of little avail. One of the real contributions of the late Morris Jastrow to the study of religion was the examination of this particular piece of the liver which was regularly used in Babylonian divination rites. With access to many divination tablets at the Museum of the University of Pennsylvania, Jastrow indicated his genius by purchasing sheep livers at a butcher shop and, by laying the lobus caudatus upon the diagram, observing the different markings which were points of departure for divination instructions. The whole liver was not used for this, but only the finger-shaped lobe called *yothereth hakkavedh,* to which eleven references are found in the Pentateuch.[177] The size, the shape, the configurations and the bends of this upper lobe were all of divinatory significance.

The official antagonism of Hebrew religion to divination is well known. The eleven references noted are all post-exilic; their writers had probably seen hundreds of instances of the use of the lobus caudatus in Babylonian rites. They probably discovered that Jews differed little from other religionists in tendency to superstition and in adoption of bizarre methods of portending the future. In their enthusiastic opposition to all things Babylonian and to divination in particular, they rigidly ordered the burning of the one piece of the sheep used for the purpose, thereby supposedly making it impossible for that particular form of superstition to be practised by godly Jews. The necessity for some such provision arose from the fact that, in the Hebrew tradition, 'olahs [178] and shelems [179] were wont to be performed when consulting an oracle.

The banquet is mentioned many times as the culmination of the zevach.[180] The flesh of the animal was boiled, apparently by the priests, and eaten at the place of worship by priests and people.[181] The flesh of the todhah must be eaten the same day that Yahweh's portion was burnt for him. The flesh of other shelems might be eaten on the same day or on the next day, but any remainder must be burnt the third day.[182] The details of the zevach banquet are never described as are the banquets of the Greek thusias, and much is left to the imagination. References to "making merry" after the feast are strongly reminiscent of the conclusion of the Greek thusias.[183]

References to regular zevachs are not nearly as frequent or as specific as those to regular 'olahs (p. 141 f.). Annual zevachs were recognized as part of the old tradition.[184] Solomon's devotion was expressed by his offering zevachs three times each year.[185] There is only one reference to a regular morning zevach.[186]

5. OUTGROWING AND SUBLIMATION OF 'OLAHS AND ZEVACHS

The incorporation and development of 'olahs and zevachs as part of Hebrew worship had marked opposition from the early days.[187] With the development of Jewish spiritual life the effectiveness of animal sacrifices steadily decreased for three reasons.

(1) Every physical rite is constantly attended by the danger of formalism, which is the performance of a rite or ceremony as an end in itself instead of as a physical means to spiritual apprehension. This was the ancient charge of the prophets and the later charge of the writers of Judaism who regarded sacrifices without proper moral preparation and accompaniment as instruments of evil [188] which can only result in stirring Yahweh to anger instead of being acts of worship.[189] Repentance,[190] obedience to Yahweh's will,[191] kindness,[192] justice,[193] righteous-

ness [194] and the knowledge of God [195] were of even greater importance than the sacrifices.

(2) To man's sense of the fit and the beautiful, which were inevitable results of spiritual development, the clumsiness and raucousness and offensiveness of sacrifices could not help becoming increasingly inappropriate. The necessity of keeping something of a stockyard as almost part of the temple equipment gave rise to the unlovely and filthy accompaniment which, at best, could not be depended upon to stimulate spiritual motions.

(3) The growing realization that God is not physical and therefore has no need of steaks broiled in fat and of mutton and goat's flesh, made the innumerable presentations of quantities of food increasingly absurd as well as extravagantly futile. God's strength was not like man's. It needed no constant replenishing with food.

By the time of our Lord the vast majority of Jews had been weaned from worship with burning animal flesh. It is not always realized that, as was indicated in the study of the 'olah, sacrifices were well outgrown before the final destruction of the temple. They had, however, made a permanent contribution to the spiritual development of which Judaism and Christianity have been such potent agents.

At the dawn of man's civilization the annual pesach, as in every rite in which the victim was wholly eaten, was somehow identified with the divine power which man was striving to understand and to appropriate. To eat that food and make its strength one's own was to have the first lesson in absolute dependence of man upon the God whom he worshiped. Later the rite was continued as a fitting memorial of the delivery from Egypt which made Israel's being and development possible. The rite is still continued by pious Jews, and the burden of the accompanying prayers is thankfulness that man can lean so heavily upon God.

When the 'olah disappeared entirely from religious economy, it had accomplished its work. Man had learned the first lesson of one more great factor of religion: that recognition of God's power must be accompanied by complete surrender of the worshiper to God. There is no such thing as giving oneself to God with reservations. What we can now give is not a whole bullock or ram, but the selves which were symbolically identified with the animal by the laying of the hand.[196] The Greeks never had that lesson; it is a contribution of Judaism to western religious knowledge.

The zevach or thusia, the direct descendant of the common meal which gave rise to sacrifice, also made its contribution to spiritual knowledge. Dependence upon God's power and complete devotion of oneself to God are not sufficient. From contemplation of these noble ideals man must return to the toiling and moiling which comprise so much of life.

Thanksgiving to God forms the contribution of the zevach. The Greek thusia had already begun to stress the idea.[197] It remained for the zevach to enlarge and extend and spiritualize it. When we consider the close etymological and logical and factual connection between remembering and thinking and thanking, we can understand that constant thanksgiving to God represents the highest possible development of religion. To be thankful to one for a gift is not merely to speak some formal words. The words are well and fitly spoken; they must entail constant "bearing in mind" of the fact of the gift. None but a churl would receive a gift, say, "Thank you," and then abuse or forget the giver. Genuine thanksgiving has no end. It might be thought of as constant co-operation with the giver in the tiniest and in the greatest acts of life. To be thankful is never to forget the donor.

'Olahs and zevachs, by reason of their frequent repetition, had never been identified with any historical occasion as had the pesach, and, when they were outgrown, they disappeared. When they came to an end, it was not by act of negligence. They had already given place to fasting, prayer, almsgiving and study of the Torah, the study of God's ways with man. These could never be replaced or outgrown. From time to time they might be symbolized in changing manner, but subjection of the physical to the spiritual, constant communication with God, care for those who are less fortunate than oneself, and deepening and widening one's knowledge of God will ever remain necessary to man's being as man.

There is no word to take the place of sacrifice in the vocabulary of religion. Yahweh and Zeus and Dagon have long since ceased to have meaning for the religious man. The simple word *God* has replaced them all and has meaning greater than any of them or than all of them combined. Thusias and zevachs and 'olahs have likewise passed into discard. The simple word *sacrifice* has replaced them and has meaning greater than any of them or than all of them combined. As no man has yet fathomed or understood the full meaning of God, so none has yet exhausted the connotation of sacrifice. We may catch a glimpse of what the Jewish Psalmist meant when he sang,

God's zevach is a troubled spirit.[198]

Chapter XI. JEWISH RITES (Continued)

One of the most frequently mentioned and least frequently quoted rites of the Old Testament was the minchah. The lack of understanding of the rite is illustrated by the fact that AV ordinarily translates it as *meat offering* and DV usually renders it as *oblation of sacrifice* or some similar term. JV has come nearer to the meaning of the term by using *meal offering*.

The simplest and oldest use of the word was to denote a present, either of a generous gift to an inferior or of a tribute to a superior. So it is used at least once in a late Phoenician inscription and many times in the Old Testament.[1] Its use as an act of worship assumed a donor, a gift and a recipient. To bring a minchah to Yahweh [2] indicated recognition of his supremacy [3] and was sometimes a general expression for "to worship." [4] To fail or neglect to bring minchahs was a sure sign of religious degeneracy.[5] Yahweh was represented as smelling,[6] taking,[7] and accepting [8] or rejecting [9] minchahs brought to him.

In earlier traditions the word *minchah* was a general term for animal or vegetable sacrifice.[10] In later writings it was confined to vegetable offerings, being used once to describe the "first fruits" offering of green ears of corn dried by the fire.[11] Its especial use was for an offering composed of fine wheat flour called soleth, to which olive oil, salt and frankincense were added. The sources for study of the rite are chiefly in Leviticus and Numbers. The two principal ones are here presented. The first source is placed in two columns in order to facilitate comparison of the ritual pattern of the uncooked minchah with that of the cooked minchah.

Sources for study of the minchah

Lev. 2:4–11

> If you bring a qorban of a minchah baked in an oven, it shall be unleavened cakes mixed with oil or unleavened wafers smeared with oil. If your qorban be a minchah in a pan, it shall be of unleavened soleth mixed with oil. You shall part it in pieces and pour oil upon it. It is a minchah.

Lev. 2:1–3	Lev. 2:4–11	Lev. 6:14–18
	If your qorban be a minchah in a frying pan, it shall be of soleth with oil. You shall bring the minchah made of these things to Yahweh.	
If any one brings a minchah		
to Yahweh his qorban shall be of soleth. He shall pour oil upon it, and put frankincense upon it. He shall bring it to And Aaron's sons, the priests,		This is the law of the minchah.
	When it is presented to the priest he shall bring it to the altar.	Aaron's sons shall offer it before Yahweh before the altar.
And he shall take from it his handful of the flour and of the oil and all of its frankincense	And the priest shall take from the minchah	And he shall take from it his handful of the flour and of the oil and all the frankincense which is on the minchah
and he shall burn its azkarah on the altar an ishsheh a reach nichoach to Yahweh. The remainder of the minchah	its azkarah; he shall burn it on the altar an ishsheh a reach nichoach to Yahweh. The remainder of the minchah	and shall burn its azkarah on the altar an ishsheh to Yahweh. The remainder of it

Lev. 2:1–3	Lev. 2:4–11	Lev. 6:14–18
is Aaron's and his sons'.	is Aaron's and his sons'.	Aaron and his sons shall eat. All the males of the sons of Aaron shall eat of it. With unleavened bread in the holy place in the court of the tent of meeting shall it be eaten.
It is most holy	It is most holy	It is most holy as the chattath and the asham. It shall be a statute forever
of the ishshehs.	of the ishshehs.	concerning the ishshehs.
		Every one who touches them is holy.
	No minchah which you shall bring to Yahweh shall be made with leaven.	It shall not be baked with leaven.
	You shall burn no leaven or any honey in any ishsheh of Yahweh.	I have given it as their part of ishshehs.

Lev. 6:23. Every minchah for a priest shall be wholly burnt; it shall not be eaten.

Ritual pattern of the minchah

I. Presentation by layman to priest
   1. Pouring oil on it
   2. Placing frankincense upon it
   3. Presentation to priest
II. The "offering"
   1. The priest takes a handful of uncooked flour and oil or
            a piece ("memorial") of cooked cake
          takes all the frankincense
   2. Burns on the altar: an ishsheh, a reach nichoach
III. Eating the remainder
   The priest who offers the minchah solemnly eats the remainder in
   the holy place.

Soleth, the basic constituent of a minchah, was the finest wheat flour obtainable. It was not used for ordinary purposes except by those who were known for luxurious living;[12] it was reserved for honoured guests.[13] It was naturally the flour demanded for a minchah to Yahweh and for all religious purposes,[14] and must be unleavened.[15]

A minchah might be offered alone,[16] or it might accompany a 'olah or a zevach.[17] It might be cooked or uncooked. If cooked, it might be prepared in one of three ways, baked in an oven, or baked on a flat plate over an open fire, or fried. These differences altered details of the rite but the ritual pattern was basically the same, and very simple.

For an uncooked minchah[18] the unleavened soleth was salted; oil[19] was poured upon it and grains of frankincense laid upon it.[20] If it was baked in an oven, the salted soleth was made into cakes or wafers upon which oil was smeared. If it was baked on a flat plate over an open fire, the soleth was mixed with oil and apparently baked in a single piece. After baking, it was broken into small portions upon which oil was poured. If it was fried it was apparently not broken before presentation.

After pouring the oil upon the minchah and placing some frankincense upon it, the worshiper solemnly presented it to the priest. If it was treated as a 'olah, or if it accompanied a 'olah,[21] the priest had only to place the minchah upon the fire. Otherwise, the minchah was treated as a zevach.[22] The priest removed all the frankincense and a handful of the uncooked soleth or a piece of the cooked cake. This azkarah,[23] as it was called, was then burnt upon the altar as an ishsheh, a reach nichoach. The remainder was solemnly eaten by the priest in a holy place. The meaning of the word azkarah has occasioned some difficulty.

Three Hebrew words from the same root are translated in the Septuagint by four words from the same Greek root. The Hebrew words are zeker, zikkaron and azkarah. The four Greek words are anamnēsis, mneia, mnēmē and mnēmosunon. All are indiscriminately rendered into English by memorial, *memory* and *remembrance*. Confusion of these terms by Greek and English translators has made understanding of the Hebrew words difficult.

Zeker [24] occurs twenty-three times and invariably describes a sign, a trace, a name, a remembrance, a vestige, a proof of something which has itself disappeared. We should use *zeker* in such a statement as, "Signs of an ancient civilization were found there." It is unfortunate that the word *memorial* was ever used to render the word.

Shades of distinction between words sometimes disappear and the words begin to become synonymous. By this tendency *zikkaron*,[25] in later writings, was used five times as practically synonymous with *zeker*. Once it is used as "proof of right of participation"; Sanballat and his associates are warned away as having no "part or right or *zikkaron*" in Jerusalem. The *zikkaron* would have been some past connection with the city. The word is ordinarily used to describe a planned or erected commemoration of an event. The meaning approximates, but does not coincide with the English *memorial*.

One curious use is that of the minchah of the suspicious husband. A husband who suspected his wife's fidelity was permitted to take her to a priest for examination. He provided a "minchah of jealousy" made of barley meal without oil or frankincense. While holding this in her hand, after drinking a concoction made of holy water and floor sweepings, the woman was bidden to confess whether she was guilty or innocent of acts substantiating her husband's suspicion. The minchah was called the "minchah of zikkaron"; its purpose seems to have been to stimulate the woman's memory lest she forget, and to stimulate her conscience lest she lie. *Zikkaron,* in this instance, was rather a reminder than a commemoration; there is no English word which would accurately translate it. With the exception of DV the English translations render the word by *memorial*. DV renders it once by *oblation searching out adultery,* and once by *sacrifice of remembrance.*

The word *azkarah* is used to describe the frankincense of the "bread of presence," [26] which was a sort of zevach-minchah, reserved for a week after being offered, instead of being eaten and burnt immediately. All other occurrences of the word were in connection with the minchah.[27] *Azkarah*, which must be transliterated because of the lack of a suitable word to translate it, was the technical term for that part of the minchah which was burnt, as it was for the frankincense of the bread of presence. This deliberate rejection of *zeker* and *zikkaron* in favour of a word used in no other connection may have been accidental, but it was more likely because neither of the rejected words expressed the idea.

The use of *azkarah* to describe the portion of the minchah which was burnt has occasioned much speculation issuing in the suggestion that the purpose of the rite was either to make the worshiper remember Yahweh, or to make Yahweh remember the worshiper. Neither of these suggestions is very profound. A deity which needed constant reminders to prevent his forgetting would not be much of a deity. A worshiper would hardly need reminding, in the midst of his worship, that he was worshiping. The function of the name *azkarah* was much deeper than either of these.

The primary meaning of the root of *azkarah*, as of the root of the Greek words which are in the same category, is not "to remember," but it is "to focus attention upon" or "to put the mind upon." The causative stem would be "to direct attention to," "to call attention to," "to fix attention upon." It would imply direction of thought upon a past event or upon a present fact or upon a basic truth. *Azkarah*, the substantive of this stem, would be "that which fixes the mind upon."

Descended from vegetable sacrifices, a minchah must accompany every ishsheh [28] and could be an ishsheh in its own right. The original purpose of the ishsheh was to carry flesh food to the deity which assimilated it not by digestion, but by olfaction; the ishsheh was a reach nichoach. While the minchah was regarded as a genuine ishsheh, it was not an animal ishsheh. It was quite possible that need was felt to establish identification between the two. This could be expressed neither by *zeker* (memento) nor by *zikkaron* (commemoration). It would be exactly expressed by *azkarah*.

The use of this substantive was exclusively sacrificial and was confined to that part of the minchah which belonged to Yahweh and was treated exactly the same as a portion of the zevach and all of the 'olah which likewise belonged to Yahweh. Therefore it is specified that the azkarah is an ishsheh, a reach nichoach.[29] It can be said to furnish the point of contact between the minchah and the 'olah or the zevach. No Greek or Latin or English word renders this idea. *Memorial* will serve probably better than any other word if it is sharply distinguished from *memento* or *remembrance* or even *commemoration*.

Except when the minchah was offered as accompaniment of, or substitute for a 'olah, the remainder was solemnly eaten with unleavened bread [30] by the priests at or near the altar.[31] In the post-exilic period the minchah was considered as a regular daily rite. Mention is made of the "morning minchah" [32] and of the "evening minchah," [33] usually translated as the "evening sacrifice" or "evening oblation." It is not always remembered that this sacrifice of cakes was essential to every 'olah and zevach and could even be offered without either 'olah or zevach.

2. FIRST FRUITS AND LIBATIONS

One of the best known of the uncooked minchahs was that prescribed at harvest time. No part of newly ripe grain was to be eaten in Israel [34] until ripened ears had been beaten, the grain dried [35] and brought to a sanctuary [36] to be presented to the priests for a t'nufah [37] (p. 148). On the dried corn was placed oil and frankincense to be burned, with a portion of the corn, as an azkarah.[38] The remainder of the corn became the fee of the priests, who were to offer a 'olah of two bullocks, a ram and seven lambs, with their appropriate cooked minchahs.[39] This occasion marked the annual "feast of first-fruits,"[40] one of

the three annual feasts prescribed by old tradition.[41] An Elisha
story tells of a stranger who brought to the prophet a first fruit
offering of twenty barley loaves and some full ears of corn,
which were immediately distributed by the prophet to the
people.[42]

With each 'olah and zevach, as with each Greek thusia, a
libation of wine was poured upon the burning animal or portion of animal. The amount of wine prescribed was equal to the
oil of the accompanying minchah, a quarter hin (1.6 American
quarts) per lamb,[43] a third of a hin (about 2 quarts) per ram,[44]
and a half hin (about 3.2 quarts) per bullock.[45]

3. PURIFICATIONS FOR WORSHIP

The most complicated rites in the Old Testament were not sacrifices or acts of worship; they were concerned with removal of
disqualifications for worship and were therefore indispensable
as preparation for worship. In some instances a short time intervened between this preparation and the actual worship; in other
instances the worship followed the preparation almost immediately. These preparation rites were probably descended from
primitive rites for purification and removal of taboo, which
might be ceremonial or moral.

Judaism, unlike many modern religions, was not an indis-
criminate collection of more-or-less like-minded people; it was
the activity of a group whose solidarity depended upon its cult.
The importance of the individual arose from the fact that he
was a member of the house of Israel and therefore a contributor
to the status of that house. The centre of the life of the group
was the sanctuary; through this Yahweh visited his people and
the people approached Yahweh. He who incurred taboo or
uncleanness of any kind tainted the whole group; and the sanctuary was the focus of the taint. "The man who is unclean and
does not purify himself shall be cut off from the group because
he defiled the sanctuary of Yahweh." [46] As the altar shared the
defilement of him who incurred uncleanness, so he who had

incurred the uncleanness must provide for the purification of
the altar. He could then be permitted to share in the worship,
to offer a 'olah or a zevach.

Some defilements were irremovable and must be punished by
permanent excommunication or execution. Such were neglect
of purification,[47] eating blood,[48] killing a sacrificial animal without offering sacrifice,[49] eating Yahweh's part of a zevach,[50]
offering a 'olah or zevach to other gods than Yahweh,[51]
"Molech" worship,[52] failure to keep pesach if able to do so,[53]
neglect of parents,[54] adultery and other sex irregularities,[55] and
"presumptuous sins." [56] The presence of any who had incurred
one of these taboos gave permanent defilement to the group
and therefore invalidated its worship. How meticulously these
prescriptions were kept is a study in itself.

Some are apt to consider most, if not all, of these as illustrations of extreme bigotry which has been fortunately antiquated
if not wholly outmoded. A study of them, however, reveals
deep insight into the basic principles of religion proceeding
from the intimate relation between the physical and the spiritual. As man increases his control of physical causes and effects,
he finds it increasingly easier to neglect spiritual causes and
effects. He is apt to lose sight of the reality of the eternal or to
forget that his grasp of the eternal depends upon his right use
of the temporal, and that wrong use of the temporal automatically cuts one off from contact with the eternal. Ancient Jews
were moving in the right direction when they realized that
proper relation of man to God depends upon right worship,
right family relations, and gratification of the basic animal
urges of hunger and sex as means to an end and never as an end
in itself.

For him who recognized the importance of right purpose
and the intimate relation between the physical and the spiritual,
but who by reason of frailty, and not of wilfulness, had endangered the worship of the group, provision was made for restoration of the purity of the worship; in that restored purity the
offender could participate. The favorite expression of this res-

toration of purity was "it shall be forgiven for him" (or them").[57]

It is hard for many twentieth-century protestants to understand or sympathize with these ideas. They no longer regard worship as the great human priority for which, if necessary, every other relationship and possession must be surrendered. They regard excommunication as a piece of vestigial superstition invoked only by victims of arrested development or by obscurantists.

To those who regard worship as of primary import, as the ancient Jews regarded it, any disqualification would be the greatest misfortune, necessitating special attention for its removal. Since worship was essentially a group act, only the group, acting through its appointed officers, could determine whether disqualification existed, how it was to be removed and when that removal had been accomplished. All this sounds strange to those who regard worship as a stimulating means for voluntary associates and who are more concerned with securing attendants at this vaguely defined worship than they are with the quality of the attendants or the character and function of the worship.

Three Hebrew verbs occur frequently in descriptions of this process of removal of disqualification for worship, *chatah*, *asham* and *kipper*. The first two are used sometimes distinctly and sometimes interchangeably. The third has been the subject of so much confusion and misunderstanding that it will need detailed explanation.

In both Hebrew and Arabic the root *chatah* denoted the idea of failing or missing or lacking. In any instance of such failure the result would be to fall short of some given requirement. The Hebrew verb to describe this act was *chatah*; the substantive was *chattath*. These will both be transliterated and treated as English words because no single English word renders them. The idea connoted is sometimes a simple occasion of quarantine as in the instance of leprosy.[58] Chattath sometimes describes an unconscious mistake from which the group, or some members of it, might conceivably suffer; such a mistake was a "sin of ignorance." It sometimes denotes taboo incurred, avoidably or unavoidably, in the course of performance of the necessary duties of life, such as coming into contact with a corpse, even for purpose of burying it. It sometimes denotes voluntary, moral defection, which is what the average modern person means by *sin*. The translation *sin*, common in all versions of the Bible, is therefore inadequate to render *chattath* as an act which issued in cultic disqualification. *Sin-offering* is equally inadequate to render *chattath* as the means by which removal of cultic disqualification was achieved or signified.[59]

In both Hebrew and Arabic the root of *asham* connotes responsibility for an act or condition which violates some standard.[60] This standard may be either aesthetic or moral. In *chattath* the emphasis is upon the act; in *asham* the emphasis is upon responsibility for the act. The difference between sin and guilt loosely describes the difference between the two words, which are sometimes distinguished and sometimes interchanged.[61] As the word *chattath* describes both the act which has produced taboo and the agent in the rite for effecting or signifying the removal of the taboo, so *asham* describes both the guiltiness of the person committing the act and the means of effecting or signifying the removal of that guiltiness. And as *sin-offering* is an inadequate translation of *chattath*, so *transgression-offering* and *guilt-offering* are inadequate translations of *asham*, which will also be transliterated and treated as a common English word.[62]

The ritual of the chattath is found in Lev. 4. The text of this definitely post-exilic rite is printed in four columns for purpose of comparison of the chattaths performed respectively for "the anointed priest," for the whole group, for an official of the group and for a commoner. The first two columns describe one kind of rite, the other two columns another. These will be referred to respectively as chattath A and chattath B. The ritual of chattath B is not complete: no provision is made for disposal of the body of the victim. This is supplied in Lev. 6:25–30, which may originally have followed chapter iv immediately and have become displaced, or it may have resulted from an afterthought. This is a problem for textual critics to attack.

THE LAW OF THE CHATTATH

Leviticus 4   CHATTATH A

3. If the anointed priest
   chatah unwittingly

   to make the people asham;
   for his chattath
   which he has chatahed

   he shall bring
   a bullock
   without blemish
   for a chattath to Yahweh.

4. And he shall bring the bullock
   to the door of
   the tent of meeting
   before Yahweh,
   And he
   shall lay his hand
   upon the bullock's head
   before Yahweh.
   And he shall kill the bullock

   before Yahweh.

5. And the anointed priest
   shall take
   some of the bullock's blood
   and bring it
   to the tent of meeting

13. If the whole group of Israel
    chatah unwittingly
    and the affair be concealed
       from
    the eyes of the assembly
    and they have violated
    one of the prohibitions
    of Yahweh
    not to be committed,
    and are asham;

14. when the chattath which
    they have chatahed
    is known,
    the group shall bring
    a bullock

    for a chattath,

    and bring him
    before
    the tent of meeting

15. And the elders of the group
    shall lay their hands
    upon the bullock's head
    before Yahweh.
    And he (they?) shall kill the
       bullock

    before Yahweh.

16. And the anointed priest
    shall bring
    some of the bullock's blood

    to the tent of meeting.

6. And the priest shall dip his
   finger
   in the blood
   and sprinkle some of the blood
   seven times before Yahweh
   before the veil
   of the sanctuary.
7. And the priest shall put
   some of the blood

   upon the horns of the altar
   of sweet incense
   before Yahweh
   which is in the tent of meet-
      ing;
   and he shall pour all the blood

   at the base of the 'olah altar
   at the door of the tent of meet-
      ing.
8. And he shall remove all the fat
   of the chattath bullock,
   the fat covering
   the entrails,
   and all the fat which is
   on the entrails,
9. and the two kidneys,
   and the fat on them
   which is by the flanks,
   and the yothereth hakkavedh,
   with the kidneys
   he shall remove
10. as it was removed from the
      bullock
   of the zevach of shelems.
   And the priest shall
   burn them on the 'olah altar.

17. And the priest shall dip his
    finger
    in the blood
    and sprinkle
    seven times before Yahweh
    before the veil.
18. And the priest shall put
    some of the blood

    upon the horns of the altar

    before Yahweh
    which is in the tent of meet-
       ing;
    and he shall pour all the blood
    of the bullock
    at the base of the 'olah altar
    at the door of the tent of meet-
       ing.
19. And he shall remove all the fat
    from him

    and
    burn it on the altar.

20. And he shall do with the bul-
       lock
    as he did with the chattath
       bullock;
    so shall he do with this one.
    And the priest shall
    make purification for them

    and it shall be forgiven them.

11. And the bullock's skin
and all his flesh,
with his head and
with his legs and his dung,
12. the whole bullock he shall
carry
outside the camp
to a clean place
where the ashes are poured
out,
and burn him
on the wood with fire,
Where the ashes are poured
out
he shall be burnt.

21. And the bullock he shall carry

outside the camp

and burn him

as he burned the first bullock;
it is a chattath for the group.

CHATTATH B

22. When a ruler
has chatahed and unwittingly

violated
one of the prohibitions
of Yahweh his God
not to be committed
and is asham;
23. or if his chattath which
he has chatahed
come to his knowledge,
he shall bring his qorban
a kid of the goats,
a male without blemish.

27. If a commoner
chatah unwittingly,

violating
one of the prohibitions
of Yahweh
not to be committed
and is asham;
or if his chattath which
he has chatahed
come to his knowledge,
28. he shall bring
a kid of the goats,
a female without blemish
for the chattath
which he has chatahed.

24. And he
shall lay his hand
upon the goat's head,

and he shall kill it
in the place where they kill
'olahs
before Yahweh.
It is a chattath.

29. And he
shall lay his hand
upon the head of the chattath

and he shall kill the chattath
in the place of the 'olah.

25. And the priest shall take
    some of the blood
    of the chattath
    with his finger
    and put it
    upon the horns of the 'olah
        altar.
    And he shall pour all its blood

    at the base of the altar.

26. And all the fat he shall

    burn on the 'olah altar,
    like the fat of the
    zevach of shelems.

    And the priest shall
    make purification for him
    from his chattath,
    and it shall be forgiven him.

30. And the priest shall take
    some of its blood

    with his finger
    and put it
    upon the horns of the 'olah
        altar.
    And he shall pour all its blood

    at the base of the altar.

31. And he shall remove all the
        fat

    as the fat is removed from
    the zevach of shelems.
    And the priest shall
    burn it on the altar,

    for a reach nichoach
    unto Yahweh.

    And the priest shall
    make purification for him,

    and it shall be forgiven him.

Leviticus 6

25. This is the law of the chattath: in the place the 'olah is killed the chattath shall be killed before Yahweh. It is most holy.
26. The priest who performs the chattath shall eat it; it shall be eaten in the holy place in the court of the tent of meeting.
27. Whatever shall touch the flesh of it shall be holy; and when any of its blood is sprinkled upon a garment, thou shalt wash that upon which it was sprinkled in the holy place.
28. The earthen vessel in which it was sodden shall be broken; if it be sodden in a brasen pot, that shall be scoured and rinsed with water.
29. All the males among the priests shall eat of it. It is most holy.
30. No chattath of which any of the blood is brought into the tent of meeting to purify in the holy place shall be eaten; it shall be burnt with fire.

The law of the asham assumes the chattath as well known. The ritual is not described in detail, but must be inferred from the two short references in Lev. 5:6–13; 7:1–7, which read as follows:

Leviticus 5

6. He shall confess what he has chatahed and bring his asham to Yahweh for his chattath which he chatahed, a female, a lamb or a kid for chattath; and the priest shall make purification for him from his chattath.

7. If he is not able to provide a lamb, he shall bring for the asham which he chatahed two turtle doves or two pigeons, one for a chattath, one for a 'olah.

8. He shall bring them to the priest, who shall offer the one for the chattath first and wring its neck but not divide it.

9. He shall sprinkle some of the blood of the chattath upon the side of the altar; the rest of the blood shall be wrung at the base of the altar; it is a chattath.

10. With the second he shall perform a 'olah according to rule. The priest shall make purification for him for his chattath which he chatahed, and it shall be forgiven him.

11. If he is not able to provide two turtle doves or two pigeons, he shall bring for his qorban for what he chatahed a tenth of an ephah of soleth for a chattath.

12. He shall bring it to the priest, who shall take his handful from it as its azkarah, and he shall burn it on the altar for an ishsheh to Yahweh; it is a chattath.

13. And the priest shall make purification for him for his chattath which he chatahed, and it shall be forgiven for him; it shall be for the priest as a minchah.

Leviticus 7

1. This is the law of the asham; it is most holy.

2. They shall kill the asham where they kill the 'olah, and they shall dash its blood around the altar.

3. And he shall bring all its fat, the rump and the fat covering the entrails.

4. And the two kidneys and the fat on them, on the flanks; and he shall remove the yothereth hakkavedh in addition to the kidneys.

5. The priest shall burn them on the altar, an ishsheh to Yahweh; it is an asham.

6. Every male of the priests shall eat it in the sanctuary; it is most holy.

7. The asham is like the chattath; there is one law for them; it shall belong to the priest who purifies with it.

Underlying these purification rites was the principle that the flesh of the animal whose blood was used for specific purification might not be eaten by him who occasioned the need for purification. Therefore the flesh of the animals whose blood was used for chattath A could not be eaten by anyone. A chattath by the "anointed priest" involved the whole priesthood. The "anointed priest" was possibly the high priest. A chattath for the whole congregation involved the whole group by definition.

A bullock was required for every chattath A. A kid, a male for an officer and a female for a commoner, was prescribed for chattath B. A ram or a lamb was prescribed for an asham. In certain instances, a poor man could substitute two turtle doves or two pigeons, one for a chattath, the other for a 'olah. For a still poorer person, a minchah without oil or frankincense would suffice. The presentation and killing of the animal were the same as in a sacrifice.

The blood rite was the chief feature of the purification. In chattath A the blood of the bullock was to be taken into the sanctuary "before the veil." There the priest was to dip his finger into the blood and sprinkle seven times before Yahweh. (The Hebrew verb means "to sprinkle" and not "to dash" or "to pour" as in the 'olah and zevach.) [63] He was then to anoint the horns of the incense altar with blood and pour the rest of the blood around the base of the altar.

In chattath B and in the asham the blood was not taken into the sanctuary for the sevenfold sprinkling. The horns of the altar were to be anointed and the rest of the blood to be poured around the base of the altar.

In chattath A the fat, the kidneys and the yothereth hakkavedh [64] were dissected and burned on the 'olah altar, just as in the zevach. In chattath B only the fat is mentioned but the instruction is to do as in the zevach of shelems; it may be inferred that the process was the same as in chattath A.

In chattath A the remainder of the animal was carted "outside the camp" to be burned. Inasmuch as the whole priesthood had shared the taint of the high priest, and the whole group, priests and laymen, had shared the taint of "group inadvertence," no one could eat any of the flesh of the animal. In chattath B and the asham the flesh of the animal must immediately be eaten solemnly by the priests inside the sanctuary. Therein the chattath and the asham differed from the zevach of shelems, the flesh of which was eaten by all who were ceremonially clean; [65] all zevachs were sacred meals shared by worshipers with Yahweh. The lugubriousness of the chattath and asham contrasted strongly with the joy of the 'olah and the zevach.

A common expression, in the three central books of the Pentateuch, to describe the process of purification, both the simple ceremony preliminary to every sacrifice and the more elaborate ceremony of the chattath and the asham, is the Hebrew word *kipper* (pronounced *kippaire*) which in AV is usually translated "make atonement for," but which will be rendered by a simple transliteration. The substantive *atonement* was introduced into the English language about 1513 by compounding a preposition, a cardinal number and a participial suffix, at-one-ment. It therefore describes a union of two separated beings. Within a dozen years it was adopted by William Tyndale for his translation of the Bible. The verb *atone* seems to be an instance of back formation and was coined about 1555. First used as a transitive verb, by 1617 it had gathered up the idea of appeasement. By 1662 it described placation in the modern sense of that term. Its whole use is post-reformational.

The verb was invented too late for incorporation into the classic English translations of the Bible, but the substantive is found in AV about seventy-five times, usually in the phrase "Make atonement." It occurs once in 2 Samuel, twice in Chronicles, once in Nehemiah, over sixty times in the three central books of the Pentateuch and once in the New Testament,[66] where both DV and AV replace it by *reconciliation*.

Reconcile is an exact translation of the Greek *katallassein,* which literally means "to down the otherness" and is therefore synonymous with the etymological meaning of the English word *atone.* A complicated problem arises when we note that *katallassein* is never used by LXX translators to render the Hebrew word *kipper.* Thus the idea of reconciliation is excluded from explanation of *kipper* by men who spoke both Hebrew and Greek. Sixteen centuries later, *reconciliation* had become the principal explanation of the word with which it had never been equated. How this transformation took place does not concern us here.

Our problem is to try to understand the meaning of the Hebrew word *kipper.* Three methods of procedure illuminate the meaning of a word. They are (1) comparison of the word with words from the same root in cognate languages, (2) study of translations of the word into other languages, and (3) study of the context in which the word was originally used.

(1) In Syriac the root of *kipper* is used for "to wipe" or "to wipe away." In Babylonian one form of the root may mean "to glisten"; another form means "to wipe away." In Arabic the root occurs in three verb stems, one of which means "to cover a thing so that it cannot be seen." One may ask whether the stress is on the act of covering or upon the fact of making unseen. In English the word "cover" is used with the sense of "to neutralize" as, e.g., in the expression "to cover one odour with another." To understand this phrase one does not become meticulous and ask who smelt the odour which was being covered. When we note that *kaphar,* the first stem of *kipper* in Hebrew, means "to cover" and that the third stem *kipper* means "to wipe away" in several semitic languages including Hebrew, we realize that the English use is similar.

(2) The two earliest translations of the Old Testament, those into Greek and Latin, present the meanings ascribed to Hebrew words at the time the translations were made. The Greek translations came from Jewish scholars at Alexandria. The translations of the Pentateuch may have been completed by the third

century before our era; the rest of the Old Testament followed within the next two centuries. These translations are of primary importance in the endeavour to ascertain the meaning of Hebrew words.

The Latin translations were made for Christians when Greek ceased to be easily understood in western Europe. They may have been commenced as early as the third century of our era; they were completed by Jerome who died in 420. Jerome learned Hebrew in order to make corrections in the interest of accuracy. His edition, the Vulgate, went through many successions of alteration and explanation until the present form was fixed in 1592. At least some of Jerome's work, probably a great deal of it, is preserved in our Vulgate.

A few of the Greek translations [68] use words plainly denoting cleansing or purification. The great majority of them employ *hilaskesthai* or its compound *exilaskesthai*. The classic use of *hilaskesthai* to describe prayer or invocation has already been noted; [69] it renders *kipper* only three times, each of which concerns the forgiveness of sins. The Moffatt translation of *cancel* is admirable.

The compound *exilaskesthai* would literally mean "to pray out." It seldom occurs in classic Greek and is unquestionably identified by the LXX translators with *kipper*. In classic Greek both the simple and compound forms of the verb take a direct, personal object in the accusative case, usually the name of a god. In LXX it does not take a direct object but, in an attempt to make a literal rendition of the Hebrew, is followed by a phrase commencing almost invariably with *peri* and, like *kipper* itself, never with the name of God for an object.

The reason for this may proceed from the fact that the Greek words which unquestionably imply purification could also be used of magic rites in which the purification was an automatic result of the physical rite. This would offend a pious Jew who regarded God as the only agent of purification. The physical rites, preserved from primitive days, were adapted as the appointed means whereby God would effect his purification. Judaism had made long strides in the direction of spiritual concepts. This idea is admirably expressed by *exilaskesthai* which makes plain that, when men performed these rites, they were praying God to purify themselves and his sanctuary in order that they might render him the worship which alone insured and mediated his protection. Thus the Greek speaking Jews of Alexandria tried to render their Hebrew into a language understanded of the people.

This was also the understanding of the Latin translators whose work throws much light upon the problem.[70] Of the eighty occurrences of *kipper,* forty are translated by words meaning "to pray." Twenty-seven are translated by words meaning "to cleanse" or "to purify." The Latin *expiare* and *placare* do not always connote the ideas expressed by the modern English words *expiate* and *placate,* but both have the meaning of "to purify" in many instances,[71] and the instances may be more numerous than we suppose. Neither Greek nor Latin translators seem aware of the idea of reconciliation.

The information contributed by the two English versions DV and AV upon the meaning of *kipper* comes from comparison of the two. AV uses thirteen words to render *kipper*; DV uses twenty. DV uses the comparatively new word *atonement* thirteen times; AV, coming twenty-five years later, uses it sixty-one times. AV uses *reconcile* six times, even when it is not appropriate; DV makes no use of the word, but uses the word *expiate* thirteen times. This sixteenth-century word, transliterated directly from Latin, described cleansing by religious rites as contrasted with secular washing. This is illustrated by the phrase *expiate the altar,* which is certainly not improved by the clumsy AV phrase *make atonement for the altar.*[72] AV may have rejected the word *expiate* because its translators had rejected the idea of cleansing by religious ceremony. In many instances DV is superior to AV.[73] The chief difference between the two translations of *kipper* is in DV's use of *pray for,* or some similar expression, in thirty-eight instances in which AV uses *make atonement for*.[74]

(3) Study of the way the verb is used in Hebrew gives a great deal of help toward understanding it. *Kipper* takes a direct object fifteen times.[75] A priest may *kipper* the temple or the sanctuary or the altar. Four times it is said that Yahweh will *kipper* iniquity. The object is never a person and is never God. In other instances of its use *kipper* is followed by the preposition *for* or *upon* or *concerning*. None of these prepositions is ever followed by the word *God*. Kippering, whatever it was, was done in the presence of God but it was never addressed to God. The object kippered upon was always a person about to worship or something used in worship. The method of kippering was to dash or to pour blood upon the altar,[76] or to pour it around the base of the altar,[77] or to smear it upon the kapporeth.[78] In the complicated treatment of one who had recovered from leprosy,[79] the patient was kippered by having oil poured upon his head. Oil was also used in addition to blood in rites of consecration and sanctification.[80]

The basic purpose of kipper rites may be seen in the prescription for Yom Kippurim on the tenth day of the seventh month, when the priest is directed to "kipper for you to cleanse you, that ye may be clean from all your sins before Yahweh." [81]

In addition to the regular purification rites before every 'olah and zevach,[82] many occasions demanded special rites. These rites are sometimes described by themselves with no reference to the worship for which they prepared; whether that worship followed immediately or at a later time is not said. Sometimes the rites are described as specifically preliminary to the worship. Sometimes they are simply mentioned with the worship; it may be assumed that they were performed before the worship, since every specific description of them is as preliminary. For convenience of reference the biblical sections describing them are appended.

I. Purification described without reference to worship

    1. Acts of inadvertence unwittingly committed. Lev. 4. Num. 15:22–28.
        (1) For priest or whole group: bullock for chattath A.
        (2) For ruler or commoner: kid or lamb for chattath B.

    2. Withholding of evidence and discovering that it should not have been withheld. Lev. 5:1.

    3. Contact with carcase of animals. Lev. 5:2. 11:39–40.

    4. Contact with person who is asham. Lev. 5:3.

    5. Taking oath and discovering later that it should not have been taken. Lev. 5:4.

        (1) Confession
        (2) Female lamb or goat for chattath or asham
        OR
        Two doves
          one for chattath
          one for 'olah
        OR
        Minchah for chattath

    6. Contact with a corpse. Num. 19. Taboo water for chattath.

    7. Intercourse with slave woman betrothed and not yet freed. Lev. 19:20–21.
    Man brings ram for asham. Both are punished.

    8. Profanation of sacred things. Lev. 5:14–16; 22:14–16.
        (1) Restoration of cost of thing profaned plus one-fifth of that value for fine: paid to priest.
        (2) Ram for asham.

    9. Financial wronging of neighbor. Lev. 6:1–7; Num. 5:6–8.
        (1) Restoration to neighbor of full amount, plus one-fifth of that amount as interest.
        (2) Ram as asham.

II. Purification followed immediately by worship.

    1. "Bloody issues" after healed. Lev. 15.
        (1) Dove for chattath.
        (2) Dove for 'olah.

    2. A woman after childbirth. Lev. 12:1–8.
    After forty days for son. After eighty days for daughter.
        (1) Pigeon or dove for chattath.
        (2) Lamb or dove or pigeon for 'olah.

    3. Leprosy after it is pronounced healed. Lev. 13–14.
        (1) Examination for healing. Lev. 13.
        (2) First purification with birds, etc.
        (3) Second purification, one week later.
            a. Lamb for asham.
            b. Cleansing with oil.
            c. Lamb for chattath.
            d. Lamb for 'olah.

Leprosy of house or garment requires only first purification.
4. Accidental breach of vow by Nazirite. Num. 6:9–12.
   (1) Dove for chattath.
   (2) Dove for 'olah.
5. Conclusion of vow of Narizite. Num. 6:15–17.
   (1) Ewe lamb for chattath.
   (2) Lamb for 'olah.
   (3) Ram for shelem.

III. Elaborate purifications in connection with consecrations.

IV. Special purification for each day of new moon and annual 'olahs
listed on pages 141–142.

V. The annual "Day of Purifications," *Yom Kippurim.*

A few of these rites need particular discussion; others can be
comparatively easily understood. The first five are plain enough
from references already made. It should be observed that all the
occasions requiring a chattath or an asham were acts of "inadvertence" or acts unwittingly committed. In every instance the
writer seems to be thinking of an act of which the offender was
not conscious when it was committed. He withheld evidence
or took an oath and learned later that he had made a mistake.
The assumption is that he would not have committed the act if
he had known all the facts.

We of the present day are apt to reason that, if an act is accidental and not intentional, it may be an unfortunate mistake
but no one can be blamed for it. We have a colloquial phrase,
"It was just one of those things." The ancient Jew realized that
he had nevertheless committed an act which should not have
been committed and for which he had consequent regrets.
Although he was morally inculpable, he was "inadvertently"
responsible for the consequences of his act. He might be more
careful in the future. In the meantime he must be cleansed from
whatever fault he had committed. We laugh at, or at least indul-
gently smile at the technique of purification; we also are prone
to shirk our responsibilities as contributors to a total picture of
the group of which we are members.

The priest and the levite in the parable of the Samaritan [83]
were not avoiding duty; these temple officers were doing

exactly what the Law of Moses required them to do when they came into sight of what, to all appearances, was a corpse. To have done otherwise would have removed them from their work for at least a week and would have endangered confidence in them as guides. "Whoever, in a public place, touches one slain with a sword, or a corpse or a human bone, or a grave, shall be unclean seven days." [84] For removal of this taboo it was necessary to make two applications of a concoction called "taboo water." [85]

This taboo water was prepared as follows: In the presence of a priest, "outside the camp," a red cow was slain. The priest took some of her blood with his finger and flipped it seven times in the direction of the sanctuary. The cow, "her skin, her flesh, her blood, her dung," was then burned while the priest threw cedar sticks, hyssop [86] and a scarlet cloth into the flames. Cedar and hyssop were aromatic and had a definitely practical use; the scarlet cloth had some connection with the idea of blood. The ashes of the fire were then gathered and stored and mixed with living, i.e., flowing water. [87] The conclusion of the rite is: this is a chattath. [88] He who had touched a corpse must remain taboo for a minimum of a week. On the third day, and again on the seventh day, he must be ceremonially cleansed by having taboo water sprinkled upon him.

The whole rite is reminiscent of primitive days. One thinks of an ancient Roman practice. The blood streaming from a horse sacrificed on the fifteenth of October was saved and mixed with the ashes of unborn calves which had been torn from their mothers and burned on the fifteenth of April. At the Parilia on the twenty-first of April the mixture was thrown on heaps of burning bean straw while taboo people leaped over the smoke and flames for purification. [89]

The specific sacred or holy things which might be profaned are not listed in either of the passages. Lev. 22:14–16 mentions eating of holy things unwittingly. The flesh of chattath B was reserved for priests to eat in the sanctuary, as was the bread of presence. Whatever the profanation, it was regarded as damaging that which had been dedicated to Yahweh. The offended must make good the cost of what he had damaged and must add one-fifth of that price as a fine. When he had made the restitution, and not until then, he must bring an asham for removal of his taboo. The asham was not a substitute for honesty or a remedy for committing acts which the offender knew were wrong.

This was particularly true of those acts which had worked financial or property loss to a neighbor. Once more, complete restitution must be made, plus one-fifth of the value as interest. Only then could the offender bring an asham. Restitution itself was not sufficient. The wrong act had left a taboo stain on the offender and had endangered the worship of the group.

"Bloody issues," possibly of venereal character, are not specifically discussed. The phrase "his flesh" [90] is frequently a euphemistic expression. Plainly the issues were not regarded as involving serious moral taint. A chattath of a dove, to be followed by the 'olah of a dove, would indicate an easily removable taboo with worship immediately following.

Likewise a woman who had given birth to a child had a mild taboo, easily removable after a chattath which could be very small if necessary, and followed immediately by a small 'olah. The act of giving birth was accompanied by blood and therefore conveyed taboo, which could be removed forty days after the birth of a son and eighty days after the birth of a daughter. It is not necessary to suppose that the taint proceeded from some sort of impurity inherent in sex processes.

Just how life is communicated is still a question. To modern folk such a question awakens only curiosity to be satisfied by laboratory experimentations. To ancient peoples all things connected with life were occasions of wonder and mystery to be approached with due humility and reverence. The ancients believed, as we do not, that some processes were beyond the power of human explanation. Such processes were attributed to the power of the deity who was always considered greater than man. The presence of the inexplicable was invariably an occasion of caution and care.

We have gone to the opposite extreme and regard the presence of the inexplicable as but a challenge to investigation upon the assumption that simple physical explanations for every phenomenon are ultimately inevitable. The superhuman is dismissed from mind except as a quantitative factor. From such assumptions, sometimes unconscious, proceed comments to the effect that sex processes, in days of ignorance, were considered impure *per se*. Recovery from such ignorance can lead to loss of all reverence for sex processes and to regarding them merely as means of amusement to be varied whimsically. The technique of ancient Judaism may have been crude. Its assumptions were basically religious.

Leprosy of biblical days was not the disease which is so feared today. There is but one biblical reference to uncured leprosy, that of Uzziah.[91] Of the case of Gehazi, the servant of Elisha, no ultimate outcome is recorded.[92] Every other instance was cured, and a cure was so normal an expectation that detailed prescriptions were given for its recognition and for the consequent religious rite.

The symptoms described as leprosy may be called abnormal white patches which could appear on a garment,[93] or on the walls of a house,[94] or on a person.[95] Distinction was made between true and false symptoms of which the priest was the judge. During the attack of the symptoms the victim must dwell "outside the camp," alone, with torn clothes, bared head, and veiled upper lip, crying out, "Taboo, taboo."[96]

When the victim thought his whiteness had disappeared the priest went out to examine him and give final judgment concerning his cure. If he considered the abnormalities had disappeared he took two clean birds. One of these he killed in an earthen vessel over living water.[97] Into the blood and water were dipped the living bird and a bit of cedar wood, hyssop and scarlet cloth. With these the leper was sprinkled seven times. The living bird was let go; no instructions were given for the carcase of the slain bird. The leper returned to camp and lived "outside his tent" for another week.

This ancient ceremony seems to be based upon the primitive concept of transference of taboo or evil, which is the reason for all fear of taboo; it is "catching" and therefore unpredictable. Nothing was known about "leprosy," the generic term given to the strange set of symptoms; but the basic nature of taboo suggested a means of purification. If in some way the taboo could be transferred to something which gave no expectation of being seen again, it would be no longer an occasion of fear.

The sprinkling with the blood of the slain bird, using the live bird as an aspergillum, may have been a composite rite. The transference of evils to animals, especially to birds, was known among primitive peoples.[98] After the transference the bird was allowed to fly away. This leprosy ceremony seems to have stemmed from the ancient custom and to have been incorporated into the blood rite as part of it.

At the end of the week the healed man shaved himself completely, washed his clothes and bathed. The next day an asham of a ram lamb was performed for him. Into the blood of the asham lamb the priest was to dip his finger and with it touch the right ear, the right thumb and the right great toe of the patient. He then touched the same ear, thumb and toe with oil and poured oil upon the patient's head. A chattath B of a ewe lamb was then performed, followed by a 'olah of a ewe lamb. The patient was then clean. A poor man could substitute two turtle doves for the two lambs.

Leprosy of a house was apparently some sort of mildew. A priest must be called to examine it and, if he pronounced it leprosy, he must close the house seven days. If the mildew was still present, the affected stones must be removed and cast "into an unclean place" outside the city.[99] They must be replaced and the house must be scraped and plastered. If the leprosy broke out again the house must be razed and carted outside the city "to an unclean place." If the replacement of the stones and the scraping and plastering were sufficient, the house was to be cleansed, exactly as the leprous man, with the two birds. No chattath or asham was necessary; the house was not a member of the congregation and did not contribute to the worship of the group.

Very little is known of the Nazirites.[100] The vow of ascetic life which they took seems to have been only temporary. The legislators were familiar with the frailty of human nature; provision was made for breach of the vow. This accidental breach must be purified by a chattath of a dove to be followed immediately by a 'olah of a dove. The small chattath and 'olah would indicate the relative importance of the vow. At the conclusion of the period for which the vow was taken, a more elaborate ceremony was required. A chattath B of a ewe lamb was followed by a 'olah of a lamb and a shelem of a ram with the accompanying minchah and libations. The former ascetic had returned to his place in the religious life of Israel.

In post-exilic Judaism entrance upon temple service was marked by solemn ceremonies which indicated that the participants were being set apart for life. One can see the sharp distinction between orders of clergy and laity which were inherited and developed by historic Christendom. Two orders are well marked, each with its appropriate ceremony of induction or ordination or consecration, the levites and the priests.

The earliest historical reference to the levites is in Ezekiel [101] who suggested that those levites [102] who had been unfaithful should, as punishment, be degraded to the status of servants or ministers to the zadokite priesthood. When priestly Judaism had become an accepted economy, levites were recognized, not as degraded priests doomed to menial service, but as men selected to be honored above laymen as participants in clerical dignity, although not actually performing principal sacrificial duties.[103] To them was committed the charge of the temple, its furnishings and sacred utensils.

The ceremony of consecration was a bit complicated; it consisted of the following parts:

(1) The candidates were sprinkled with "water of chattath."

(2) They were completely shaved.

(3) They washed their clothes.

(4) They were formally presented to the congregation who laid their hands upon them. No instructions are given for this extensive and complicated act.

(5) The high priest offered them for a t'nufah.[104] No intimation is given how this physical feat was accomplished.

(6) The levites laid their hands on two bullocks.

(7) One of these was then killed and offered as a chattath. The kind of chattath is not indicated but the rite of consecration to the priesthood specifies a chattath A.

(8) The other bullock was offered for a 'olah.

(9) The levites were once more (*sic*) presented to the high priest to be offered as a t'nufah.

The two elements of the service are plainly purification and setting apart for temple service.

The consecration of priests was much more impressive. An elaborate description of their vestments is given in Exodus 28. This is followed in Exodus 29 by the prescription of the details of the rite by which they were consecrated. Leviticus 8 describes the details which were said to have accompanied the carrying out of these prescriptions. The rite was as follows:

(1) The candidates were formally presented to the congregation and washed (apparently completely).

(2) The vestments of their office were placed upon them and oil poured upon their heads.

(3) A bullock was presented and after the candidates had laid their hands upon his head, he was offered as a chattath A.

(4) A ram was then offered as a 'olah.

(5) A second ram was killed called the "ram of consecration."

    a. The blood of this ram was then tipped on the candidates' right ears, right thumbs and right great toes and sprinkled upon the altar.

b. The blood and anointing oil were sprinkled upon the candidates' vestments.

c. The fat, the rump, the yothereth hakkavedh, and the right shoulder of the ram, a loaf of bread and a (minchah?) wafer were placed in the hands of the candidates to be a t'nufah and then burned as an ishsheh.

d. The breast of the ram was given "to Moses" as his portion. This would probably signify that the breast was the portion of the officiating priest.

e. The flesh of the ram was then boiled "at the door of the tent of meeting" and eaten by the candidates. What they could not eat was immediately burned.

(6) For each of the seven succeeding days a bullock was offered as a chattath, probably a chattath A.

A chattath was offered as preliminary to the majority of the regular rites.[105] The chief difficulty in picturing these rites is the tax upon the imagination to make allowance for the time and space required for the numerous slaughters. The addition of preliminary chattaths would make time and space even more crowded. The regular morning and evening 'olahs and the additional sabbath day 'olahs required no further preliminary preparation than that for every 'olah and zevach. No chattath was required for the pesach for the simple reason that the pesach was a family rite practised long before any priesthood came into being and needing no altar.[106] Despite post-exilic efforts to "sacerdotalize" the rites of the feast, it remained the one sacrifice of Israel which survived the fall of the temple and the priesthood and has continued so today.

For every day of annual and new moon 'olah rites a chattath of a kid was the necessary preparation. The eight day feast of Booths, the most elaborate festival of the year, was appropriately prefaced, five days earlier, by the most solemn purification rites of the year.

The name of this day of solemn preparation was *Yom Kip-*

purim,[107] which is translated *Day of Atonement* in all the
English versions of the Bible except that of Moffatt, who calls
it *Expiation Day*. A literal translation would be *Day of Purifications*. The ritual of the day is found in Leviticus 16. Two
accounts are apparently combined in this chapter, the older one
going through verse 10 and the other following immediately
after. The two accounts are placed in two columns for purpose
of comparison.

THE TEXTS FOR THE RITUAL OF *YOM KIPPURIM*

Leviticus 16

3. Aaron shall enter the sanctuary with a bullock for a chattath and a ram for a 'olah.
4. He shall don the linen tunic;
he shall wear the linen
breeches; he shall be girded
with a linen girdle;
he shall wear the linen turban.
He shall bathe himself and
don them.
5. He shall take for the group
of the Israelites
two male goats for a chattath
and a ram for a 'olah.
6. And Aaron shall present the
bullock of the chattath which
is for himself and shall purify
himself and his house.

11. And Aaron shall present the
bullock of the chattath which
is for himself and shall purify
himself and his house. He
shall kill the bullock of the
chattath for himself.
12. And he shall take a censer full
of live coals from the altar before Yahweh, and his hands
full of sweet incense beaten
small, and bring it within the
veil.
13. And he shall put the incense
upon the fire before Yahweh,
that the cloud of incense may
cover the place of purification,
that he die not.

14. And he shall take of the blood of the bullock and sprinkle it with his finger upon the place of purification on the east, and before the place of purification he shall sprinkle some of the blood seven times.

7. And he shall take the two goats and set them before Yahweh at the door of the tent of meeting.
8. And Aaron shall cast lots upon the two goats, one lot for Yahweh, another for Azazel.
9. And Aaron shall present the goat upon which the lot fell for Yahweh and offer him for a chattath.

15. Then shall he kill the goat of the chattath which is for the group and bring his blood within the veil and do with his blood as he did with the blood of the bullock, and sprinkle it upon the place of purification.
16. And he shall make purification for the sanctuary because of the uncleannesses of the Israelites, and because of their transgressions and all their sins. So shall he do to the tent of meeting which dwells among them in the midst of their uncleannesses.
17. And no one shall be in the tent of meeting when he goes in to make purification in the sanctuary, till he comes out after making purification for himself and for his house, and for all the group of Israel.
18. And he shall go out to the altar which is before Yahweh and make purification for it. And he shall take of the blood of the bullock and of the blood of the goat and put it around on the horns of the altar.

19. And he shall sprinkle some of the blood upon it with his finger seven times and cleanse it and sanctify it from the uncleannesses of the Israelites.

10. And the goat upon which the lot fell for Azazel shall be set alive before Yahweh

20. And when he has completed the purification of the sanctuary and the tent of meeting of the group and of the altar,

21. he shall bring the live goat and Aaron shall lay both his hands upon the head of the live goat

to make purification for him to send him away for Azazel

and shall send him away by the hand of a man who is in readiness

into the wilderness.

into the wilderness.

22. And the goat shall bear upon him all their iniquities into a solitary land; and he shall let go the goat in the wilderness.

23. And Aaron shall enter the tent of meeting and shall doff the linen vestments which he donned when he entered the sanctuary, and shall leave them there.

24. And he shall bathe his flesh in water in a holy place and shall put on his vestments and come out and perform his 'olah and the 'olah of the people and make purification for himself and for the people.

25. And the fat of the chattath he shall burn on the altar.

26. And he who sent away the goat for Azazel shall wash his clothes and bathe his flesh in water and then he shall come into the camp.

27. And the bullock of the chattath and the goat of the chattath whose blood was brought in to make purification in the sanctuary, shall be carried forth outside the camp; and their skins and their flesh and their dung shall be burned with fire.

28. And he who burns them shall wash his clothes and bathe his flesh in water; and then he shall come into the camp.

As might be expected, the first ceremony was a chattath A of a bullock for the high priest, who doffed his regular festal vestments and replaced them with linen ones.[108] After killing the bullock he first took a censer with coals from the perpetual fire of the 'olah altar and flooded the "holy of holies" with clouds of incense smoke, possibly to recall the old tradition of Yahweh's presence in the cloud. He then returned with the blood of the bullock and flipped it with his finger upon the spot reserved for that purpose, the *Kapporeth* or place of purification.[79] The carcase of the bullock was left until later.

This purification of the high priest was followed by a chattath A for the people. The subject of this chattath A was not, as might be expected, a bullock, but a goat chosen by lot from two goats, presented and designated as "Yahweh's goat." With the blood of this goat he returned to the "holy of holies" to perform the purification for the people. With the blood of the bullock and the goat he then purified the 'olah altar by smearing the horns of the altar and flipping the blood with his finger toward the altar seven times.

The second goat was then brought and the high priest laid his hands upon it[109] for transference of the year's "sins of inadvertence," both his own and those of the people.[110] A man was standing by to take this goat and lead him away "to the wilderness for Azazel." Who or what this Azazel was is not known by anyone.[111] He may well have been a depotentiated deity or some wood demon once honored by more primitive dwellers of the land and long forgotten except for his annual reception of a goatful of sins. The word may not be a proper name; it may signify the simple removal of the sins to the wilderness.

Doffing his linen vestments, the high priest then bathed himself and donned his regular vestments to perform a 'olah of a ram.

The carcases of the bullock and goat used for the chattaths were carted "outside the camp" and burned. Both the goat leader and the carcase burner had to bathe themselves before returning to camp.

This elaborate purification, with the simple 'olah following,[112] was a fitting preparation for the eight day feast of Booths which came five days later.

The lesson of all these purifications is simple. Approach to the presence of God is a group act in which each individual participates by reason of his constituent membership of the group. Faults on the part of the group or its constituent members automatically invalidate the approach. If the faults are deliberate, or responsibly committed, any consequence must be rectified before the approach can be made. If the faults are unconsciously committed any untoward consequences must be rectified and they who committed the faults must at least direct their minds to the seriousness of their acts.

Ancient, priestly, Judaism, by its crude purification rites, made a permanent contribution to religion, appreciated long after the rites had ceased. One is reminded of the words of our Lord suggesting that right worship is definitely impaired or even invalidated by wrong conduct,[113] or of the words of his great interpreter St. Paul who spoke of the responsibility of every individual for every other individual and for the group of which all are members,[114] and of the constant necessity of that group to be "holy and without blemish." [115] Our Lord and St. Paul both spoke as Jews who had penetrated to the heart of the religion of the people they both loved.

Chapter XII. THE CHRISTIAN SACRIFICE

In his short ministry in Palestine Jesus gathered a small group of followers. Many may have attached themselves to the group, but a few he specifically invited to follow him.[1] The nucleus was composed of about a dozen who were called "apostles," "those who were sent."[2] To these he gave instructions for extending his work [3] and described the kind of character necessary for that work.[4] One account describes the appointment of seventy others to do the same work and with similar instructions.[5] St. Paul knew a tradition which recorded the appearance of Jesus after his resurrection to more than five hundred.[6] After the ascension of the Lord the group was said to number one hundred twenty.[7]

To the men and women of this group, and to these only, Jesus appeared after his resurrection. Even these had not wholly understood the purpose of their Leader; [8] they had to wait for ten days before it was clear to them. From that time they began to understand that their function was to preserve and extend the Christ life as far and as long as possible.

The term *Christ life* is used rather than *Christian life,* which is frequently interpreted as living by a set of rules. The Christ life was one of power and peace which naturally and enthusiastically developed a certain character. It was described as a life infused by the Spirit of God which made men easily understood and which was definitely contagious. It was also a life which, both in our Lord and in his followers throughout the centuries, aroused bitter opposition from all who desired to maintain any kind of system which was slightly or greatly profitable to themselves, or which ministered to their pride.

Within a few years this life began to appeal to Greek speaking Gentiles. Many opposed the admission of these to the Christ group, which had been composed entirely of Jews. They were foiled in their attempt to insist that all converts to the Christ life must first become Jews,[9] and the life was established as interracial. Jewish Christianity [10] seems to have continued for a couple of centuries as a sort of esoteric sect recognized by neither Jews nor Greek Christians. Judaism was nevertheless the milieu in which Christianity was born; from it came the first enthusiasm. Early leaders of gentile Christianity were fond of calling themselves the true Israel, free from the meticulous peculiarities of Judaism and of Jewish Christians.

2. THE SUBLIMATION OF SACRIFICE

From the destruction of Jerusalem in 586 B.C. and the consequent migration of Jews, first to Babylon and Egypt, and then gradually throughout the Mediterranean world, animal sacrifices had played a dwindling part in Jewish life. After a lapse of two or three generations the temple had been rebuilt and sacrifices renewed; but by the time of Jesus hardly one Jew in ten had ever seen a sacrifice. The ideal of sacrifice, however, had been preserved and developed. Prayer and fasting and almsgiving and reading of the Torah were not only accepted as surrogates for 'olahs and zevachs; they were capable of much further spiritual development and were free from the necessarily revolting features which accompanied killing and burning of beeves and sheep and goats, without much spiritual inspiration. The one sacrificial rite which Judaism preserved to the present day was the non-professionally sacerdotal feast of the pesach, none of which was burnt for Yahweh; therefore, it needed neither priest nor altar. By the time of our Lord the ideas which grew from animal sacrifices were all on their way to spiritual development. When Jerusalem was destroyed, forty years after the ministry of Jesus, they disappeared and no one has desired their renewal.

In the Greek speaking gentile world sacrifices were still familiar. The hellenistic world was dotted with altars and temples where thusias expressed the only form of worship. Every Greek in Egypt, in Asia Minor and in Greece itself, was familiar with the worship of the gods by burning steaks on an

altar and participating in the feast which marked the climax of
the rite. The widespread continuance of these physical ceremonies probably contributed to the slow process of their sublimation and to their final abandonment when Christianity
had utilized all their spiritual value and left them as hollow
rites. The word *thusia* became almost synonymous with *worship*.

A review of the four purposes of the various forms of sacrifice may help to understand how the word itself was finally
baptized and how it became the word *par excellence* to describe the character of Jesus, the ideal of Christian character
and of Christian worship.

(1) In Babylonian and Roman rites the liver of a victim was
carefully examined for omens. In order to do this the animal
had first to be killed. Even a sheep can make trouble enough
for one who wants to remove his liver. In Babylonia, after
examination of the omens, the carcase was burnt; in Rome it
became the property of the priests to be eaten or sold as they
wished.

The search for omens was a religious act. An omen refers to
future time. If one could ascertain whether a proposed action
met the approval of the deity, one could govern oneself accordingly. Modern homilists often accuse ancients of seeking to
control the will of a god and thus make him do the will of the
devotee, but the quest for omens shows the reverse to be true.
One planned a certain action but sought first to learn whether
the god favoured it. He sought to do the will of the god,
although the expression was not used. To be sure, the favour
of the god was supposed to be the success of the undertaking,
but all spiritual concepts have developed from material beginnings. If an ancient devotee was a bit selfish, he was not so different as some may like to suppose from the modern who prays
for success for his undertaking and who, if the undertaking
fails, may even dismiss the god from his employ as ineffectual.
The ancient who was willing to desist from an undertaking
had far more respect for his deity than has the modern who

conditions his devotion to the deity upon that deity's obedience to the behests of him who prays.

Among the Hebrews omens and oracles were entirely separated from sacrifice and were sought in other ways. Today omen seeking has been relegated to the realm of superstition. They who really practise religion now seek to learn the will of God not merely for some proposed act, but for their whole lives. When they pray, "Thy will be done," they are thereby committing themselves to do that will as far as is humanly possible with the help of the grace of God in every act of life.

We dare not enter into the problem of the authorship of the Epistle to the Ephesians but, when that author bade his readers "understand what the will of the Lord is," [11] he was writing in the spirit of the Pauline school and in the spirit of all ancient sacrificial thinking. When he continued his exhortation by bidding them sing and give thanks (the Greek is *make eucharist*) always for all things to the Father, he was using a word familiar to all Asia Minor towns for over two centuries to describe a special, joyful thusia. Sacrifice, as a means of learning the will of God, had been raised to the nth power.

(2) The thusia, paralleled by the Jewish zevach, was the commonest sacrificial rite of the Greek world. It was frequently, if not always, preceded by taking omens. Descended from the common meal of earlier men, it always connoted the meal at which the gods, as the honoured guests, received the steaks which were sublimated into smoke that they might ascend to the dwellers in the sky. The basic principle of the common meal is fellowship, partnership, co-operation. When the banquet is given in honour of a superior guest, the meal must needs indicate the proper honour due that guest, as well as the desire to do his will. When that honoured guest was a god, the honour became worship. It was but a step for the common meal of worship to receive the spiritual significance of the worshipers' co-operation with God their Creator. When monotheism was recognized as the first premiss of all true religion, the sacrifice set forth the ideal of complete co-operation with God. The text

for such worship was, "Hallowed be thy Name; thy will be done by us."

(3) The pesach rite, which has continued to the present day, has expressed, for many centuries, complete reliance of a devotee upon the power of God, and therefore the resolve to apprehend that power by conduct of which God approved. In other similar rites in which the victim was wholly eaten by the worshipers, these ideas were but faintly expressed and were not predominant or reasoned out. The germ of the idea may be seen in totemistic rites.

In the pesach these ideas were articulated in the prayers which accompanied the ceremonies. Yahweh had saved his people in their exodus from Egypt when they faced the angry waters of the Red Sea and were pursued by the seemingly invincible army of Egypt. Yahweh had promised to continue his saving and protecting power so long as they trusted him and did his will. In the pesach they expressed gratitude for these blessings and would fain make the power their own.

(4) The 'olah was peculiar to Judaism. The Greek holocaust was a prophylactic against evil demons and was carefully distinguished from the thusia which was an act of worship offered to the gods of the sky. The very word *holocaust* was avoided by translators of the Septuagint who seem to have coined a word to translate *'olah,* their highest act of worship. The 'olah marked a distinct spiritual development as compared with the zevach. In the zevach the deity was honoured by being offered the choice parts of the animal. It was natural to reason that he would be more greatly honoured by being given the whole animal. The solemn laying of the devotee's hand upon the head of the victim was a ritual identification of the two; it was as if the devotee had said, "Thus I give myself to God." The 'olah expressed the complete surrender or devotion of the worshiper to him who had created heaven and earth and who ordered the goings and comings of those who did his will and kept his laws.

These four purposes, therefore, were expressed in sacrifices:

(1) To learn the will of God.

(2) To co-operate with God and do that will.

(3) To rely upon God for protection when doing his will.

(4) To surrender oneself entirely to God and his will.

There is still no other word than *sacrifice* to embody all these ideas.

It is always easy to content oneself with performance of physical rites and to neglect the effort which is ever necessary for spiritual concepts. It is not surprising, therefore, that even some religiously minded men sought the value of sacrifice in the physical acts and identified it with the physical killing and burning of the victim. It is not surprising that many spiritual leaders of Judaism lifted reproving voices to the rites and stressed the neglected spiritual purpose.[12] These men recognized that no man naturally seeks to do God's will and to know it at all times, to lay hold of God's saving and protecting power, and to devote himself completely to God. The question was, "Is this possible?"

It became increasingly evident to men that no sacrifice had really achieved the ideal which it proclaimed. Men sought the will of God for specific acts but were quite conscious that they often wanted their own desires and tried to persuade God to grant them, even if they flouted his will. Many times they leaned upon God's power, but many other times they trusted themselves or consulted their fears. Often they gave to God the worship due the Creator of the universe, and quite as often they forgot God in their daily living. They honestly tried to surrender themselves to him, but realized that their surrender was restricted and conditioned and irregular.

3. THE CHRISTIAN APPLICATION OF THE TERM *Sacrifice*

Animal sacrifices gave rise to a spiritual ideal for men who never attained it. The perfect sacrifice would be that ideal. Therefore the word easily lent itself to describe the Christian ideal in three respects.

(1) It proclaimed the eternal character of God as revealed in Jesus.

(2) It proclaimed a human character completely surrendered to God to worship him and to do his will. This was likewise revealed by Jesus.

(3) It proclaimed the worship by which men might learn God's will and lay hold upon the only Power by which they might accomplish that ideal. This took the form of adoration of God through the Christ life and incorporation of that life in the worshipers. This worship was traced directly to Jesus.

The peculiar content of Christian belief proceeds from the life of Jesus. The peculiar content of historic Christian action has been continuation and communication of the power of that life by simple proclamation and reasoned explanation of the story, by adoration and incorporation through group worship, and by observable behaviour in contact both with those who believe it and with those who reject it.

Belief in Jesus was not primarily acceptance of ethical precepts; many of these had been enunciated by the rabbis. They were accepted by his followers as axiomatic because they described his character and his acts, which taken together may be called his life. That life is one of the most bewildering and compelling which the world has ever seen. Jews, Christians and unbelievers, semitists, hellenists, physicians, rotarians, psychologists, lawyers, historians, novelists and politicians have all addressed themselves to the fascinating and provoking problem of unraveling the secret of the character of this man who demands explanation more than any man in history. It is small wonder that a life which demands explanation ten thousand miles away, and after nineteen hundred years, should have so profoundly impressed those who came into immediate contact with it that they gladly followed him to learn the secret of his power, or opposed him because he thwarted their ambitions.

Following Christ commenced with devotion to the magnetic and powerful man and friend whom Jewish peasants gladly accepted as the Messiah whose kingdom they were eager to see established. They knew his family and his trade and his habits. They ate and drank with him. They saw him rejoice at banquets and sorrow at burials. They saw his remarkable works and followed him from town to town into Jerusalem where they saw him suffer and die.

This, however, was but half the story. The character of Jesus presented a bewildering problem. Despite his manifest and patent finiteness, his character and personality were just as patently free from the limitations arising from this humanity. His life was dominated from the beginning by a clearly cut purpose from which nothing was able to deflect him. Every circumstance was evaluated and every choice determined by its relation to this purpose. He called this "possession of the single eye," and declared that a man thus equipped would find his path sufficiently illuminated to make errors of evaluation and choice unnecessary and even impossible. "If thine eye be single, thy whole body shall be full of light. But if thine eye be evil, thy whole body shall be full of darkness. If, therefore, the light that is in thee be darkness, what a darkness!" [13] Thus his life was one of integrated actions rather than an aggregate of uncoordinated reactions. He called this doing the will of God and urged men to pray, and consequently to pledge themselves to live, that God's kingdom would come by their doing God's will, and thus hallowing the Father's Name.

His choices were never impeded by hesitation but rather ennobled by calm decision which set them out in clear relief. Consequently, fear had no place in this man's soul; anxiety never concerned him. The hours on the Cross were wholly without regrets, for no choice of his could ever have been otherwise. In the throes of the death thirst he could calmly say, "Father, into thy hands I commend my spirit." [14] This quality was recognized not as an achievement resulting from long exertion of effort, but as being natural, simple and uninterrupted from the beginning. It was an example of being, not of becoming. Such an one could not be holden of death, the last product of finiteness, but must needs rise triumphant and thus cap the climax of victory.

Here was the wonder of wonders: a finite man whose personality was wholly unimpaired by limits of finiteness, and in whom the eternal chasm between finite and infinite had been definitely bridged. God and man had become one; herein lay the hope of man's salvation. Such a phenomenon was unique, arousing adoration, demanding explanation and pleading for perpetuation so long as the world doth stand. To the adoration, explanation and perpetuation of the Christ life the Christ group was pledged "until the whole earth should be filled with the knowledge of the Lord as the waters cover the sea." [15]

Many books have been written and many expressions have been coined to describe the life and character of Jesus. To early Christians who knew how men groped for God by sacrifice, this word appealed as best describing him whom they worshiped and tried to follow. He is the one true, pure, immortal sacrifice. His life was regarded as an entity from his miraculous conception and humble birth through his active ministry. It reached the climax in his blessed passion and precious death, and attained its triumphant denouement in his mighty resurrection and glorious ascension.

The climax of that sacrifice was always seen in the passion and death upon the Cross, which was interpreted by three scenes, the first at the beginning of his ministry, the second in the upper room before he left for Gethsemane, the third in Gethsemane just before his seizure.

(1) The first is known as "The Temptation," [16] which, in three scenes, describes the human tension between self preservation and ambition on the one hand, and devotion to the will of God on the other. Jesus is portrayed as understanding the appeal of hunger and ambition but calmly disregarding them when their gratification involved neglect or flouting of God's will. "And angels came and ministered to him."

(2) The second scene is placed just before he left the upper room. Once more the tension was between human visions of grandeur and doing God's will.[17] The disciples had given way to ambition and he said, "Ye are they which have continued with me in my temptations, and I appoint unto you a kingdom as my Father hath appointed unto me. Simon, Simon, Satan hath desired to have you that he may sift you as wheat, but I have prayed for thee that thy faith fail not. And when thou art converted strengthen thy brethren." Simon himself had to be plunged into the despair of self preservation before he laid hold on that strength.

(3) The third scene is in the Prayer in Gethsemane immediately before his seizure, when there came the final tension between self preservation and doing God's will.[18] He had long known what the outcome of the opposition of the priests and Sadducees would be. Only a fool courts suffering and execution; a very brave man may meet them calmly if they lour as inevitable consequences of doing his duty. Self preservation, the first law of nature, is the last consideration in the spiritual realm. "He that will save his life shall lose it; and he that shall lose his life for my sake shall find it." [19]

The calmness of Jesus was different from that of the brave man who steels himself to conquer his fear; this man knew no fear. He was not courting suffering; it was being thrust upon him as the work of men who were opposing the will of God which he had revealed. He could still make his escape if he wished. And so he prayed, "Father, I certainly don't want to drink these dregs, but I want to do your will. And if doing your will involves drinking these dregs, I shall do your will." "And there appeared an angel from heaven, strengthening him." The spiritual side of his sacrifice was complete; the physical acts had yet to come.

He had foreseen all this and had assured his disciples of it; he had also assured them that he would return the third day. Their faith in him was tremendous, so great that they did not disband after his crucifixion. When, on the morning of the third day, the young man at the tomb told the women to go and announce to the disciples, even to Peter, that he had risen, he assumed that they knew just where to find those disciples.[20] When the two men discovered at Emmaus that their companion had been Jesus, who had been known to them in the breaking of bread, they hurried back to Jerusalem and knew just where to find the disciples.[21]

The appearances after the crucifixion convinced the disciples that Jesus had risen and that the Christ life was triumphant. Their own relation to the Christ life had yet to be clarified, but their faith in him had been vindicated. Their last view of their Lord was just before the ascension, which represented the final triumph of Jesus. Their reasoning was slow and varied in character but their conviction was unshakeable and they finally came to the inspiring conclusion: The Christ life, the Christ sacrifice is eternal.

We are familiar with the story of how the little group grew by leaps and bounds. Within three days after the crucifixion his disciples' faith in him was confirmed by the resurrection. Within three months all Jerusalem and its environs were agog with the story. Within three years all Palestine had been stirred. Within three decades the Roman world was dotted with groups of followers of Jesus. Within three centuries Christianity became the official religion of the Roman Empire.

To describe the relation between Christ and the Church and its members the New Testament uses five metaphors, two of which are attributed to our Lord himself. These are the metaphors:

(1) The foundation and the building.[22] Christ is the Foundation; the building is the Church, of which individual members are the stones, which are integrated into an entity.

(2) The Groom and the Bride.[23] Christ is the Groom, and the Church is the Bride.

(3) The Shepherd and the sheep.[24] Christ is the Shepherd and individual followers are the sheep which form a flock or fold for which he cares and which he guards.

(4) The Vine and the branches.[25] Christ is the Vine and each individual is a branch. Bad branches are lopped off; good ones are pruned to enhance the life of the vine.

(5) The Head and the body.[26] The individuals of the Church form a body with differently functioning members. Of this body Christ is the Head. Because each member is endowed with choice, it is possible for the body to be split or chaotic.

In all these metaphors the common feature is the integration of two factors, each of which is necessary to the proper functioning of the other. A foundation without a building would be futile; a building without a foundation would be dangerous. One cannot be a groom without a bride, or a bride without a bridegroom. A shepherd without sheep would have nothing to do; a flock of sheep would be scattered without a shepherd. A vine stock without branches would be ineffective; it might not even live; the branches, detached from the stock, would die. Separating a head from a body causes both to die.

The members of the Church are therefore literally members of Christ. They are linked with him as the stones of a building are linked with the cornerstone. More than this, they are linked with him and with each other as the branches of a vine or the members of a body which all share the same blood, the Blood of Christ.

This vital interpretation of the Christ life was elaborated by St. Paul, whose letters to the gentile churches set forth the transformation effected in men by the Christ life. He himself had experienced this transformation and never lost the inspiration of it. His own physical handicaps remained. He was so little that they called him "Shorty" or "Tiny" (*Paulos* means just that), but his very nickname has become holy and has completely overshadowed his real name Saul. He was so nearly blind that he did not recognize the High Priest who struck him.[27] Whether this near blindness was his "thorn in the flesh"[28] we cannot say, but it may have been. Five times thrashed with whips, thrice beaten with rods and once stoned,[24] he knew well enough that his impression upon strangers was of one who was "weak in bodily presence and contemptible in speech." [30] Despite these handicaps, and possibly by reason of them, he became the outstanding missionary and interpreter of the Christ life. For nineteen centuries the enthusiasm of his transformed life has enkindled and inspired millions of Christians to study and live the Christ life. His picture of that life is preserved in one of his letters.[31] "Oh, the depth of the riches of the wisdom and knowledge of God . . . Of him and to him and through him are all things: to whom be glory forever. . . . I beseech you therefore brethren, by the mercies of God, that ye present your bodies a living sacrifice, holy, acceptable unto God. This is your rational [32] worship. And be not conformed to this world, but be ye transformed by the renewing of your mind."

By our nature as finite men we have sinned, as have our ancestors from the beginning. Men have always been imperfect in recognition of God by worship, by learning and doing his will, and by leaning upon him for power to do these things. Our surrender to God has been, at best, faulty. This natural, human trait is called by St. Paul "the old man," whose highest concept of doing God's will had been keeping arbitrarily given laws. Union with Christ effects the death of this old man which is buried by baptism which, from the beginning, was the means of entrance into the Christ group. As men come from baptism they commence to share the resurrection life of Jesus, the great triumph over finiteness. The nature of this risen life is joy and peace. "I am crucified with Christ; still I am living; no longer the old "I" lives, but Christ now lives in me and I am now living by the faith of the Son of God who loved me and gave himself for me." [33] "The works of the flesh are plain, which are adultery, hatred, envyings (and fifteen others). . . . They which do such things shall not inherit the kingdom of God. But the fruit of the Spirit is love, joy, peace, longsuffering, gentleness, goodness, faith, meekness and temperance. There is no law against these. And they who are Christ's have crucified the flesh with its longings and desires." [34]

This does not imply that we are exempt from the inconveniences and sufferings of the finite body; it means that these things not only have no effect upon the life of the Spirit, but they may even be the means of exhibiting the power of that life. When the Lord Christ had proclaimed his inflexible determination to do God's will, there remained before him greater suffering than any man has been called to endure. St. Paul could rejoice in his own sufferings and say, "For the sake of his Body the Church, I fill out in my flesh what is lacking of the sufferings of Christ." [35]

Christ's sufferings were as much a part of his sacrificial life as any other event. Conception, birth, ministry, suffering, death, resurrection and ascension were all blended into one triumphant whole. Since his sacrifice, which continues today in heaven, millions of men and women have shared with him the results of human finiteness. He suffered *for* us but not *instead of* us. For us men and for our salvation he was incarnate and suffered and was crucified; he rose and ascended into heaven. We are still living in the flesh although the longings and desires of the flesh need not rule our choices. They will not rule those choices if we are living the Christ life with the same Power with which he lived it. "If we suffer with him, we shall also reign with him." [36] Where he has ascended we may also in heart and mind thither ascend and with him continually dwell. The Christ life is the Christ sacrifice and leads to eternal triumph. This is the Christian sacrifice, the ideal toward which we are moving and which we can exhibit when we meet the tensions of life as he met them unless we let that old man come to life again in us.

A laboured effort was made by the writer of the Epistle to the Hebrews to interpret the work of Christ in terms of Jewish purifications, especially in terms of the Day of Purifications before the annual Jewish New Year Festival. After the destruction of the temple, zevachs and 'olahs and purifications could no longer be made. How were men to worship and purify themselves? Two answers were forthcoming.

The synagogue had already set the pace and led the way for assurance to orthodox Jews that study of the Torah, accompanied by prayer, fasting and almsgiving, would be an adequate surrogate for the worship which had engaged them for centuries and for the purifications which it necessitated.

For Christian Jews the writer of *To the Hebrews* tried to do a piece of exegesis. His eager spirit and his complete devotion exceeded his knowledge of ancient rites and his ability to use words properly. He even called purifications *thusiai,* which in both pagan Greek and the Septuagint, had always been used exclusively for acts of worship. Nevertheless, his purpose was lofty.

For a generation Christians had been meeting the objection that Jesus could not be the Messiah because of his ignominious execution. They were already familiar with the application, unknown in rabbinic circles, of the Twenty-Second Psalm and the Servant sections of Isaiah as explaining the death of the Messiah. The author of *To the Hebrews* tried to explain the work of Jesus in terms of Jewish purifications.[37]

Whether he was Jew or Greek, he recognized blood as the well nigh universal symbol of life, and blood rites as the cultic expression of purifying power. He proposed to go farther than the ABC's of Christian teaching and carry his readers to maturity of thought.[38] Taking familiar *kipper* rites as his point of departure, he pictured Jesus as the great High Priest, the agent *par excellence* of purification, which was to include sins of conscience as the ultimate of which physical taboos were symbolic.[39] Thinking of the disgusting parade of unclean carcases to the smouldering offal in the Valley of Hinnom, he came to the triumphant conclusion:

> We have an altar whereof they have no right to eat which serve the tabernacle. For the bodies of those beasts whose blood is brought into the sanctuary by the High Priest for sin, are burned outside the camp. Wherefore Jesus also, that he might sanctify (*kipper*) the people with his blood, suffered outside the gate. (Calvary was outside the city limits). Let us go forth therefore

unto him outside the camp, bearing his reproach. For here we
have no continuing city but we seek one to come.⁴⁰

The argument is simple. Christians who are united with
Christ must expect to share his whole life of sacrifice, both the
reproaches and the humiliations, as well as the eternal triumph
to which the Christ life leads.

The third Christian category which is described by sacrifice
is worship. The first Christians were Jews. As Jews they continued their devotion to the synagogue worship on the Sabbath. This was based upon singing of Psalms, reading prayers
and chapters from the Old Testament, and recitation of the
shema, the equivalent of a creed.⁴¹ On the first day of the week,
either at a house or at a public meeting place, an additional rite
was conducted, called the "Breaking of Bread." The oldest testimony to this rite is that of St. Paul.⁴²

In his first letter to the Corinthians he assures his readers that
he is telling them what he himself had been taught. We have
therefore a tradition already well formed and received and written within thirty years after the ministry of Jesus. Many were
still living who could verify or deny that tradition but it seems
to have been generally accepted.

He refers to a rite which he calls "The Lord's Banquet" (a
more accurate translation than *supper*), thus using a title
which we saw applied to the banquet after the Greek thusia.⁴³
He traces the origin of this rite to the last meal which Jesus ate
with his disciples before the crucifixion, when he took bread
and a cup of wine, blessed them, called them his Body and
Blood, and gave them to the disciples with the injunction to do
this "for a memorial" of him.

The Greek word translated *memorial* (*anamnesis*) may well
have reminded the author of the portion of the minchah and
the incense of the Bread of Presence which were burned on the
altar. This portion, called the azkarah, was rendered into Greek
usually as *anamnesis.* This was neither a memento nor a token
nor a commemoration nor a memorial in our sense of that
term, but a peculiarly sacrificial term denoting some sort of

identity between the thing so described and that to which it referred. Except on special occasions when it was substituted for a 'olah, the minchah was not burned on an altar. Instead, a small piece of it, or the incense on the Bread of Presence, was burnt; the remainder was eaten by a priest. From the fact that the azkarah was burnt, the minchah was called an *ishsheh,* a *reach nichoach,* a burnt offering of sweet savour,[44] a title given only to 'olahs and zevachs.

The Bread and the Wine which were blessed at the Lord's Banquet became an azkarah of the sacrifice of Jesus. St. Paul insisted that, in Hebrew rites, "they who eat thusias are partakers of the altar." The same would be true of Greek thusias. Thus he lays down a general principle that Christians cannot be partakers of the Lord's table and also partakers of the tables of pagan deities. (The Lord's Table was another Greek sacrificial expression.) [45] A Christian cannot worship God and pagan deities. Thus, within thirty years of our Lord's ministry, the Christian feast was treated as in the same category as Hebrew zevachs and Greek thusias; it was a sacrificial act of worship, an azkarah, participation in our Lord's passion, death, resurrection and ascension. The Greek word for participation was *koinōnia;* in Latin this was *communio,* from which comes our word *communion.* The sacred participation in, or holy communion of, our Lord's humanity was one of the earliest names for the Christian feast and has remained to the present, although many who use it, and many who avoid the use, do not realize its tremendous sacrificial significance when they interpret it as a "sweet communion with one another."

It may well have been that the last meal of Jesus with his disciples was a *qiddush,* a Jewish family meal with religious meaning, eaten on the eves of sabbaths and of great festivals. St. Paul the Pharisee, who must have eaten hundreds of qiddushes in his Jewish and early Christian days, made not the slightest reference to this fact in his interpretation of Holy Communion except to use the phrase "cup of blessing" and "breaking of bread" in order to draw a sharp contrast. "The

cup of blessing which *we* bless is a participation in the Blood of
Christ; the Bread which *we* break is a participation in the Body
of Christ." They who eat this Bread and drink of this Cup
worthily become participants in the Body and Blood of Christ,
participants in the Christ life and power, in the Christian sacrifice.

Our purpose at this time is not to trace the history of the
doctrine of the Lord's Banquet which, from earliest days, has
been the peculiar worship of the Christian Church. It is to
indicate that, since sacrificial language has been used from the
first to describe the holy participation in the sacrifice of the Son
of God, it is not surprising that this sacrificial interpretation has
continued throughout historic Christendom. It has been variously interpreted and just as variously misinterpreted by men
who did not understand the meaning of ancient sacrifices and
purifications or of the Epistle to the Hebrews, whose author was
not always clear in his understanding despite his commendable
purpose and zeal.

Within a hundred years after St. Paul the Greek word
eucharistia had become a name of the Banquet and of the Bread
and Wine which constituted it.[46] This word we remember as
in use for at least two centuries before Christ as a technical term
to describe an elaborate act of thanksgiving culminating in a
thusia. By the year 200 the Christian Church was composed
chiefly, if not wholly, of Greek-thinking Gentiles who had no
hesitancy in applying the word *thusia* to describe best the Christian worship which by that time was widespread in the Roman
Empire. When Christian thought was translated into Latin,
sacrificium was the normal word to express this idea. From this
comes our word *sacrifice*.

It is not surprising, as the centuries rolled by and Jewish
thought became strange, and Greek almost unknown, to Christian thinkers of the West, that philosophers made mighty
efforts to explain just how the Bread and the Wine became the
azkarah of the humanity of Jesus. Nor is it surprising that, in
trying to explain the process by aristotelian philosophy which

came to be commonly accepted by the thirteenth century, they used some exceedingly extravagant expressions which were denied by expressions quite as extravagant. Zeal is not always tempered with knowledge and with accurate thinking and expression.

In the course of centuries Christian thinking, Christian worship and Christian living became separated from each other, to speak mildly, and all three were corrupted. Sacrifice became an academic word, wholly misunderstood by thinkers of the West who knew neither Greek nor Hebrew. It is not surprising that rugged reformers became zealously convinced that something had to be done by them. And since their zeal was not accompanied by love and extensive information, it is not surprising that they frequently did the wrong things in lively sincerity. Nor is it surprising that defenders of the western System should assume as their first premiss that this System must be maintained and developed and that they should try to fortify their arguments with this determination.

Anglican reformers, while rejecting the imperial System of the West, tried zealously to maintain the Order upon which that system was built. These also were men who had just been introduced to Greek and Hebrew, and they must not be wholly blamed if their finite information and their equally finite reasoning were sometimes faulty and negligent of facts not yet discovered or, being discovered, were not clearly understood.

The purpose of these chapters has been to clarify the meaning of sacrifice in ancient religions which formed the milieu in which Christianity had its rise and to make plain that this is the only word which adequately describes the work of Jesus, the purpose and content of Christian worship and the basis and ideals of Christian living. Thus we can hope to hear the great voices singing. The kingdoms of this world have become the kingdom of our Lord and of his Christ; and he shall reign forever.

THE HALE LECTURES

The Right Reverend Charles Reuben Hale, D.D., LL.D., Bishop of Cairo, Bishop Coadjutor of Springfield, was born in 1837, consecrated Bishop on July 26, 1892, and died on Christmas Day in the year 1900.

In his will he bequeathed to Western Theological Seminary, now Seabury-Western Theological Seminary of Evanston, Illinois, a fund to be held in trust "for the general purpose of promoting the Catholic Faith, in its purity and integrity, as taught in Holy Scripture, held by the Primitive Church, summed up in the Creeds, and affirmed by the undisputed General Councils, and, in particular, to be used only and exclusively for . . . the establishment, endowment, printing, and due circulation of a yearly Sermon . . . and . . . of Courses of Lectures."

The subjects of these Lectures were to be:

(*a*) Liturgies and Liturgics.

(*b*) Church Hymns and Church Music.

(*c*) The History of the Eastern Churches.

(*d*) The History of National Churches.

(*e*) Contemporaneous Church History, i.e. treating of events happening since the beginning of what is called "The Oxford Movement," in 1833.

The Trustees of the Seminary accepted the generous bequest of Bishop Hale and have endeavoured faithfully to carry out its provisions. A full list follows of the Hale Lectures thus far delivered and published.

VOLUMES IN THE HALE LECTURES

The Doctrine of the Atonement. By the Rev. Leonard Hodgson, D.D., Regius Professor of Divinity in the University of Oxford, Canon of Christ Church, Oxford. 1950.

Witness to the Light. By the Rev. Alec R. Vidler, D.D., Priest of the Oratory of the Good Shepherd, Warden of St. Deiniol's Library in Hawarden, Hon. Canon of Derby Cathedral. 1947.

Men and Movements in the American Episcopal Church. By the Rev. E. Clowes Chorley, D.D., L.H.D., late Historiographer of the Church. 1943.

Personalities of the Old Testament. By the Rev. Fleming James, D.D., Ph.D., Professor of the Literature and Interpre-

tation of the Old Testament, Emeritus, Berkeley Divinity
School, affiliated with Yale University Divinity School. 1938.

The Church in Japan. By the Rt. Rev. Henry St. George Tucker,
Bishop of Virginia; a former Presiding Bishop of the Protes-
tant Episcopal Church; formerly (1912–1923) Bishop of
Kyoto. 1937. (Published under the title *The History of the
Episcopal Church in Japan.*)

The Praise of God. By the Rev. Winfred Douglas, Mus.D., late
Canon of St. John's Cathedral, Denver, Colorado. 1935. (Published under the title *Church Music in History and Practice.*)

The Social Implications of the Oxford Movement. By the Rev.
William George Peck, Rector of St. John Baptist, Hulme,
Manchester, England. 1932.

Pastoral Psychiatry and Mental Health. By the Rev. John Rath-
bone Oliver, M.D., Ph.D., late Associate in the History of
Medicine at the Johns Hopkins University. 1932. (Published
under title *Psychiatry and Mental Health.*)

Christ in the Gospels. By the Rev. Burton Scott Easton, Ph.D.,
S.T.D., late Professor at the General Theological Seminary.
1930.

New Horizons of the Christian Faith. By the Rev. Frederick C.
Grant, D.D., Th.D., Professor of Biblical Theology at Union
Theological Seminary, New York City; formerly Dean of the
Seabury-Western Theological Seminary, 1927–38. 1928.

Some Aspects of Contemporary Greek Orthodox Thought. By
the Rev. Frank Gavin, M.A., Ph.D., late Professor at the General Theological Seminary. 1921.

The Ethiopic Liturgy. By the Rev. S. A. B. Mercer, D.D., Ph.D.,
Professor Emeritus of Trinity College in the University of
Toronto. 1915.

Biographical Studies in Scottish Church History. By the Rt.
Rev. Anthony Mitchell, D.D., Late Bishop of Aberdeen and
Orkney. 1913.

The National Church of Sweden. By the Rt. Rev. John Words-
worth, D.D., LL.D., Late Bishop of Salisbury. 1910.

Church Hymns and Church Music. By Peter C. Lutkin, Mus.D.,
A.G.P., Late Dean of the School of Music, North-western
University. 1908.

NOTES

CHAPTER I

1. Comparison of Luke 4:23 with Luke 2:46 indicates the use of words three centuries ago. In both AV and DV the translations are:

2:46 sitting among the doctors
4:23 physician, heal thyself.

Today the word translated *doctor* would be *teacher*; *physician* would be *doctor*.

2. 1706, the date given by the *Oxford Dictionary* as the earliest instance of this meaning of sacrifice, refers naturally to literary use.

3. This underlies the dictum of many that *do ut des* (I give that thou mayest give) is the basic meaning of sacrifice. To read a modern connotation into an ancient term does not make for accuracy.

4. This fact, first emphasized by H. C. Trumbull in *The Blood Covenant*, 1st ed. 1885; 3rd ed. 1893, p. 286, is of primary importance.

CHAPTER II

1. The biological differences between man and the beasts are discussed by Prof. Julian Huxley in the first chapter of *Essays of a Biologist* (1923).

2. The spiritual significance of the prolongation of human infancy was first made clear by John Fiske in 1874 in *Outlines of a Cosmic Cosmology,* vol. 2, pp. 324–363.

3. The tendency to treat religion as a separate process of life, increasingly irrelevant to other activities and to find an independent origin of worship, goes hand in hand with that scepticism of the value of religious acts which issues in omitting the acts entirely or sublimating them into other social acts. Life, to early man, was a single, complex unit. He was eager to do anything to protect and strengthen it. Magical, scientific and religious acts may have been, at first, segregated because they had to do with invisible processes and required greater knowledge and experience for performance. "Not everybody could do it." This contrasts with the modern American attitude which looks for expertness principally in physical things and processes. In the fields of education, politics and religion one man's opinion is as welcome as another's.

4. An excellent discussion of the

relation of magic to science and religion is given by Prof. Robert H. Lowie in *Primitive Religion* (1925), pp. 136–152.

CHAPTER III

1. The most nearly complete study of totemism is Sir James Frazer's *Totemism and Exogamy* (1910) in four volumes. The totemistic thesis underlies his monumental work, *The Golden Bough,* expanded to thirteen volumes in the third edition.

2. The derivation of θυειν is that of Emile Boisacq in *Dictionnaire étymologique de la langue grecque,* p. 360. My suggestion that θεος is a cognate is based upon the form *dhou* which the root has in related languages. See Boisacq, pp. 339–340.

3. The variety, significance and extent of all bull cults of all kinds are excellently described and illustrated by A. B. Cook in *Zeus,* vol. I, pp. 441–718.

CHAPTER IV

1. Divination in Babylonia and Assyria is discussed in detail by Morris Jastrow in *Aspects of Belief and Practice in Babylonia and Assyria,* pp. 143–206.

2. Dt. 18:10. 1 Sam. 15:23. 2 Kg. 17:17. Jer. 14:14. Ezk. 12:24; 13:6–7; 21:21–23.

3. Ex. 29:13, 22. Lev. 3:4, 10, 15; 4:9; 7:4; 8:16, 25; 9:10, 19.

4. Acts 1:26.

5. The most satisfactory discussion of the "ark" is by W. R. Arnold in *Ephod and Ark* (Harvard Theological Studies, 1917).

6. Ex. 18:15. Dt. 17:9–10. Jdg. 1:1–2. 1 Sam. 9:9. 1 Kg. 22:5–6. 2 Kg. 22:13–14 refer to the recognized custom of "enquiring of the LORD" for guidance in decisions.

7. The verb προφητευειν was used with the meaning of "interpret" in early Greek literature. Cf. Pindar *Frag* 118; Euripides, *Ion* 369; Herodotus vii, 111; Aristotle 391. a. 16 (de Mundo 1:2). It is used to describe the possible mantic ravings of the seeress of Apollo by Pausanias II, 24:1.

8. The best source for the study of taboo is, of course, J. G. Frazer's *Taboo and the Perils of the Soul* in *The Golden Bough.* One may differ frequently from the author's interpretations and deductions, but the book remains the best collection of facts available.

9. The three volumes of Edward Westermarck's *History of Human Marriage* (5th ed., 1922) are indispensable for a thorough study of marriage rites and customs.

10. Lev. 13 and 14. See Chapter XI, pp. 187 ff.

11. Lev. 22:4. Num. 19:11–22. Chapter XI, pp. 184 f.

12. See next chapter, especially pp. 48 f.

CHAPTER V

1. Dt. 12:23. The Hebrew and Greek words (*nephesh* and ψυχη) here translated *life,* are both frequently rendered *soul.* Early man considered the blood as the seat, the principle and the vehicle of the soul. Because the liver was supposed to be

a mass of clotted blood, the soul was located in that organ.

2. Hesiod, *Theogony*, 154 ff.

3. Ioul., *frag. epist.* I 375. Quoted by A. B. Cook, *Zeus,* vol. ii, p. 1053.

4. Sixty years ago Henry Clay Trumbull astonished the scholarly world by his book *The Blood Covenant* in which he made a remarkable collection of instances, from all over the civilized world, from ancient and more recent times, illustrating the mutual and common use of blood. The references selected for this study may be verified, unless otherwise noted, from the careful index of the second edition of this book (1893). Most of the relevant illustrations are in the first chapter but the whole book is filled with useful information. See also H. W. Robinson, Article *Blood* in ERE II, p. 716b.

5. F. B. Jevons, *Introduction to the History of Religion*, p. 191. Frazer, *The Dying God,* pp. 92 ff.

6. Homer, *Odyssey* xi, 34 ff.

7. Pausanias ii, 24:1.

8. Franz Cumont, *Oriental Religions in Roman Paganism,* pp. 66–68. Georg Wissowa, *Religion und Kultus der Römer,* pp. 267–269.

9. See *Blood bathing* in Index of Trumbull's *The Blood Covenant.*

10. Aeschylus, *Seven against Thebes,* 42 ff.

11. J. G. Frazer, in *Taboo and the Perils of the Soul* (3rd ed., pp. 239–251), has made an extensive collection of instances of blood taboo. From these he has made generous excerpts, without references, in *The Golden Bough* (pp. 227–230), the single volume which he abridged from the twelve-volume work.

12. Lev. 13:10.

13. Gen. 9:4. Lev. 3:17; 17:10, 11, 14; 19:26.

14. Acts 15:20; 21:25.

15. Koran v:4.

16. J. G. Frazer, *The Magic Art,* ii, 367.

17. id. ii, 16.

18. id. ii, 44.

19. Frazer, *Taboo and Perils of the Soul,* p. 104.

20. id., p. 115.

21. id., p. 176.

22. id., p. 219.

23. Frazer, *The Magic Art,* ii, pp. 107–109.

24. Frazer, *The Dying God,* p. 180.

25. Frazer, *Taboo and the Perils of the Soul,* p. 15.

26. Frazer, *The Dying God,* p. 176.

27. Ignatius Goldziher, *Muhammadanische Studien,* ii, p. 328.

28. Ex. 12:7, 22.

29. Ex. 24:8.

30. Zech. 9:11.

31. Gen. 17:10–14. Ex. 4:25–26.

32. Ex. 29:19–21.

33. Num. 35:31–33.

34. Lev. 14:52.

35. Ex. 24:8.

36. Lev. 8:30.

37. Lev. 4:6. Num. 19:4.

38. Ex. 29:16.

39. Ex. 24:6; 29:16. Lev. 1:5, 11; 3:2, 8, 13; 7:2, 17:6, 11. Num. 18:17. 2 Kg. 16:13. 2 Ch. 29:22. Ezk. 43:18.

40. Lev. 4:7.

41. Lev. 5:9.

42. Ex. 29:12. Lev. 4:7, 18, 25, 30, 34; 8:15; 9:9; 16:18.

43. Lev. 16:14–15. See Chapter XI, note 79.

44. 2 Kg. 16:15.

45. Lev. 1:4; 4:20; 5:6; 8:34. Num. 8:19 and many others.

46. Heb. 4:16.

47. Chapter XI, pp. 168–196.

CHAPTER VI

1. *Iliad.* i, 37–42.
2. id., i, 472–474.
3. *Odyssey,* iii, 419.
4. *Suppliants,* 117, 128.
5. *Argonauts,* i, 1093, 1139.
6. *Iliad,* xxiii, 864.
7. *Odyssey,* ix, 554.
8. *Iliad,* ii, 420.
9. Jane E. Harrison, *Prolegomena to the Study of Greek Religion* (3rd ed., Cambridge University Press, 1922), p. 10. Miss Harrison's study made a genuine contribution to the study of the history of religions, and of the Greek religions in particular. While some of her conclusions have been questioned by scholars, minor differences of opinion have not affected the general recognition of the value of her penetrating examination of the sources.
10. By the time of Pausanias, who wrote in the latter part of the second century A.D., the distinction was not so sharp. The Greek verb θυειν, possibly under the influence of Latin generalization, possibly because of the natural tendency to carelessness or inaccuracy in use of words, and possibly because of natural changes in connotation of words used through many centuries, had become extended in meaning and was often used as a general term for sacrifice. See Pausanias ii, 24:1; iv, 9:3; ix, 8:1, et al.
11. The winds were invoked by σφαγια, which were also used in oaths. In oaths the idea seems to be: If I break my oath may I become like the animal which we have just slain and hacked. The cult of Zeus Meilichios furnishes a strange and difficult instance of fused cults. See J. E. Harrison, *Prolegomena,* pp. 15–28,

and A. B. Cook, *Zeus,* vol. ii, pp. 1091–1160. The Olympian Zeus had plainly ousted the older being Meilichios as a separate divinity, but the holocaust rite of Meilichios remained the central feature of the fused cults. Similar instances are frequent in the attachment of the rites of pagan divinities to the cults of Christian and Moslem saints and holy days (e.g. Christmas and New Year rites).

12. For the study of Roman cult one must examine Georg Wissowa, *Religion und Kultus der Römer* (1902), J. B. Carter, *The Religious Life of Ancient Rome* (1911), W. Warde Fowler, *Roman Festivals* (1st ed. 1899, 3rd ed. 1911, reprinted 1916), and Fowler's masterpiece, the Gifford Lectures of 1910–1911, published as *The Religious Experience of the Roman People* (1911). Wissowa's work will be referred to as RK, Carter's by the author's name, Fowler's first book as RF, and his second book as RE.
13. Carter, p. 19.
14. RE, p. 210.
15. RF, pp. 95–97. RE, p. 173.
16. One wonders how far this fact contributed to the development of the western rites without any communions.
17. RE, pp. 180, 186. For absence of blood taboo in Rome: RE, p. 33.
18. RF, pp. 242–250.
19. RF, p. 71. Ovid, *Fasti,* iv, 629–676.
20. RF, pp. 79–85. RK, pp. 165–166. Ovid, *Fasti,* iv, 721–782.
21. Ovid, *Fasti,* iv, 733 ff. Ovid (1st century A.D.) participated in the Parilia.
22. Karl Kircher, *Die sakrale Bedeutung des Weines im Altertum,* pp. 82–87. Gen. 49:11. Dt. 32:14.
23. RE, p. 180.

CHAPTER VII

1. Livy, VIII, vi:13–xi:1.
2. W. W. Fowler, RE, p. 107.
3. RE, pp. 44, 112. Georg Wissowa, RK, pp. 354–355.
4. A general survey of these can be made from the eight articles *Vows* in ERE, vol. XII, pp. 644–660. The articles, each by a specialist, include the following peoples and religions: Hindu, Buddhist, Chinese, Greek, Roman, Hebrew, Jewish, Teutonic and Christian. Enough instances are given to enable one to secure a basic understanding of the subject.
5. *Iliad,* vi, 93 ff. and 274 ff.
6. id., viii, 287–291.
7. Xenophon, *Anabasis,* iii, 2:12. ετι νυν αποθουσιν, "they are still sacrificing away."
8. These have been carefully studied and fully described by W. H. Rouse in his *Greek Votive Offerings* (Cambridge, 1902). The article by the same author in ERE, vol. XII, pp. 641a–643b, is based upon this book.
9. Rouse gives a list of such offerings in pp. 394–408 of his book.
10. Rouse, op. cit., pp. 57, 89, 92, 122, 185, 214, 230, 234, 254, 262, 265, 295, 296, 328, 329, 330.
11. Fowler, RE, pp. 200–206. Wissowa, RK, pp. 319–323. Article by A. C. Pearson, *Vows,* Roman, in ERE, vol. XII, pp. 653a–654b.
12. Virgil, *Aeneid,* i, 334.
13. Fowler, RE, p. 209.
14. This same primitive reasoning might well explain the disposal of the bodies of Greek σφαγια rites. The blood, the life, of the animal had been used for distasteful prophylactic and apotropaic rites and purposes. The body was not fit for food;

it might be burned on an εσχαρα or pitched into the sea; it was taboo.
15. Gen. 28:20–22. In Gen. 31:13 the vow is closely associated with smearing oil upon the stone for ratification.
16. 1 Sam. 1:22, 28.
17. 2 Sam. 15:7.
18. Lev. 7:16; 22:18, 21; 23:38.
19. Acts 18:18.
20. Acts 21:24; 23:12–13.
21. Ps. 22:25; 50:14; 56:12; 61:5, 8; 76:11; 116:13, 16; 132:2.
22. Prv. 7:14; 20:25; 31:2. Eccl. 5:4.
23. Nah. 1:15.
24. Num. 6:1–21. AV and DV spell Nazarite. RV and JV spell Nazirite. AV and DV were under influence of a tradition preserved in Matt. 2:23, connecting the ascetic (spelled Naz*arene*) with the city Nazareth.
25. Jer. 35.
26. Jos. 6:17–7:26.
27. Jud. 11:30–40.
28. 1 Sam. 15:1–33.
29. The story is sometimes misunderstood because of the translation in AV, which uses the word *curse,* or its cognate *accursed,* to translate Hebrew *charam.* This word occurs twenty-eight times in OT; eleven of them are in the Jericho story. In AV it is translated five times as *devoted,* once as *a dedicated thing,* once as *forfeit,* four times as a proper name *Hormah,* twice as *curse* (one of these is in the Jericho story), ten times as *an accursed thing,* once as *utterly destroyed,* and twice as *utter destruction.* DV uses Latin *anathema,* a transliteration of the Greek word. JV uses the phrase *the devoted thing,* following RV. The error of the AV translation is thus avoided by the one

older translation (DV) and by all the later official translations.

30. The fact that *charam* is not used does not alter the meaning of the story.

31. The meaning of *devotio* is lost by the almost uniform translation of *utterly destroyed* in AV and largely in RV and JV. DV uses *slain,* which describes the fact but loses the religious significance.

32. Reference to this kind of qorban is found in Mark 7:11.

33. Rom. 9:3.

34. Luke 21:5, where it is translated *gifts.*

35. Acts 23:12, 14 (bis), 21.

36. 1 Cor. 12:3. Miss J. E. Harrison, in *Prolegomena* (pp. 138–143), shows the close relation between votive offerings and curses.

37. 1 Cor. 16:22. Gal. 1:8, 9. Rouse, in *Votive Offerings,* pp. 322–334, gives a whole chapter to discussion of votive formulas.

CHAPTER VIII

1. The chief sources for knowledge of the Bouphonia are as follows: Aristophanes, *The Clouds,* 984–985, and the Scholion, which quotes a passage from one Androtion, who is usually identified with the opponent of Demosthenes; Pausanias, i, 24:4, and i, 28:11; Porphyry, *De abstinentia,* ii, 10 ff.; Porphyry, *De abstinentia,* ii, 29, quotes Theophrastus, but the quotation does not appear in any known collection of Theophrastus. Contributions to discussion and interpretation of the feast have been made by the following: W. Robertson Smith, *Religion of the Semites,* pp. 304–306; J. G. Frazer, *Spirits of the Corn and the Wild,* vol. ii, pp. 4–7; L. R. Farnell, *Cults of the Greek States,* vol. i, pp. 56–58; P. Stengel, *Opferbräuche der Griechen,* pp. 203–221; Jane E. Harrison, *Prolegomena,* pp. 111–114, and *Themis,* pp. 141–147, 173–174; A. B. Cook, *Zeus,* vol. iii, pp. 570–605.

2. *Zeus,* vol. iii, p. 582.

3. Instances of ritual connection of yoking to a plough with (1) resuscitation, (2) rain magic, and (3) various features of dionysiac cults cannot be studied here. The present purpose is not examination of all the details of the Bouphonia, but the study of the feast as illustrative of a sacrificial rite in which no part of a victim was offered to a god or burnt upon an altar.

4. Frazer, *Totemism and Exogamy,* vol. i, p. 19, and vol. iii, pp. 67, 81.

5. See note 10, chapter VI; also Mt. 22:4. Mk. 14:12. Lk. 15:23. Acts 10:13.

6. The text of the treaty between Magnesia and Miletus is printed in SIG, 588. Otto Kern, in *Inschriften von Magnesia,* 98, and SIG, 589, preserve the decree concerning the bull festival. Few students of Greek religions have given it sufficient attention. J. G. Frazer gave two pages to it in *Spirits of the Corn and Wild,* ii, pp. 7–9. Miss J. E. Harrison examined it in more detail in *Themis,* pp. 150–157. Dr. A. B. Cook (*Zeus,* i, p. 717) says simply, "Both a bull and a ram figured in the rites of Zeus Sosipolis at Magnesia on the Maiandros." Kern (*Die Religion der Griechen,* iii, p. 177) suggests that the bull feast was established as a thank offering because of the peace between the two cities. "Das Fest für

diesen Gott ist im Herbst des Jahres 196 nach dem Friedenschluss mit Milet gestiftet, wie im Delphinion von Milet gefundede Inschrift erwiesen hat."

7. The works of Neilos are preserved in Migne PG, vol. 79, not vol. 71, as quoted in the excellent article on *Ancient Arabs* by Theodor Nöldeke in Hastings ERE, vol. I, pp. 659–673. The same article gives references to other sacrifices similar to that described by Neilos. Serious attention to the camel sacrifice was first called by W. Robertson Smith in *Religion of the Semites*, first published in 1889.

8. The quotation is the paraphrased translation of Robertson Smith, op. cit., p. 338.

9. In the article on *Ancient Arabs* in ERE, vol. i, p. 665b.

10. Transliteration of semitic consonants is not always easy because of the number of gutturals in semitic languages. The common transliteration of the Hebrew *chet* by *h* is here abandoned in favour of the simpler *ch*.

11. The verb *pasach* occurs seven times in the Old Testament. In 1 Kg. 18:21 the Hebrews are asked, "How long halt ye between two opinions?" The exact translation would be, "How long do ye continue to *pasach* upon two branches?" Yahwism and baalism were two conflicting cults; the Hebrews were apparently trying to follow both, hopping from one to the other. Five verses later, when the baalim did not hear the prayers for fire, the devotees performed in an enthusiastic way described by a different stem of *pasach*: "they *pasached* at (or upon) the altar." LXX renders this as διετρεχον (they ran across), but LV translates as *transilie-*

bant (they kept leaping across). DV translates as "leaping over"; AV goes one better and translates as "leaping upon." JV comes to the rescue and translates "dancing in halting wise about." In 2 Sam. 4:4 the fate of Mephibosheth was, "he fell and was *pasached*." All the English versions, following LXX and LV, translate "He fell and became lame." Isa. 31:5 likens Yahweh's care for Jerusalem to hovering birds (so DV and JV; AV has *flying birds*). "He will protect and rescue it; he will *pasach* and save it." The thought is that Jerusalem is safe because Yahweh is passing to and fro over it, hovering to watch and save it. All English versions translate "pass over." The thought is that Jerusalem was safe because Yahweh was continually passing to and fro over it, hovering to watch and save it.

In Ex. 12:13, 23, 27, Yahweh *pasached* the houses of the Hebrews to protect them from the death which was being meted out to the children of the Egyptians. The popular interpretation of *pasach* (pass over) in this place is that Yahweh skipped or omitted the houses of the Hebrews. The connotation of *pasach* is that he was hovering over them to protect them. The burden of the feast of the pesach is the protection of Yahweh who was the sole source of strength.

The Greek translators were not sure what *pasach* meant. They rendered as follows: Ex. 12:13, LXX, σκεπαζειν; LV, transire; DV, pass over; AV, pass over; JV, pass over. Ex. 12:27, LXX, σκεπαζειν; LV, transire; DV, pass over; AV, pass over; JV, pass over. Ex. 12:23, LXX, παρερχεσθαι; LV, transire; DV, pass through; AV, pass through; JV, pass through. 2 Sam. 4:4, LXX, χωλαίνειν; LV, claudus fieri; DV, become lame; AV, become lame; JV, become lame. 1 Kg. 18:21, LXX, χωλαίνειν; LV, claudicare; DV, halt; AV, halt; JV, halt. 1 Kg. 18:26, LXX, διατρέχειν; LV, transilire; DV, leap over; AV, leap upon; JV, dance in halting wise. Isa. 31:5, LXX, περιποιεσθαι; LV, transire; DV, pass over; AV, pass over; JV, pass over.

They did not even try to render the noun *pesach*, which had become a technical term and lost all etymological significance. They therefore transliterated the word, varying the spelling, as πασχα and φασεκ. LV usually uses *phase* and DV retains the transliteration.

12. It must be remembered that the writers of the Old Testament were not trying to initiate or create religious customs. They addressed themselves not to establishment of new rites, but to explanation and interpretation of rites which they found. When the Deuteronomist sanctioned centralization of cult at Jerusalem, he was not trying to inaugurate anything; he was endorsing a movement which had already started. When he prescribed observance of the pesach he may, as some think, have suggested that the feast was being neglected. However, his whole treatment of it indicates that it was already familiar.

13. See the index volume of *The Golden Bough* under "doorposts."

14. Ex. 12:25. Hebrew *'avodha* and Greek λατρεια, which uniformly renders it, correspond exactly to English *service*, which may refer to domestic or military or naval service, but which is also a technical term for a religious performance of almost any kind.

15. Ex. 12:27. *zevach* in Hebrew is almost identical with θυσια. Its earliest uses always described an act in which part of a victim is burnt for a deity and part eaten by the worshipers. Long usage extended its references until it eventually came to describe any kind of religious service.

16. Dt. 16:2, 5, 6.

17. Ex. 12:21. 2 Ch. 30:15, 17; 35:1, 6, 11.

18. Ex. 12:48. 2 Ch. 30:18.

19. Ex. 12:48. Nm. 9:2, 4, 5, 6, 10, 13, 14. Dt. 16:1. Jos. 5:10. 2 Kg. 23:21, 22, 23. 2 Ch. 30:1, 2, 5; 35:16, 18, 19. Ezr. 6:19. Cf. the use of ποιειν in Greek (ch. 9, note 14). This has exactly the same significance and uniformly translates Hebrew *'asah*. LV, of course, translates by *facere*. DV uniformly uses *keep*. AV continues this except in the 2 Kg. passages where it has *hold*.

20. Ex. 12:11, 27, 48. Lev. 23:5. Num. 28:16. Dt. 16:1. 2 Kg. 23:21. 2 Chr. 30:1–5.

CHAPTER IX

1. Zech. 9:13. When I have raised up thy sons, O Zion, against thy sons, O Greece.

2. Zeus (*Iliad*, i, 424) and Poseidon (*Od.*, i, 26) both journeyed all the way to Ethiopia for a banquet.

3. (1) θυειν is used by Homer of a raging wind (*Od.*, xii, 400), of a raging river (*Iliad*, xxi, 234; *Od.*, xii, 408) and of men raging in mind (*Iliad*, i, 342). The form θυνειν is used of soldiers raging in battle (*Iliad*, ii, 446; v, 250; xx, 493). The abstract θυσις is used by Plato as "raging" (*Crat.*, p. 419E).

(2) θυμός, ordinarily translated *spirit* or *soul*, stems from the same root. Its primary meaning is that of the *fume* or *vapour* which animates a man, makes him courageous and enkindles his desires, which are called επιθυμιαι, the things upon which a man concentrates his θυμός. The θυμός may go out from a man and leave him fearful and depressed. (3) θυσια, the act of burning a part of a victim for a god, is peculiar to Greek. θεος, a god, and θειος, divine, may derive from the same root. See E. Boisacq, *Dictionnaire étymologique de la langue grecque*, pp. 337–339.

4. Such words as *fumes, perfume* and *fumigate* have maintained the idea expressed by Latin *fumus* (smoke). In the English *to fume* the idea of violence is expressed.

5. Ex. 3:2; 19:16.

6. Isa. 6:4.

7. Acts 2:3–4.

8. This does not imply that man, in his "pre-human" days, was not carnivorous. The earliest days of primitive civilization are far removed from the animal ancestor of man.

9. SIG, 604, line 8.

10. *Od.*, iii, 7, 8, 59.

11. *Iliad*, xxiii, 147.

12. id., vi, 93, 115.

13. id., i, 447.

14. In Homer the two most familiar verbs thus used are ερδειν and ρεζειν, both variants of the later εργειν, *to work* or *to effect*. θυειν and ιερευειν and their compounds are used early and frequently.

Pindar used once the active of δωρειν, to present, in the phrase εδωρησαν θεων καρυκα λιταις θυσιαις (*Ol.*, vi, 78). "They presented the herald of of the gods with supplicatory thusias." Homer used διδοναι, *to give*, in the clause "to give sacred things to the gods" (ιρα θεοισι εδωκε, *Od.*, i, 67).

In classic days two of the commonest words of the language, αγειν and ποιειν, are so frequently used that many theological writers try to argue that ποιειν had some sort of "sacrificial significance." E.g., Darwell Stone in *A History of the Doctrine of the Eucharist*, vol. I, p. 9. Such arguments show profound and pathetic ignorance of Greek. αγειν, emphasizing the process, and ποιειν emphasizing the result, are the natural verbs to describe any sort of action which effects something, good or bad.

τελειν and some of its compounds are often used with the idea of completion or going through with. θεραπευειν, *to minister to*, is used by Plato and Thucydides. προσφερειν, *to offer*, which is used in the New Testament, is once used by Aristotle (Fr 108) in the clause "we do not offer anything mutilated to the gods." παρεχειν, *to provide*, is common in the inscriptions. ιερουργειν, *to do a sacred work*, is used by later writers, e.g., Apollodorus, *Bib.*, ii, 7:7.

15. *Iliad* xxiii:206. cf. *Iliad* i:423. *Od.* i:22.

16. *Iliad* i:457–473; ii:421 ff. *Od.* iii:447 ff; xii:359 ff.

17. *Od.* i:146; iv:52; vii:172; x:182, 369.

18. *Iliad* ix:171–172. Aeschylus, *Eumenides*, 626. Sophocles, *Oed. Tyr.*, 239–240. *Oed. Col.*, 1599. Euripides, *Elec.*, 791–792.

19. *Od.* ii:261.

20. *Oed. Col.*, 159.

21. *Works and Days*, 337.

22. *Od.* iv:761.

23. Apollonius of Rhodes, *Argonautica*, i:409, 425.

24. *Od.* xii:357–358.

25. Guilelmus Dittenberger, *Sylloge Inscriptionum Graecarum* (1st ed.), 67[4] & 68[2]. These two fourth century B.C. inscriptions found at Dodona were omitted from the more nearly complete and better known 3rd edition.

26. Pausanias viii:38, 4. Many modern prayer books have such petitions.

27. *Od.* xiii:180–187.

28. *Iliad* ii:306. *Od.* xiii:24–28; xv: 222, 261. Apol. Rhod. *Arg.* i, 351–354, 402–407.

29. *Iliad* ii:402.

30. *Od.* x:518:540. Sophocles, *Antigone,* 998–1023. Failure to seek such omens was ruled negligence and was apt to be occasion for anger on the part of the god, who would doom the undertaking and cease to help men until they repaired the oversight and offered a thusia to ascertain his will (e.g. *Iliad* xii:8). See note 70.

31. Plutarch, *Lycurgus* v:3.

32. Apollodorus, *Bib.* II, 8:iv.

33. *Iliad* iii:103–106; 264–301.

34. SIG 289,[14] 384,[19] 388,[9] 466.[9]

35. SIG 384, 391. Xenophon, *Anabasis* iii:2, 9; v:1:1.

36. Apol. Rhod. *Arg.* iv, 1185–1188.

37. *Od.* iii:179; ix:552–553; xi:130–132. Apol. Rhod., *Arg.* ii:685–719.

38. Apol. Rhod., *Arg.* ii:156.

39. *Corpus Inscriptionum Atticarum* ii, 352b.

40. Michel 258.

41. Polybius v, 14:8. In Michel 730 (SIG 982) is a phrase ευχαριστη-ριων σκελος. Most of the letters constitute a very probable restoration.

42. Pindar, *Pyth.* v:86. *Isthmian* iv:30 (in Donaldson's edition). Many later scholars, e.g., Sandys, break the third *Isthmian* into two odes. By this division the quotation would be *Isthmian* v:30.

43. Michel 190, 325, 334, 372, etc. The first three are in SIG 533, 656, 731. Other references to SIG are 545, 798, 800. These inscriptions commence in the third century B.C., and extend through the first two centuries of the Christian era. The use of ευχαριστια becomes increasingly frequent and always with the same technical and official significance.

44. Michel 55, 56, 394, 475. SIG 748, 798. The quotation from Michel 475 has only four letters in the original; the last six letters are supplied as restoration, but the suggestion is so apparent that the quotation may be used.

45. Michel 516, 546, 993.

46. Michel 993.

47. SIG 559.

48. SIG 336, 547, 590, 834.

49. SIG 285.

50. SIG 374, 485, 540, 587, 613, 731, 912, 1099, 1102.

51. SIG 346, 615, 711, 721.

52. *Iliad* iii:273; xix:254. *Od.* iii: 446; xiv:422.

53. *Phoenissai* 1525. *Orestes* 96.

54. J. G. Frazer, *Spirits of the Corn and the Wild* (3rd ed.), vol. ii, 48–137. One need not assume with Frazer that this implied totemistic hypotheses and that it was but a method of placating the spirit which was about to be eaten. The harvest was plainly from the earth powers. Before these were considered personal, return of the firstfruits would prevent the life cycle from breaking. After the powers were considered personal, the firstfruits were gifts to them. Any totemistic development comes later.

55. A further extension of the same principle is seen in the dedication of the first born of flocks to a god.

56. *Iliad* x:294. *Od.* iii:437.

57. *Bibliotheka* i, 9:27.

58. *Ol.* vii:80. Sandys, *in loco* in the Loeb Classical Library, misses the idea entirely in his strange translation of this passage as "reeking sacrifices of flocks that pass in procession."

59. Thucydides i, 20:3; vi, 56:2. SIG 271 (Michel 679).

60. Plutarch, *Theseus*. xxxvi, 2. SIG 372, 589, 695, 762, 1045 (Michel 378).

61. Pindar, *Nem.* vii, 46.

62. *Iliad* i:317.

63. Michel 735.

64. Splanchna rites are discussed by Paul Stengel in *Opferbräuche der Griechen*, pp. 73–91.

65. *Od.* xx:252. SIG 57 has two references to roasting of the splanchna.

66. The inscriptions indicate careful regulations of the fees of the priests. The conventional phrase is "the priest takes his fee," which is then specified. It regularly included the skin and the right leg of the animal. Other specifications are the tongue and the shoulder (Michel 714), the tongue and the splanchna with a portion of the meat (Michel 708) and the ears (Paton-Hicks, *The Inscriptions of Cos* 37). SIG 1002 and 1013 (Michel 708) indicate that the splanchna belonged to the priests. In SIG 1015 (Michel 453), 1016 (Michel 724) and 1044 (Michel 854) one-quarter of the splanchna become the property of the priests.

67. *Prolegomena*, p. 55.

68. *Iliad* i:63.

69. *Iliad* iii:274; xi:773. *Od.* iii: 445.

70. That the technical term ιεϱα is not applied to the splanchna in Homer, is no reason for assuming that it necessarily did not have this connotation in homeric times. No one supposes that any poet exhausts every use of every word in a vocabulary.

71. Xenophon recognized four methods of divination: birds, oracles, portents and thusias. *Anabasis* v, 2:9; vi, 1:22. *Cyropaedia* iii, 2:3. *Memorabilia* i, 1:1–3. Sophocles was familiar with all four methods. *Antigone* 998–1023. The inscriptions give many references to obtaining omens from thusias. SIG 347 (Michel 610), 717 (Michel 459), 735.

72. The adjective ιεϱος presents even more difficulties than ϑυσια. Dictionaries all give two different words spelled alike, with different meanings and possibly derived from different roots. One is said to mean *strong, mighty, vigorous*; it is used frequently in Homer and continues, with decreasing frequency, to the time of Theocritus. The other is rendered *divine*, and was likewise used from homeric to post-classical times. The problem is whether it originally meant *divine* and was applied to the splanchna because these came to be associated with the gods, or whether the adjective referred primarily to the splanchna and, because these formed the seat of abundant life, power and vigour, the word which described them was applied to the gods who came to personify these qualities. Men came to know divinity through cultus; they did not devise cultus as appropriate to divinity. In all ancient psychological thinking, the liver was the seat of the soul and of life and of emotions which are now popularly referred to the heart.

73. Diodorus 50. A. B. Cook, *Zeus,* vol. II, pp. 338 and 891.

74. Miss J. E. Harrison (Themis, pp. 140–157) directed attention to the significant importance of δαις as describing primarily a "distributed meal of flesh food."

75. Michel 679 (SIG 271).

76. SIG 1106.

77. SIG 736.

78. Apol. Rhod. ii:701.

79. Michel 499.

80. *Od.* iii:450.

81. *Od.* iv:767.

82. SIG 1021. In Pausanias v, 15: 10, this officer is called θεηχολος.

83. SIG 589.

84. SIG 237 and 238.

85. SIG 1046.

86. SIG 271, 289. Michel 678, 858.

87. SIG 338, 647, 725, 931.

88. SIG 1157.

89. Michel 810.

90. Michel 865.

91. SIG 57.

92. SIG 982 (Michel 730). Michel 711.

93. Michel 865. Pausanias viii, 42:12.

94. Pausanias v, 15:10. SIG 1021.

95. SIG 1021. Michel 865.

96. SIG 633.

97. SIG 1021.

98. Michel 694.

CHAPTER X

1. E.g., Uriah the Hittite in the army of David. 2 Sam. 11:1–16.

2. Ezk. 16:3.

3. Cf. G. B. Gray, *Sacrifice in the Old Testament,* p. 101.

4. 1 Kg. 16:31–32.

5. 1 Kg. 18:17–40.

6. 2 Sam. 5:11.

7. 1 Kg. 5:1–18; 9:11.

8. 1 Kg. 11:4–8.

9. 2 Kg. 21:3–6.

10. Records of even the good kings are punctuated by the sad refrain, "Nevertheless the high places were not removed; the people still sacrificed and burnt incense in the high places. Cf. 1 Kg. 14:23–24; 15:13–14. 2 Kg. 12:3. 14:4, etc. In one tradition Hezekiah tried to destroy other cult sites and to centralize the worship at Jerusalem. After his death his work was undone by Manasseh. Finally Josiah attacked the problem in earnest and with some success. Within ten years after his death Jerusalem fell to Babylon; eleven years later it was destroyed.

11. The Aramaic papyri describing this community and its temple were first published in English by A. H. Sayce and A. Cowley in 1906. They were included in *Aramaic Papyri of the Fifth Century B.C.* (Oxford, 1923), in which Dr. Cowley collected all the pre-christian papyri, with translations and notes.

12. Amos 5:25–26. Jer. 7:22–23. It is interesting that this tradition was preserved by the priests of Anathoth, the city of Jeremiah, to which Solomon had banished some of the davidic priests in the purge with which he began his reign.

13. E.g., Samuel and Elijah.

14. 1 Sam. 15:22. Isa. 1:11–17. Jer. 14:12. Hos. 6:6. Amos 5:22. Mic. 6:6–8.

15. The sources for study of Canaanite-Phoenician religion are of four kinds: (1) Occasional references in ancient literature, e.g., the Old Testament, and Egyptian and Babylonian inscriptions. (2) North Semitic Inscriptions. The first part of the *Corpus Inscriptionum Semiticarum*

(1881) is devoted to Phoenician inscriptions. Some forty-five of these are in Mark Lidzbarski's *Handbuch der Nordsemitischen Epigraphik* (1898) and in G. A. Cooke's *North Semitic Inscriptions* (1903). Both Lidzbarski and Cooke publish also the most important inscriptions discovered and studied during the last twenty years of the nineteenth century. Those inscriptions most valuable for our purpose are CIS i:165, 166 and 167 (Cooke 42, 44 and 43, respectively), which list tariffs for punic sacrifices and may therefore be assumed to be a fairly complete list of those rites. (3) Archaeological discoveries. Among the most important publications and the most useful for our purpose are: F. J. Bliss & R. A. S. Macalister, *Excavations in Palestine* (1902); R. A. S. Macalister, *Excavation of Gezer* (1909); H. Vincent, *Canaan d'apres l'exploration recente* (1907). These results are given in popular form in the following: P. S. P. Handcock, *Archaeology of the Holy Land* (1916); G. A. Barton, *Archaeology and the Bible* (many editions); Wm. F. Albright, *The Archaeology of Palestine* (1949). This little Penguin book is the best introduction to the subject. It is written in popular style and presents a concise history of palestinian excavations, an excellent critical evaluation of the work which has been done, and the bearing of this work upon Old Testament and New Testament study. (4) Secondary works: The most important are: S. A. Cook, *Religion of Ancient Palestine* (1908); W. W. Baudissin, *Adonis und Esmun* (1911); R. A. S. Macalister, *History of Civilization in Palestine* (1912); Ed. Meyer, Article *Phoenicians* in EB; M. Jastrow, Article *Canaanites*

in EB; L. B. Paton, Articles *Canaanites* and *Phoenicians* in ERE.

16. G. A. Cooke NSI 7:2.

17. id. 12:4.

18. id. 29:10.

19. id. 40:1.

20. id. 11c.

21. id. 39:1.

22. id. 51:1; 55:1.

23. E.g., Ex. 23:17; 34:23. Isa. 1:24; 3:1; 10:16, 33; 19:4.

24. Jos. 3:11, 13. Ps. 97:5. Mic. 4:13. Zch. 4:14; 6:5.

25. 2 Kg. 10:21.

26. 1 Sam. 5:2.

27. 2 Kg. 5:18.

28. 2 Kg. 19:37.

29. G. A. Cooke NSI 5:16–18; 20A:4.

30. id. 5:17.

31. id. 5:18.

32. id. 5:15–17; 33:2.

33. id. 29:3; 38:2; 46:1; 57:1.

34. For discussion of the altar, G. B. Gray, *Sacrifice in the Old Testament*, pp. 96–147.

35. This inscription, discovered in 1868, provides the oldest north semitic inscription we have. It was apparently done for Mesha, King of Moab, at the time of Ahab in the middle of the ninth century B.C., about a hundred and fifty years after the time of Solomon. The article *Moab* by W. H. Bennett in DB gives a photograph of the stone and a transcription of the text.

36. By Lidzbarski, Cooke, Bennett, etc.

37. *bamah* (במה) is rendered by LXX by the following words meaning "altar": βωμος—Isa. 15:2; 16:12. Jer. 7:31; 48:35 (LXX 31:35); 32:35 (LXX 39:35). Hos. 10:8. Amos 7:9. βουνος—1 Sam. 10:13. Ps. 78:58 (LXX 77:58). ϑυσιαστηριον—2 Ch. 14:4. It is transliterated in the

following instances: βαμα—1 Sam. 9:12, 13, 14, 19, 25; 10:5. 1 Ch. 16:39; 21:29. 2 Ch. 1:13. αβαμα—Ezk. 20:29. It is rendered by the following words meaning "height": υψος—2 Sam. 1:19; 22:34. υψηλον (or the plural υψηλα)—Jer. 19:5. Hab. 3:19. Ps. 18:33 (LXX 17:34). Fifty-one times in Kings and Chronicles.

38. E.G., 1 Sam. 9:12. 1 Kg. 3:4.

39. See pp. 130–131.

40. Qorban occurs only in Leviticus and Numbers and twice in Ezekiel. In the Ezekiel passages it is omitted from the Greek translations. In the pentateuchal passages it is regularly translated δωρον, gift. In Latin it is rendered oblatio. AV translates it as offering; RV prefers oblation; DV uses both terms. In Mk. 7:11 the word is rendered korban, and then translated δωρον. Etymologically the word is related to the verb karav, and means "something brought near." This could be the meaning of the phrase "a qorban to Yahweh" in Lev. 1:14; 17:4; 27:9, 11, etc. By the time of the LXX translation, the gift theory of sacrifice had become the accepted explanation of all such rites.

41. Fourteen times in Num. 7.

42. References are to the English versions, which follow the Vulgate in chapter division and differ from the Hebrew and from many Greek versions. For purposes of convenience the equivalents are here listed. Vulgate and English: Lev. 6:1–7; 6:8–30. Hebrew and most Greek: Lev. 5:20–26; 6:1–23.

43. See p. 67.

44. SIG 997:9; 1025:33.

45. id. 1025:31; 1027:9.

46. Xenophon, Anabasis vii, 8:4. Cyropaedia viii, 3:24.

47. The LXX translations of 'olah are as follows: καρπωμα & καρπωσις 19 times; ολοκαρπωμα & ολοκαρπωσις 16 times; ολοκαυτωσις 66 times; ολοκαυτωμα 162 times. θυσια was used, or rather misused, three times. Ex. 29:42. Num. 23:15. Job 1:5.

48. Lev. 6:15, απαν. Lev. 6:16, ολοκαυστος. Dt. 33:10, διαπαντος. 1 Sam. 7:9, ολοκαυτωσις. Ps. 50:18 (51:21 MV), ολοκαυτωματα.

49. Dt. 33:10.

50. 1 Sam. 7:9.

51. Ps. 51:19 (51:21 MV).

52. Lev. 6:22–23 (6:15–16 MV).

53. So Briggs-Driver-Brown Hebrew English Lexicon, p. 78.

54. Uebersicht über die Bildung . . . der Nomina, p. 190.

55. Antiquities iii, 10:7.

56. The occurrences of the phrase are as follows: Gen. 8:21. Ex. 29:18, 25, 41. Lev. 1:9, 13, 17; 2:2, 9, 12; 3:5, 16; 6:15, 21; 8:21, 28; 17:6; 23:13, 18; 26:31. Num. 15:3, 7, 10,, 13, 14, 24; 18:17; 28:2, 6, 8, 13, 24, 27; 29:2, 6, 8, 13, 36. Ezk. 6:13; 16:19; 20:28, 41.

57. This translation of RV and JV is more accurate than the cumbersome "tabernacle of the congregation" of AV, and certainly better than "tabernacle of the testimony of DV. The underlying thought was that in this place they met Yahweh.

58. Num. 10:10.

59. 2 Ch. 29:27–28.

60. 2 Kg. 3:27.

61. Gen. 22.

62. Ex. 29:15. Lev. 8:18. Num. 8:12.

63. Ex. 29:19. Lev. 3:2, 8, 13.

64. Lev. 4:4, 15, 24, 29, 33; 8:14. Num. 8:12. 2 Ch. 29:23.

65. Lev. 8:22.

66. Lev. 16:21.

67. Num. 27:18, 23. Dt. 34:9.

68. Num. 8:10.
69. Lev. 24:14.
70. This explanation is elaborated by Alfred Bertholet in his commentary on Lev. 1:4.
71. Ezk. 44:11.
72. Lev. 1:16.
73. E. Schürer, *History of the Jewish People in the Time of Christ*, translated by P. Christie (1891). Dic. II, vol. i, p. 283.
74. Ex. 30:17–21; 40:30.
75. This corresponds also to the elaborate descriptions of Ezk. 40:38–42, where the "north gate" is named as the place "where they wash the 'olah."
76. Gen. 8:20.
77. Gen. 22.
78. Ex. 18:12.
79. Ex. 24:5.
80. Num. 23:2.
81. Jos. 8:31.
82. Jdg. 6:26.
83. Jdg. 13:16–23.
84. 1 Sam. 7:9–10.
85. 2 Sam. 6:17–18.
86. 1 Kg. 3:4–15.
87. 1 Kg. 8:64.
88. 1 Kg. 18:31–38.
89. 2 Kg. 5:17.
90. 1 Sam. 9:9.
91. This is the basic meaning of judging cleanness, e.g., in the leprosy laws of Lev. 13–14.
92. The uses of *zaraq*, with Greek equivalents, are as follows: Of sprinkling ashes or dust—πασθαι, Ex. 9:8–10; καταπασσειν, Job 2:12; ριπτειν, 2 Ch. 34:4. Of scattering hot coals—διασκορπιζειν, Ezk. 10:2. Of gray hairs "sprinkled" in the hair—εξανθειν, Hos. 7:9. Of the cultic use of blood—κατασκεδαννυσθαι, Ex. 24:8; ραινειν, Ezk. 36:25; περιρραντιζειν, Num. 19:13, 20; δεχεσθαι, 2 Chr. 30:16; περι-

χειν, 2 Chr. 29:22; προσχειν, Ex. 24:6; 29:16; Lev. 1:5, 11; 3:2, 8, 13; 7:2, 14; 8:19, 24; 9:12, 18; 17:6; Num. 18:17; 2 Kg. 16:13, 15; 2 Chr. 29:22 (*bis*); 35:11; Ezk. 43:18.
93. Ex. 24:6, 8.
94. SIG #63, 1002, 1004, 1007, 1010, etc.
95. G. A. Cooke, NSI #43.
96. id. 42.
97. Lev. 16:27. Num. 19:5.
98. The cultic significance of skins is discussed in Robertson Smith's *Religion of the Semites*, pp. 435–440, and many times in J. G. Frazer's *The Golden Bough* (see in General Index Volume for references).
99. The widespread use of perpetual fire among primitive peoples is reviewed by J. G. Frazer in *The Magic Art*, vol. ii, pp. 253–265.
100. P. 105.
101. SIG 1025, line 35.
102. Pp. 105 f.
103. Lev. 8:7–9.
104. The occurrences of *badh*, the Hebrew word for linen as material for clothing, are as follows: Ex. 28:42; 39:28—Directions for making vestments. Lev. 6:10 (6:3 MV) (*bis*); 16:4 (quater), 23, 32—The 'olah and day of *kippurim*. 1 Sam 2:18—The child Samuel had a linen ephod. 1 Sam. 22:18—The priests of Nob. 2 Sam. 6:14 (= 1 Ch. 15:27)—David. Ezk. 9:2, 3, 11; 10:2, 6, 7; Dan. 10:5; 12:6, 7—A messenger from Yahweh.
105. Ezk. 44:18, 19.
106. It is difficult for a traditional Christian today, such as a Roman Catholic or an Anglican, to interpret the literature of the first three centuries apart from the eucharistic concepts of his Church. The difference between a 'olah of Samuel's day and one of the fifth century was probably as great as between a eucharist of

Justin Martyr's day and a solemn high mass. Despite the differences, there is little difficulty in relating them as different stages of the same developing rite.

107. The publication of the first volume of Edward Gibbon's *Decline and Fall of the Roman Empire* (1776) was probably the first instance of avowed study of sources without bias. It is not surprising that Gibbon did not attain his announced ideal. Has any historian really attained it?

108. Num. 23:1–2, 14–15.

109. Jdg. 21:4–5. 1 Sam. 7:9, 10.

110. Jos. 8:31. 1 Sam. 6:14, 15. 2 Sam. 6:17–18 (= 1 Ch. 16:1–2). Ps. 66:13, 15.

111. Gen. 22.

112. Num. 6:11, 14, 16. Jdg. 11:31, 39.

113. Ex. 24:5.

114. 1 Kg. 8:64 (= 2 Ch. 7:1).

115. Ex. 29:16, 25. Lev. 8:18–21.

116. Lev. 12:6.

117. Lev. 14:19, 31.

118. Lev. 15:15, 30.

119. Num. 28:3–4. Ezk. 46:13.

120. Ex. 29:39. Lev. 9:17. Num. 28:4, 23. 2 Kg. 16:15. 2 Ch. 2:4. Ezk. 46:15.

121. Ex. 29:39. Num. 28:3–8, 23. Ezr. 3:3.

122. Num. 28:10; 29:6.

123. The expression *'olah tamidh*, probably meaning "continual *'olah*, cannot refer to another kind in addition to those already listed. It is apparently an adjectival expression describing the continuity of *'olahs*. Its occurrences are: Ex. 29:42. Num. 28:3, 31; 29:6, 38. 1 Ch. 16:40. 2 Ch. 24:14. Ezr. 3:5. Neh. 10:33. Ezk. 46:15.

124. Num. 28:11–13. 1 Ch. 23:31. 2 Ch. 2:4; 31:3. Ezr. 3:5. Neh. 10:33.

125. Num. 23:1–3, 14.

126. Job 42:8.

127. Lev. 23:18.

128. Num. 28:11, 27.

129. Num. 28:17–25.

130. Num. 29.

131. 1 Kg. 3:4.

132. 2 Ch. 29:32.

133. Ezk. 9:4. An angel is bidden to go through the city and "set a mark" (AV, RV & JV, following LXX) upon the forehead of certain persons who were thereby immune from destruction. DV translates "mark a Thau," following LV which renders the Hebrew more faithfully than LXX does. The *tau* was the last letter of the Hebrew alphabet and, in the days of Ezekiel, was made like a cross tilted a bit at an angle. The prophylactic upon the heads of the chosen ones was no more or less than the sign of a cross.

134. As an anthropologist rather than a student of religion, E. B. Tylor could hardly be expected to distinguish between cultic rites. He was giving uncritical academic approval to a familiar religious theory when he made the statement which has frequently been credited with being the first enunciation of the gift theory. "As prayer is a request made to a deity as if he were a man, so sacrifice is a gift made to a deity as if he were a man." *Primitive Culture* (1874), ii, 375.

135. *Religion of the Semites*, p. 371 ff.

136. See p. 128 and note 47.

137. See p. 123.

138. The word translated as "to kill" is *shachat*.

139. 1 Sam. 20:6, 29.

140. 1 Sam. 9:11–24.

141. Gen. 31:54; 46:1.

142. 1 Sam. 9:13; 13:8–12.

143. 2 Sam. 6:18.

144. 1 Kg. 8:62.
145. 1 Kg. 12:32.
146. 2 Kg. 5:17.
147. Jdg. 16:23–25. Cf. p. 193.
148. Num. 25:1–3.
149. See pp. 122, 136.
150. Ex. 29:27. Lev. 7:31–34; 9:21. Deut. 18:3.
151. *t'rumah* and *t'nufah* were not distinct from each other in the minds of LXX translators, who used the same Greek words to render both Hebrew words. The three most familiar words are απαρχη, αφαιρεμα and αφορισμα. The first of these is equivalent to "first fruits"; the second is "that which is lifted"; the third is "that which is designated." *t'rumah* was used not only to express the priest's fee from sacrifice, but also to describe the money tithes exacted by the P code. *t'nufah* is also used of bread (Lev. 23:17), of gold (Ex. 38:24) and of brass (Ex. 38:29).
152. 1 Sam. 2:13–14.
153. Num. 15:3. As zevach in Lev. 7:16; 22:21, 23. 1 Sam. 1:21. Jon. 1:16. As 'olah in Lev. 22:18. Ps. 66:13. For the vow (*nedher*) in Hebrew, see ch. 7, pp. 66 f. *n'dhavah* (gift) was a name applied to all kinds of voluntary offerings which were not made in performance of any kind of duty. The precious metals, jewelry, wood, cloths, etc., for the tent of meeting were so described (Ex. 35:20–29; 36:3), as were those of the second temple (Ezr. 1:4; 8:28). First fruit offerings (Dt. 16:10), offerings for Josiah's giant pesach (2 Ch. 35:8), and offerings for the temporary altar which was pictured as erected before the second temple (Ezr. 3:5) were all so named. Yahweh's love for Israel was a *n'dhavah* (Hos. 14:5). Any prayer or 'olah or zevach could be so considered if they

were over and above all requirements. The translation "freewill offerings" of AV and "voluntary offerings" of DV are both accurate.
154. Ex. 12:27; 23:18.
155. 2 Chr. 35:7–12.
156. This form of greeting was common to semitic peoples. In an inscription of the 4th century B.C. (CIS ii, 137), written in Egyptian-Aramaic characters on a piece of pottery, is a description of a dream in which the writer saw an apparition enter the room and pronounce the word *shalom* (greetings) before pronouncing the dream message to be interpreted. One is reminded of St. John 20:21, where Jesus is described as appearing to the eleven disciples and prefacing his message by the same word, which loses some of its significance in the conventional translation, "Peace be with you."
157. CIS i, 165, lines 3, 5, 7, 9, 11.
158. See p. 102 and chapter IX, note 35. The plural form σωτηρια is always used in Greek literature and inscriptions.
159. The uses of σωτηριον in the Old Testament are as follows: τα του σωτηριου—Ezk. 43:27; 45:17; 46:12. σωτηριον—Singular, Lev. 6:12 (6:5 MV); 7:14, 33; Num. 6:14: 15:8; Am. 5:22. Plural, Ex. 20:24; Num. 29:39; 2 Ch. 7:7. σωτηριου—1 Ch. 16:1, 2; 21:26; 2 Ch. 29:35; Ezk. 45:15; 46:12. θυμα σωτηριου—Ex. 29:28. θυσια (or θυσιαι) σωτηριου —Ex. 24:5; 32:6; Lev. 3:1, 3, 6; 4:10, 26, 31, 35; 7:11, 20, 21, 29 (bis), 32, 34, 37; 9:4; 10:14; 17:5; 19:5; 22:21; 23:19; Dt. 27:7; Jos. 8:31; 22:23, 27; Num. 6:17; 7:17, 23, 29, 35, 41, 47, 53, 59, 65, 71, 77, 83, 88; 10:10. θυσια αινεσεως σωτηριου— Lev. 7:13, 15. Wanting in LXX—Lev. 7:18.

160. ϑυσιαι ειρηνιχαι, 1 Sam.
10:8. 1 Kg. 8:63, 64. Prv. 7:14. ειρηνιχαι as substantive *terminus tech-
nicus* without ϑυσιαι. 1 Sam. 11:15;
13:9. 2 Sam. 6:17; 24:25. 1 Kg. 3:15;
8:64; 9.25. 2 Kg. 16.13.

161. τελεια is used in Jdg. 20:26;
21:4. Both are in B. A reads σωτηριον.

162. Tables C and D list the uses of
todhah in Hebrew and present translations into Greek and Latin and into
the three best known English versions
of the Bible, and the Psalter translations of the Book of Common Prayer.

163. This is illustrated by the objective use of the word. Twenty-three
of the thirty-one occurrences of the
word are objective. Fifteen times it
is the object of a verb, and eight
times of a preposition.

A. *todhah* as unquestionably something to be sacrificed. 10 times.
   1. piel of *qatar,* "to burn" (in
      worship). Amos 4:5.
   2. piel of *shalam,* probably best
      translated as "to shelemize,"
      "make a shelem of." Ps. 56:13.
   3. *zavach,* "to zevachize," "make
      a zevach of." Lev. 22:29. 2
      Chr. 33:16. Ps. 50:14, 23;
      107:22; 116:17.
   4. After the preposition *'al,* "for."
      Lev. 7:12 (bis).

B. *todhah* as probably something to
be sacrificed, possibly something
spoken.
   1. hiphil or piel of *bo,* "to bring."
      4 times. 2 Chr. 29:31 (bis).
      Jer. 17:26; 33:11.

C. *todhah* as probably spoken, possibly something sacrificed. 6 times.
   1. *nathan,* "to give." Jos. 7:19.
      Ezr. 10:11.
   2. With the preposition *b,* "with."
      Ps. 69:31; 95:2; 100:4; 147:7.

D. *todhah* as something spoken,
therefore to be heard. 3 times.
   1. With the preposition *b,* "with,"
      in the phrase "with the voice
      of." Ps. 26:7; 42:5. Jon. 2:10.

164. The Greek αινεσις, which
renders twenty-two of the thirty-one
occurrences of *todhah,* appears sixty-
five times in LXX and, in every instance, describes an act or attitude
addressed solely to Yahweh and
marked by song and gladness. Twen-
ty-four translations of *todhah* in AV
are in words having to do with
thanksgiving; twenty-eight instances
are so rendered in JV. In DV the
word *praise* preponderates.

The only two instances in which
any other idea than that of praise or
worship is attached to the word are
in the three English versions, DV,
AV and JV, all of which use *confession* or *confess* to render the term in
Jos. 7:19 and Ezr. 10:11. The Greek
gives αινεσις for the Ezra passage
and εξομολογησις for the Joshua
passage. The English versions all reflect the influence of the Latin.

The Latin *confessio,* which accurately renders εξομολογησις, means
"acknowledgment," but it is quite as
applicable to connote the natural su-
periority of another as to describe the
moral inferiority of oneself. One can
acknowledge the greatness of God as
well as one's own faults. The phrase
"confession of faith" is familiar.

In Jos. 7:19 Achan had deliberately
disobeyed Yahweh's command in order to increase his personal possessions. He had thereby brought failure to the group. Joshua insisted that
to ignore God or to disobey his com-
mands was folly, and Achan had better acknowledge this fact and tell
what he had done. His confession had
nothing to do with forgiveness of

sin; he was stoned anyhow. He was called upon to "give glory and *todhah* to Yahweh," i.e., to recognize Yahweh's supremacy.

In the Ezra passage Ezra had come to revive a forlorn hope. He reasoned that Israel's calamities had been the result of their exogamous practices which were in violation of Yahweh's will. Trying to ignore Yahweh was futile. Israel's very existence was contingent upon recognition of his greatness and their folly in flouting it.

In both instances *todhah* is the exact Hebrew word for the situation. It describes giving to Yahweh that which is for him alone. It may not be given to another; nor may it be withheld from Yahweh without dire consequences.

165. The phrase "zevach of todhah" in singular or plural occurs as follows: Lev. 7:12, 13, 15; 22:29. Ps. 107:22; 116:17. 2 Chr. 33:16. The Greek translator of Ps. 50:14, 23 apparently had a Hebrew manuscript with the same expression. Eight of the Greek translations are "thusia of praise." The translation of Lev. 22:29 has the interesting expression "thusia prayer of thanksgiving" (θυσίαν εὐχὴν χαρμοσύνης). "Sacrifice of praise" is used in all English versions. "Sacrifice of thanksgiving" is used in AV and JV but not in DV. The phrase "zevachs and todhahs" occurs in 2 Chr. 29:31.

166. Lev. 7:15; 22:29–30.

167. The verb *hodhah*, "give thanks," occurs often, e.g., Ps. 75:1; 105:1; 107:1, etc.

168. Pp. 102 ff., 113 f. Chapter IX, notes 37–51.

169. The Old Testament references to sanctification are as follows: Ex. 19:10, 14, 15—Preparation for receiving the Ten Commandments. Lev. 19:2; 20:7—Be ye "holy," for Yahweh is holy. Num. 11:18—Before eating the flesh of miraculously sent quails. Jos. 3:5—Preparation for the miracle of crossing the Jordan. 1 Sam. 16:5—Before the zevach preceding the anointing of David. Joel 2:16—Before calling a "solemn assembly."

170. Num. 19:11.

171. See p. 40 f. In Luke 10:25–37, the lawyer who asked "Who is my neighbor?" was really asking, "Whom must I love?" He must have been shocked at the suggestion that the taboo of the Samaritan was no obstacle to his receiving the same kind of devotion as one would naturally show to temple officers. The strong contrast is between two who were always clean and one who was never clean. When the lawyer admitted that the Samaritan would be his neighbor, he was admitting that he would have to love an unclean person. See Chapter VI and pp. 184 f.

172. Prov. 15:8; 21:27. Isa. 1:11–15.

173. As, for instance, purification after childbirth, purification of one healed from leprosy and, most significant, annual purification of the whole congregation at the New Year, to be discussed under "atonement."

174. Num. 7:17, 23, etc.

175. 1 Kg. 8:63.

176. Jdg. 16:23.

177. The eleven references to the *yothereth hakkavedh* are Ex. 29:13, 22. Lev. 3:4, 10, 15; 4:9; 7:4; 8:16, 25; 9:10, 19. See p. 31. Discussion of the method of use of the upper lobe of the liver in Babylonian divination rites is summarized in *Civilization of Babylonia and Assyria* by M. Jastrow (Philadelphia, 1915), pp. 255–258. The use is discussed at length by

Jastrow in *Die Religion Babyloniens und Assyriens*, vol. ii, pp. 220–232.

178. Num. 23:2–4.

179. Jdg. 20:26; 21:4.

180. Gen. 31:54. Ex. 18:12; 32:6. Num. 25:2. Dt. 12:27. Jdg. 16:23–25. 1 Kg. 3:15. 1 Chr. 29:21–22. Ezk. 39:17.

181. 1 Sam. 2:13. Lev. 8:31. Ezk. 46:24.

182. Lev. 7:15–18.

183. Ex. 32:6. Jdg. 16:23–25. 1 Chr. 29:21–22. Ps. 27:6. Comparison of the translations of Ps. 27:6 indicates that the translators may not have realized that the banquet and the merry making or music and singing which followed it were integral parts of the zevach. The translations are as follows:

AV: Therefore will I offer in his tabernacle sacrifices of joy; I will sing, yea I will sing praises unto the LORD.

PB: Therefore will I offer in his dwelling an oblation with great gladness; I will sing and speak praises unto the LORD.

DV: I have gone round and have offered up in his tabernacle a sacrifice of jubilation: I will sing and recite a psalm unto the LORD.

JV: I will offer in his tabernacle sacrifices with trumpet-sound; I will sing, yea I will sing praises unto the LORD.

184. 1 Sam. 1:3, 21; 2:19; 9:13; 20:6, 29.

185. 1 Kg. 9:25 (= 2 Ch. 8:13).

186. Am. 4:4.

187. P. 119 and notes.

188. Prv. 15:8; 17:1; 21:27.

189. Is. 1:10–15; 61:8. Jer. 6:20.

190. Ps. 51:17.

191. 1 Sam. 15:22. Ps. 40:6–8.

192. Hos. 6:6.

193. Prv. 21:3.

194. Dt. 33:19. Ps. 4:5; 51:19.

195. Hos. 6.6.

196. P. 133 f. and note 70.

197. Pp. 102 f., 113 f., 138–140.

198. Ps. 51:17.

CHAPTER XI

1. G. A. Cooke, *North Semitic Inscriptions*, p. 42, records a short inscription from Sidon using the word *minchath* as "a present." In a number of other insciptions the word denotes a sacrificial rite of some kind, but no clue is given to its constitution. In O.T. *minchah* denotes a present from man to man in the following instances: Gen. 32:13, 18, 20, 21; 33:10: Jacob to Esau. Gen. 43:11, 15, 25, 26: Jacob to Joseph. Jdg. 3:15, 17, 18: Ehud to Eglon. 1 Sam. 10:27: Omitted by sons of Belial to Saul. 2 Sam. 8:2 (= 1 Chr. 18:2): Moabites to David. 2 Sam. 8:6 (= 1 Chr. 18:6): Syrians to David. 1 Kg. 4:21 (5:1 MV) (= 2 Chr. 9:24): Tribute to Solomon. 2 Kg. 8:8, 9: Hazael to Elisha. 2 Kg. 17:3, 4: Hoshea to Assyria. 2 Kg. 20:12 (= Isa. 39:1): King of Babylon to Hezekiah. 2 Chr. 17:5, 11: Judah to Jehoshaphat. 2 Chr. 26:8: Ammonites to Uzziah. Ps. 45:12 (45:10 MV): Tyrian to new bride. Ps. 72:10: Foreign kings to king of Judah. Dan. 2:46 (as a divine honour): Nebuchadrezzar to Daniel.

2. Gen. 4:3. Lev. 2:1. 2 Chr. 32:23. Isa. 66:20. Jer. 33:18. Joel 2:14. Mal. 2:12.

3. Isa 19:21. Mal. 3:4.

4. Num. 16:15. Zeph. 3:10.

5. 1 Sam. 2:17, 29. Joel 1:9, 13; 2:14.

6. 1 Sam. 26:19. AV, DV, and JV all translate the Hebrew word for "to

smell" by *accept*. All three versions translate the same verb *yarach* as *smell* in Gen. 8:21.

7. Jdg. 13:23.

8. Gen. 4:4.

9. Gen. 4:5. Amos 5:22. Mal. 1:10, 13; 2:13.

10. Gen. 4:3–5.

11. Lev. 2:14–16.

12. 2 Kg. 7:1, 16, 18. Part of the extravagant provision of Solomon's palace was 30 cors (nearly 3 bushels) of soleth daily. 1 Kg. 4:22 (5:2 MV).

13. Gen. 18:6.

14. Ex. 29:2. Lev. 2:1, 2, 4, 5, 7; 5:11; 6:15, 20; 7:12. 14:10, 21; 23:13, 17; 24:5. Num. 6:15; 7 (12 times); 8:8; 28:5, 9, 12, 13, 28; 29:3, 9, 14. 1 Chr. 23:29. Ezk. 46:14. The one exception was the minchah of jealousy, made of barley meal (Num. 5:15).

15. Lev. 2:4, 5, 11; 6:17 (6:10 MV). A minchah offered with a todhah was accompanied by leavened cakes. Lev. 7:13; 23:16–17.

16. As a substitute for a chattath. Num. 5:15. Also in every minchah offered for a priest. Lev. 6:21 (6:14 MV).

17. Lev. 9:17; 14:10, 20; 23:13, 18. Num. 6:15–17; 15:1–12; 28:20; 29:2–4, 9–10, 13–15.

18. The size of the minchah was determined by the amount of soleth used in its making. Lev. 6:20–23 (6:13–16 MV); 14:10. Num. 15:4–9; 28:5, 9, 20–21; 29:3–4, 9–10, 14–15. If a minchah was offered alone, one-tenth of an ephah of soleth was prescribed. If it was offered with a flesh ishsheh, the prescription was one-tenth of an ephah for a lamb, two-tenths for a ram or a ewe, three-tenths for a bullock.

The volume of an ephah is not exactly determined. In the article on "Weights and Measures," by Lauter-bach in the *Jewish Encyclopedia*, vol. 10, an ephah or bath is fixed at 36.44 litres. An American quart is about .9463 litre; an American gallon is about 3.785 litres. One-tenth of an ephah would approximate 3.644 litres, or about 3.85 American quarts (about 3.20 imperial quarts). This would be about .911 American gallon or .8 imperial gallon.

19. The normal amount of olive oil to be used was a quarter of a hin with a tenth of an ephah, a third of a hin with two-tenths, and a half hin with three-tenths. The article quoted in the preceding note sets 6.074 litres as the size of a hin, about 1.6 American gallons or 1.38 imperial gallons. A quarter of a hin would approximate 1.6 American quarts or 1.38 imperial quarts. A third of a hin would approximate 2.12 American quarts or 1.75 imperial quarts. A half hin would approximate 3.2 American quarts or 2.76 imperial quarts.

The amount of oil prescribed by Ezekiel in 46:5, 7, 11, was a hin of oil to an ephah of soleth instead of 2½ hins as in Leviticus. No oil was used when the minchah was a poor man's substitute for a chattath. Lev. 5:12.

20. *Libonah* (frankincense) occurs 20 times in OT. In Cant. 3:6; 4:6, 14, it indicates sybaritism in secular life. The other instances are all in connection with sacrifice, chiefly the minchah and Bread of Presence. They are: Ex. 30:34. Lev. 2:1, 2, 15, 16; 5:11; 6:15 (6:8 MV); 24:7. Num. 5:15. 1 Chr. 9:29. Neh. 13:5, 9. Isa. 43:23; 60:6; 66:3. Jer. 6:20; 17:26. Very little is known of this sacrificial use. Throwing scented gums on sacrificial fire was known from Greek days (p. 105). The use of frankincense with the minchah resembles

the use of it in the thusia. None was used when the minchah was a poor man's substitute for a chattath. For use of frankincense with the Bread of Presence, see note 26.

A wholly different word, *q'toreth*, was used to describe the incense offered separately upon an altar on which 'olahs and zevachs were never burned. This word occurs 45 times, all but nine of which are in Exodus, Leviticus and Numbers.

21. A minchah for a priest was treated as a 'olah and wholly burned. Lev. 6:23 (6:16 MV).

22. This is illustrated by the translations of the word into Greek, which had only one word to describe a sacrifice partly burned and partly eaten. θυσια was used 134 times to translate *minchah*. δωρον was used 29 times, largely for a *minchah* from man to man. θυσιασμα was used in Num. 18:9.

Seventeen times the translation was by one who was apparently not sure of the word and tried to transliterate it as μαναα. This led to occasional confusion with the mysterious food supplied by Yahweh during the forty years of wilderness wandering (Ex. 16:11-15. Num. 11:4-9).

No one knew anything about this strange food but tradition preserved the name *man*, which in Hebrew means *what?* Hebrew etymology explained the word by a story that, when the food was first found, it was welcomed with the exclamation, "What is it?" In Hebrew this would read *man hoo*. Thus the name was interpreted to mean "what is it?" Some of the translators seem to have been without a sense of humour; when they came to occurrences of *man*, they transliterated it as *manna*. Jerome knew a little better and

coined a Latin word *man* as a translation. No English translator has come any nearer. The DV translators tried to make it intelligible by rendering, "And they said, Manhu, which signifieth, What is this? for they knew not what it was." The AV translators made no sense at all of Ex. 16:15 and rendered, "And they said, It is manna, for they wist not what it was." The JV translators missed a real opportunity to make a contribution and, as was their wont, followed AV.

In eight instances the combination *zevach and minchah* occurs. Since θυσια was the normal translation of both words, the combination of the two in the same phrase gave difficulty to translators. The eight instances, with their translations are listed in Table B.

23. For occurrences of *azkarah* see Table E.

24. *zeker* as trace, recollection, name, remembrance, occurs as follows:

Ex. 3:15. Hos. 12:5. The name YAHWEH is God's zeker.

Ps. 30:4; 97:12. Give thanks for the zeker of God's holiness.

Ps. 102:12; 135:13. The zeker of Yahweh shall last throughout generations.

Ps. 111:4-5. Yahweh has given a zeker of his works, viz., food.

Ps. 145:7. People shall sing of the zeker of Yahweh.

Isa. 26:8. We desire the zeker of Yahweh. Isa. 26:14. The zeker of other gods is perished.

Ps. 112:6. The zeker of the righteous shall be eternal.

Ps. 34:16; 109:15. The zeker of evil doers will be cut off.

Prv. 10:7. The zeker of the just is blessed.

Hos. 14:7. The zeker of sinners returning to Yahweh shall be as the wine of Lebanon. *Zeker* is translated *smell* (DV), *scent* (AV) and *fragrance* (JV).

Ex. 17:14. Dt. 25:19. Every zeker of Amalek will disappear.

Dt. 32:26. Yahweh nearly tempted to make zeker of Israel disappear.

Est. 9:28. The zeker of the days of Purim shall never disappear.

Job 18:17. Every zeker of human individuals shall disappear.

Eccl. 9:5. Every zeker of the dead is forgotten.

Ps. 6:5. There is no zeker of Yahweh after death.

Ps. 9:6. Every zeker of destroyed cities is perished.

25. References to *zikkaron* as a planned or erected commemoration of an event are as follows:

Ex. 12:14; 13:9. The 14th of Nisan to be a z of what Yahweh did in Egypt.

Lev. 23:24. Num. 10:10. Blow trumpets over sacrifices on feast-days to make them z's.

Ex. 17:14. Record of Amalek's defeat written in a book for a z. See preceding note: Amalek's *zeker* shall perish; the record of this is a zikkaron.

Mal. 3:16. Names of righteous written in a book of zikkaron.

Ex 28:12. Stones in Aaron's ephod a zikkaron.

Ex. 28:29; 39:7. Names of Israelites on Aaron's breastplate for a zikkaron.

Jos. 4:7. Stones erected at Jordan as zikkaron of crossing.

Zech. 6:14. Crowns on head of Joshua to be a z in the temple he will build.

Num. 16:40 (17:5 MV). Censers of Korah, Dathan and Abiram made

into an altar covering, as z that none but priests may offer incense.

Ex. 30:16. Poll tax money appointed as service for tent of meeting as a zikkaron of purification.

Num. 31:54. Spoils of war presented in tent of meeting as a zikkaron.

Num. 5:15, 18. Minchah of jealousy as zikkaron to suspected wife.

zikkaron as synonym of *zeker*:

Eccl. 1:11. There is no zikkaron of past or future.

Eccl. 2:16. There is no more z of a wise man than of a fool.

Isa. 57:8. Tell tale signs "behind the door" are z of infidelity to Yahweh.

Job 13:12. "Your zikkarons are but ashes."

zikkaron as probable synonym of *zeker*:

Neh. 2:20. Sanballat and his associates have no z in Jerusalem. I.e., they have never done anything there or left any marks.

Est. 6:1. A book of zikkarons (records).

26. The "Bread of Presence" seems peculiar to Judaism. Once a week twelve loaves were baked, each loaf containing two-tenths of an ephah of soleth (nearly three pints). These were placed in two rows upon a holy table; on each row frankincense was placed as an azkarah. Each sabbath the azkarah was burned as an ishsheh (p. 129) and the bread solemnly eaten by the priests. (Lev. 24:5–9). Thus was constituted a sort of protracted or reserved zevach-minchah which was burnt and eaten a week after being offered, instead of immediately.

This was undoubtedly related somehow with the idea of the perpetual presence of Yahweh, although

Jewish writers never attempted metaphysical explanations. The concept of God perpetually present has gone far beyond physical associations. Limitations of space are harder to overcome than those of time. It was easier to symbolize the fact that Yahweh was always present than it was to symbolize his presence everywhere.

The reserved bread was called *bread of presence* (Ex. 25:30; 35:13; 39:36. 1 Sam. 21:6. 1 Kg. 7:48. 2 Chr. 4:19). It was *holy bread* (1 Sam. 21:4), or *ordered bread* (1 Chr. 9:32; 23:29. 2 Chr. 13:11. Neh. 10:34), or *continual bread* (Num. 4:7).

The table upon which it was placed was the *table of presence* (Num. 4:7) or the *table of ordering* (1 Chr. 28:16. 2 Chr. 29:18).

The Greek translations were as follows:

Loaves of presentation: αρτοι προθεσεως, Ex. 39:36. 1 Sam. 21:6. 1 Chr. 9:32; 23:29. 2 Chr. 4:19. προθεσεις αρτων, 2 Chr. 13:11.

Holy loaves: αρτοι αγιοι, 1 Sam. 21:4 (21:5 LXX).

Loaves of presence: αρτοι προσωπου, 1 Sam. 21:6 (21.7 LXX). Neh. 10:34. αρτοι ενωπιοι: Ex. 25:30.

Continual loaves: αρτοι δια παντος, Num. 4:7.

Loaves of offering: αρτοι προσφορας, 1 Kg. 7:48 (7:34 LXX).

Following the Latin rendering *panes propositionis,* DV translates as *loaves of proposition.* The other English versions render *shew bread* (AV) or *show bread* (JV), which is exactly what the *bread of presence* was not.

Eating of this bread by David and his soldiers was of sufficient importance to be incorporated into the tradition (1 Sam. 21:7) and to continue as part of the Christian tradition (Mt. 12:4. Mk. 2:26. Lk. 6:4).

27. Lev. 2:2, 9, 16; 5:12; 6:15 (6:8 MV). Num. 5:26.

28. Num. 15:1–15.

29. Lev. 2:2, 9.

30. Lev. 6:16 (6:9 MV); 10:12. When offered with a todhah it was eaten with leavened cakes. Lev. 7:13.

31. Lev. 2:2, 10; 6:16 (6:9 MV); 7:9, 10.

32. Ex. 29:41. Num. 28:8. 2 Kg. 3:20. Ezk. 46:15.

33. 1 Kg. 18:29, 36. 2 Kg. 16:15. Ezr. 9:4. Ps. 141:2. Dan. 9:21. In 1 Kg. 18:29, 36, AV inserts the word *evening* which is in neither MV nor LXX. DV omits *evening* but JV follows AV.

The *minchah tamidh,* translated "perpetual meal offering" (JV) is mentioned four times, viz., Lev. 6:20 (6:13 MV & JV). Num. 4:16. Neh. 10:33. Ezk. 46:15. Like the *'olah tamidh* (Note 123, Chapter X), it refers not to a separate rite, but to the continuity of minchahs.

34. Lev. 23:14.

35. Lev. 2:14.

36. Ex. 23:19; 34:26. Dt. 26:1–11. Neh. 10:35. Ezk. 44:30.

37. Lev. 23:14, 20.

38. Lev. 2:14–16.

39. Num. 28:26–28.

40. Ex. 23:16, 19; 34:22, 26.

41. Ex. 23:14–17; 34:23. Dt. 16:16.

42. 2 Kg. 4:42.

43. Ex. 29:40–41. Lev. 23:13. Num. 15:5; 28:7.

44. Num. 15:7.

45. Num. 15:10; 28:14.

46. Num. 19:13, 20.

47. Lev. 7:20–21; 22:3. Num. 19:20.

48. Lev. 7:26–27; 17:10–14.

49. Lev. 17:3–4.

50. Lev. 7:25.
51. Lev. 17:8–9.
52. Lev. 20:2–5.
53. Num. 9:13.
54. Lev. 20:9.
55. Lev. 18:6–29; 20:10–21.
56. Num. 15:30–31.

57. The word translated *forgive* was *salach* (סלח). Whenever this verb is used in the active voice, the subject is always God; in the passive voice the agent is always God. The removal of blots on worship could be achieved only by God; rites were the means by which he worked.

58. Num. 12:11. Aaron, seeing Miriam leprous, exclaims, "Lay not this chattath upon us," i.e., "This chattath is not our fault." The chattath may possibly denote the act causing the leprosy; more likely it refers to the leprosy itself.

59. חטאת occurs 289 times in the O.T. In LXX it is regularly translated αμαρτια, except in eight instances, as follows: αγνισμος, Num. 8:7; 19:17. αγνισμα, Num. 19:9. ασεβημα, Lam. 4:22. ιλασμος, Ezk. 44:27. ματαιος, 1 Kg. 16:2. μετακινησις, Zech. 13:1. Ps. 32:5 (31:5 LXX), עון חטאתי is rendered ασεβειαν της αμαρτιας μου. αμαρτια means primarily "missing a mark," as in archery, "to fail of a purpose," "to make a mistake." It is not equivalent to *sin* as used in modern English.

60. The commonest translations of the verb אשם and the noun אשם are πλημμελειν and πλημμελεια, which describe a false note or cacophony in music. Because the O.T. is concerned with moral and religious concepts, the verb αμαρτανειν (Lev. 4:3, 27. 2 Chr. 19:10. Isa. 24:6) and the substantive αμαρτια (Lev. 5:7. Isa. 53:10) both occur in translation.

αμαρτανειν occurs in 2 Chr. 28:13 in the articular infinitive.

61. In 2 Chr. 28:13 the two substantives are joined as if each described a different concept. In Lev. 6:4 (5:23 MV) the two verbs are so joined. The same rite is called both chattath and asham without distinction in Lev. 5 and 14. In Gen. 20:9 Abimelech reproves Abraham for bringing great chattath upon his people by lying about his wife. In Gen. 26:10 Abimelech reproves Isaac for lying about his wife and thus making it possible for his people to incur asham if one of them had lain with her. LXX translates *asham* by αγνοια.

62. In 1 Sam. 6:3, 4, 8, 17 *asham* is used to describe the voluntary fine or tribute of golden emerods and mice which the Philistines imposed upon themselves to be paid at the return of the "ark." The translators of LXX recognized that this had nothing to do with the asham rite and translated it by βασανος. Vulgate translators did not know this and rendered *asham* by *peccatum* as usual. 1 Sam. 6:15 describes the Bethshemeshites as accepting the tribute and immediately offering 'olahs and zevachs as thanksgiving.

63. The Hebrew word נזה occurs only 23 times in the O.T. In the qal stem it has the intransitive meaning of "to splash" or "to spatter" and is found only in Lev. 6:27 (6:20 MV), 2 Kg. 9:33 and Isa. 63:3. In the hiphil stem it has the transitive meaning of "to sprinkle" or "to splash" for purpose of purification. With a single exception it is found only in ritual passages as follows: Ex. 29:21. Lev. 4:6, 17; 5:9; 8:11, 30; 14:7, 16, 27, 51; 16:14, 15, 19. Num. 8:7; 19:4, 18, 19, 21. The one exception is Isa.

52:15. In DV and AV this is translated "sprinkle." In the various English revisions it is "startle." John B. Peters (in *Scriptures, Hebrew and Christian*) renders it "startle." Msgr. Ronald Knox, in his recent translation of *The Old Testament* (London: Burns, Oates and Washbourne, 1949: New York: Sheed and Ward), with characteristic brilliancy penetrates to the real meaning of the word and renders "purify," although he does not so render it in the Leviticus passages. The reason for this is apparent: the Leviticus passages are literal physical prescriptions; Isa. 52 is definitely spiritual.

64. For the significance of the yothereth hakkavedh see pp. 156 f.

65. Lev. 7:19–21; 10:16–19.

66. Rom. 5:11.

67. A short discussion of these comparisons is given by G. Buchanan Gray in *Sacrifice in the Old Testament*, pp. 68–73.

68. The Greek words which translate *kipper* are as follows:

A. Words indicating cleansing or purification: αποκαθαιρειν, Prv. 16:6. αφαιρειν, Isa. 27:9; 28:18. καθαριζειν, Ex. 29:37. Lev. 8:15. εκκαθαριζειν, Dt. 32:43. περικαθαριζειν, Isa. 6:7. καθαρισμος, Ex. 29:36. καθαρον γινεσθαι, Isa. 47:11.

B. Words from the root √ιλα(ρ): ιλασκεσθαι, Ps. 65:3; 78:38; 79:9 (Ps. 64, 77 and 78 in LXX). εξιλασκεσθαι, Gen. 32:20. Ex. 30:10, 16; 32:30. 58 times in Lev. and Num. Dt. 21:8. 1 Sam. 3:14. 2 Sam. 21:3. 1 Chr. 6:49. 2 Chr. 29:24; 30:18. Neh. 10:33. Prv. 16:14. Ezk. 16:63; 43:20, 26; 45:15, 17, 20. Dan (Th.) 9:24. ιλασμος, Num. 5:8. ιλεως γινεσθαι, Dt. 21:8. εξιλασις, Num. 29:11.

C. Other words: αγιαζειν, Ex.

29:33, 36. αθωουν, Jer. 18:23. αφιεναι, Isa. 22:14.

69. For classic instances of ιλασκεσθαι as meaning "to pray," see chapter vi, p. 52 f., and footnotes 3, 4 and 5.

70. The Latin translations of *kipper* are as follows:

A. Words meaning "to Purify" and kindred ideas: *expiare*, abstract (e.g., *ad expiandum*), Ex. 29:36. Lev. 6:30. Num. 25:13; 28:22; 35:33. Isa. 47:11. Ezk. 45:15, 17, 20. Altar or sanctuary as object, Ex. 29:37. Lev. 8:15; 16:16, 32, 33. Ezk. 43:20, 26. *super altare*, Lev. 17:11. iniquities as object, 1 Sam. 3:14. *expiatio*, Ex. 29:36. Lev. 1:4; 16:27, 30. Num. 5:8; 28:30; 29:5. *mundare*, Ex. 29:36. Isa. 6:7. *emundare*, Lev. 16:20. *dimittere*, Isa. 27:9. *redimere*, Prv. 16:6. *delere*, Isa. 28:18. Dan. 9:24.

B. Words meaning "to pray for" and kindred ideas: *orare*, Lev. 5:6, 18; 12:7, 8; 14:53; 16:6, 18, 34; 19:22. Num. 8:19, 21. *exorare*, Neh. 10:33. *precari*, 1 Chr. 6:49 (6:34 MV). *deprecari*, Ex. 30:10; 32:30. Lev. 9:7. Num. 6:11; 8:12; 15:28; 16:47 (17:11 MV); 31:50. *impetrare*, Num. 15:28. *fundere preces*, Lev. 16:10. *rogare*, Lev. 4:20, 26, 31, 35; 5:10, 13, 16; 6:7 (5:26 MV); 14:19, 21; 15:15, 30; 16:11, 17, 24. Num. 15:25; 16:46 (17:11 MV).

C. Other words: *piaculum*, Lev. 17:11. 2 Sam. 21:3. 2 Chr. 29:24. *placare*, Gen. 32:20. Ex. 30:10. Lev. 14:29. Prv. 16:14. Ezk. 16:63. *placabile (sacrificium)*, Ex. 29:33. *offere*, Lev. 7:7. Num. 5:8. *ritus sacrificii*, Lev. 8:34. *propitiari*, Gen. 32:20. Ex. 30:16. Ps. 65:3 (64:4 LV). Jer. 18:23. *propitius esse*, Dt. 21:8; 32:43. Ps. 79:9 (78:9 LV). *propitius fieri*, Ps. 78:38 (77:38 LV).

71. E.g., Livy V, 50:2 and V, 53:1.

72. Ex. 29:37. The English and American revisions retain *make atonement for the*. Moffatt restored *expiate*. Knox renders *cleanse*.

73. Two illustrations will suffice: Lev. 16:16—DV, expiate the sanctuary; AV, RV, ARV, make atonement for the holy place; Moffatt, performing expiatory rites for the holy place; Knox, purify the sanctuary. Lev. 16:20—DV, cleanse the sanctuary; AV, reconcile the holy place; RV and ARV, atone for the holy place; Moffatt, expiatory rites for the sacred place; Knox, cleanse the sanctuary.

74. The two translations may be compared by examination of Tables F and G.

75. Gen. 32:20. Lev. 16:20, 33. Dt. 32:43. 1 Sam. 3:14. Ps. 65:3; 78:38. Prv. 16:14. Isa. 22:14; 27:9; 47:11. Ezk. 43:20, 26; 45:20. Dan. 9:24.

76. Lev. 1:5.

77. Lev. 8:15.

78. Lev. 16:14. The Hebrew *kapporeth* is translated by the Greek ἱλαστήριον. Both Hebrew and Greek forms indicate "the place of (?)". "Place of purification" is here adopted instead of the clumsy renderings of the English versions, which are: *propitiatory* (DV), *mercy seat* (AV, RV, ARV), *ark cover* (JV), *cover of the ark* (Moffatt) and *throne* (Knox).

The only biblical references to it are as follows: (1) Those having to do with the construction of the "ark." Ex. 25:17, 18, 19, 20, 21, 22; 26:34; 30:6; 31:7; 35:12; 37:6, 7, 8, 9; 39:35; 40:20. 1 Chr. 28:11. (2) Those having to do with the purifications of *Yom Kippurim*. Lev. 16:2, 13, 14, 15. (3) Num. 7:89. Yahweh spoke from the *kapporeth*.

79. Lev. 14.

80. Oil is the "blood of the olive" as wine is the "blood of the grape."

81. Lev. 16:30.

OCCASIONS AND SUBJECTS OF
CHATTATHS AND ASHAMS

Act of "advertence."

Chattath A—Act of a priest: bullock; act of the congregation: bullock; consecration of levite: bullock; consecration of priest: bullock; solemn entry of high priest to duties: calf for priest, ram for people; before a festal 'olah: kid or goat; Yom Kippurim: bullock for priest, goat for people, goat to Azazel.

Chattath B—Act of a ruler: male kid; act of a commoner: female kid or lamb; contact with human corpse: taboo water; bloody issue: dove; childbirth: pigeon or dove; leprosy: lamb; breach of Nazirite vow: dove; end of Nazirite vow: ewe lamb.

Asham—Withholding evidence: female kid or lamb; contact with animal carcase: female kid or lamb; contact with asham person: female kid or lamb; taking oath wrongly: female kid or lamb; intercourse with a slave: ram; profanation of holy things: ram; wronging a neighbor: ram.

82. Pp. 137, 154 and Lev. 1:5, 3:2.

83. Luke 10:25-37.

84. Num. 19:16.

85. Num. 19:9, 13. The phrase is variously translated as follows: DV, water of aspersion *or* water of expiation; AV & RV, water of separation; ARV, water for impurity; JV, water of sprinkling; Knox, lustral water. The purpose of the water was evidently to remove the taboo from contact with a corpse.

86. Hyssop was used as an instru-

ment of purification as follows: Ex. 12:22. Lev. 14:4, 6, 49, 51, 52. Num. 19:6, 18. Ps. 51:17. Heb. 9:19. Other biblical references are as follows: 1 Kgs. 4:33. Jn. 19:29.

87. The phrase "living water" occurs in the following biblical passages: Gen. 26:19. Lev. 14:5, 6, 50, 51, 52; 15:13 Num. 19:17. Cant. 4:15. Jer. 2:13; 17:13. Zach. 14:8. Jn. 4:10; 7:38. Rev. 7:17. In all these instances DV consistently translates "living water." AV translates "springing water" in Gen. 26:19, "running water" in the other pentateuchal passages, and "living water" in the remaining verses.

88. English translators were at a loss, having little concept of the significance of the rite. They rendered as follows: DV—The cow was burned for sin. AV & RV—It is a sin offering. JV—It is a purification from sin. Knox—The ashes of this heifer that was burned to atone for men's faults. Commentators seem troubled that the burned red cow was called a chattath although it was not burned on an altar. They go so far as to suggest that copyists must have made a mistake! Very little of any chattath was burned on an altar. The chattath was not a sacrifice or an act of worship. It was an act of purification for worship.

89. See W. W. Fowler, *Roman Festivals*, pp. 71–72, 82–84, 241–250.

90. Lev. 15:2, 19.

91. 2 Kgs. 15:5. 2 Chr. 26:21.

92. 2 Kgs. 5:27.

93. Lev. 13:47–59.

94. Lev. 14:33–53.

95. Lev. 13:1–46.

96. Lev. 13:45–46.

97. The law of cleansing the leper is in Lev. 14:1–32. The presentation to the priest is noted in Mt. 8:4. Mk.

1:40–44. Lk. 5:12–14; 17:14. The cleansed leper who went back to Jesus could not have been admitted for observation by a Jewish priest. A Samaritan had irremovable taboo and could not come near a priest.

98. J. G. Frazer, *The Scapegoat* (*The Golden Bough,* part vi), 3rd edition, pp. 31–37.

99. The provisions for house leprosy were imaginarily reflected back to the days of Moses. Stone houses and a city are indications of a much later civilization.

100. See chapter vii, p. 65 and notes 24, 25. Also Num. 6.

101. Ezk. 44:10–16.

102. They may have been priests of local sanctuaries or "high places." See chapter x, p. 119 and note 10.

103. Four descriptions of the dignity of levites are given in Num. 1:47–53; 2:33–4:49; 8:5–26; 18:2–6.

104. Chapter X, pp. 148 and note 147.

105. Chapter X, p. 141 f.

106. Dt. 16:2–5 suggests that the pesach is to be eaten only in Jerusalem at designated places. The writer's zeal for centralization was evident. Ezk. 45:18–22 suggests a chattath of a bullock on the 1st and again on the 7th of Nisan for cleansing the sanctuary and the temple, together with a chattath of a bullock on the 14th to prepare for eating pesach. The elaborate pesach attributed to Josiah in 2 Chr. 35:1–19 pictures a gorgeous temple service with levites to kill the pesach lambs, and priests and levites officiating at day long 'olahs.

107. The plural form *kippurim* occurs only eight times, viz., Ex. 29:36; 30:10, 16. Lev. 23:27, 28; 25:9. Num. 5:8; 29:11. The three occurrences in Lev. are in the expression *yom kippurim.* Ex. 30:10 and Num. 29:11 de-

scribe the chattath of that day as the *chattath kippurim.* Ex. 29:36 uses the same expression as part of the rite of consecration of a priest. Num. 5:8 calls the chattath of one who has wronged his neighbor the "ram of *kippurim.*" In Ex. 30:16 the money from the census half-shekel per head is called "money of *kippurim*" because it is "an offering to Yahweh to make purification for their souls." In all these instances the translation *purification* is exact.

108. See chapter X, p. 139.

109. See chapter X, p. 134.

110. See p. 177 and note 99 for transfer of evil to animals.

111. It is practically hopeless to expect to know more about *Azazel,* a word which occurs only in Lev. 16:8, 10, 26. It may be kindred to a similar root in Arabic meaning "remove," and therefore may be a clumsy formation to express "removal." It may be a proper name of which we know nothing. Translators have been of little help. Their results are as follows: LXX, αποπομπαιος, "the sent away" (goat); LV, *caper emissarius*; DV, *emissary goat*; AV, *scapegoat*; RV, *Azazel* with alternative *dismissal*; ARV, *Azazel* with alternative *removal*; JV, *Azazel*; Knox, *the people's discharge* or *the goat discharged.*

112. Num. 29:7–11 makes *yom kippurim* a day similar to the feast of trumpets on the first day of the same month, to be marked by a 'olah of one bullock, one ram and seven lambs with accompanying minchah, and a chattath of a kid in addition to the prescribed rites of the day. How all this ceremony, a day's work in itself, could come after the crowded ceremonies of purification is hard to imagine.

113. Mt. 5:23–24.

114. Romans 14:1–15:7.

115. Ephesians 5:25–27.

CHAPTER XII

1. Mt. 4:18–22. Mk. 1:16–20; 2:14. Lk. 5:1–11; 6:13–16. Jn. 1:35–42.

2. Mt. 10:1–5. Mk. 3:13–19.

3. Mt. 10:7–15. Mk. 3:14; 6:7–13.

4. Mt. 5–7. Lk. 6:20–49.

5. Lk. 10:1–20. Some manuscripts give the number as 72.

6. 1 Cor. 15:6.

7. Acts 1:15.

8. Acts 1:6–8.

9. Acts 15.

10. F. J. A. Hort, *Judaistic Christianity,* p. 202.

11. Eph. 5:17.

12. 1 Sam. 15:22. Ps. 40:6–10; 50:8–14; 51:16–17. Isa. 1:11–12. Jer. 7:22–23. Hos. 6:6. Amos 5:25.

13. Mt. 6:22–23.

14. Lk. 23:46.

15. Isa. 11:9. Hab. 2:14.

16. Mt. 4:1–11. Lk. 4:1–13.

17. Lk. 22:24–30.

18. Mt. 26:36–46. Lk. 22:39–46.

19. Mt. 16:25.

20. Mk. 16:1–7. Lk. 24:10.

21. Lk. 24:33.

22. 1 Cor. 3:10–12. Eph. 2:20–22. 1 Pet. 2:5.

23. Rev. 21:2.

24. Jn. 10:11–16.

25. Jn. 15:1–5.

26. Rom. 12:4–10. 1 Cor. 11:3; 12:12–27. Eph. 1:22–23; 4:15–16; 5:23. Col. 1:18.

27. Acts 23:2–5.

28. 2 Cor. 12:7–10.

29. 2 Cor. 11:24–25.

30. 2 Cor. 10:10.

31. Rom. 11:33–12:18.

32. The Greek words bring out this meaning very clearly. This ϑυσια which was being urged upon the readers was the true λατρεια. With ϑυσια we are familiar as denoting a concrete act of worship. λατρεια was the abstract word for the highest kind of worship. λογικος was an adjective denoting a category in contrast with physical and therefore might be translated as "spiritual." Msgr. Knox's use of the word *rational* is good.

33. Gal. 2:20.

34. Gal. 5:19–24.

35. Col. 1:24.

36. 2 Tim. 2:12.

37. In 2:11, 17; 9:13, 14, 22, 23; 10:2, 4, 10, 14, 18, 29; and 13:12, he ingeniously uses every Greek word in New Testament usage which translated *kipper* in the Old Testament, but prefers αγιαζω.

38. 5:12; 6:1.

39. 9:14.

40. Heb. 13:10–14.

41. Dt. 6:4–9.

42. 1 Cor. 10:16–21; 11:20–30.

43. See page 105.

44. See page 165.

45. See page 108.

46. Justin Martyr uses ευχαριστια to describe the elements after consecration. 1 Apol. 65, 66. This same use is found in the Institution Office of the American Book of Common Prayer, where the instituted priest is directed to "proceed with the Communion and to administer the Eucharist to the people."

TABLE A   HEBREW SACRIFICIAL WORDS AND GREEK EQUIVALENTS

	קרבן	מנחה	עלה	זבח	שלם	תודה	אשה	חמאת	אשם	כליל	פסח	Not in Hebrew	Apocrypha
δωρον	74	29				1							
δωρον θῦσια		5											
δωρεισθαι	1												
ξενιον		3											
σεμιδαλις		3											
μαναα		17											
προσφορα		1											12
θυσια	134	3		138	5		9					17	53
θυσιασμα		2		7			1						
θυμιαμα				6			1						
θυμα				9									
θυσιαζειν				1			1						
θυσια σωτηριου					4								
σωτηριον					62								
ειρηνικα					11								
αινεσις						22							
εξομολογησις						6							
χαρμοσυνη						1							
καρπωμα			16				34						
καρπωσις			3				1						
ολοκαρπωμα			4										
ολοκαρπωσις			12										
ολοκαυτωμα			162							1			
ολοκαυτωσις			66							1			
ολοκαυστος										1			
καρπουν							1						
πυρ							1						
αμαρτια								18	2				
περι (της) αμαρτιας								88					1
βασανος									4				
πλημμελεια									26				
πλημμελειν									8				
πλημμελησις									1				
πλημμελημα									2				
αγνοια									4				
αδικια									1				
καθαρισμος									1				
απαν										1			
διαπαντος										1			
πασχα											29		
φασεχ											19		
omit in LXX	3	10				1							

	Jos 22:29	1 Sam 3:14	Ps 40:6 (39:6 LXX. 39:7 DV)	Isa 19:21	Jer 17:26	Jer 33:18	Dan 9:27	Amos 5:29
TABLE B — Occurrences of the Phrase "ZEVACH AND MINCHAH" and Translations								
LXX θυσιαι και θυσια	★							
θυσια και θυμιαμα					★			
θυμιαμα και θυσια		★						
θυσια και προσφορα			★					
θυσια και θυμα						★		
θυσια και σπονδη							★	
σφαγια και θυσια								★
θυσια				★				
LV sacrificia et victima	★							
victima et sacrificia					★			
sacrificium et oblatio			★					
hostia et sacrificium							★	★
sacrificium et victima						★		
hostia et munera				★				
victima et munera		★						
DV sacrifice and victims	★					★		
victim and sacrifice					★		★	★
sacrifice and oblation			★					
sacrifice and offerings				★				
victims and offerings		★						
AV sacrifice and offering		★	★					★
sacrifice and oblation				★				
sacrifice and meat offering					★			
meat offerings and sacrifice	★					★		
JV sacrifice and offering		★					★	★
sacrifice and meal offering			★	★	★			
meal offering and sacrifice	★					★		

TABLE C   GREEK AND LATIN TRANSLATIONS OF *todhah*

			αἴνεσις	θυσία αἰνέσεως	ἐξομολόγησις	θυσία εὐχὴ χαριμοσύνης	ᾄδειν	δόξα	θεοδοθα	ὁμολογία	gratiarum actio	hostia gratiarum	sacrificium laudis	hostia laudis	laus	laudes	laudatio	oblatio	confessio	confiteor	vota	chori laudantium	chorus referentium gratias	omitted
tōdhah	Lev	7:12	★								★													
	Jos	7:19			★															★				
	Ezr	10:11	★																★					
	Ps	50:14		★									★											
		:23		★									★											
		69:31	★												★									
		95:2				★													★					
		100:4				★													★					
		147:7				★													★					
	Isa	51:3				★					★													
	Jer	17:26	★															★						
		30:19					★								★									
		33:11						★												★				
	Amos	4:5							★						★									
hattōdhah	Neh	12:38	★																				★	
		:40	★																			★		
tōdhōth or tōdhoth	Neh	12:27							★		★													
		:31	★																			★		
	Ps	56:13	★														★							
qōl tōdhah	Ps	26:7	★												★									
		42:5			★														★					
	Jon	2:10	★												★									
zevach tōdhah	Lev	7:12		★							★													
singular or plural		:13		★								★												
		:15		★																				★
		22:29				★					★													
	Ps	107:22		★									★											
		116:17		★										★										
zvachim wthōdhōth or zivche tōdhah	2 Chr bis	29:31	★													★								
		33:16	★												★									
hōdhōth	Neh	12:46	★																	★				

TABLE D TRANSLATIONS OF *todhah* IN ENGLISH VERSIONS

A Authorized version
D Douay version
P Book of Common Prayer
R Revised version margin
J Jewish version

Book	Verse	confession	confess	praise	praises	sacrifice of praise	thanks	thank offerings	thanksgiving	sacrifice of thanksgiving	sacrifice of peace offerings for thanksgiving	victim for thanksgiving	sacrifice of thanks	offerings for thanksgiving	offering	vows	OMITTED
Lev	7:12								AD J								
Jos	7:19	A J	D	R													
Ezr	10:11	AD J					R										
Ps	50:14					D			A P	J							
	:23			A P		D	P			J							
	69:31			D					A PJ								
	95:2								AD PJ								
	100:4			D					A PJ								
	147:7			D					A PJ								
Isa	51:3								AD J								
Jer	17:26					A			J						D		
	30:19			D					A J								
	33:11					A							J			D	
Amos	4:5					D				A J							
Neh	12:38							AD J									
	:40			D				A J									
Neh	12:27								AD J								
	:31			D				A J									
Ps	56:13				AD		P	J									
Ps	26:7			D					A PJ								
	42:5			AD J					P								
Jon	2:10			D					A J								
Lev	7:12									A J							D
	:13									A	J		D				
	:15										A J						D
	22:29									A J			D				
Ps	107:22					D				A PJ							
	116:17					D				A PJ							
2 Chr	29:31 (bis)			D				A J									
	33:16			D			A			J							
Neh	12:46						D		A J								

TABLE E

HEBREW AND GREEK WORDS TRANSLATED *memorial*

References are to AV

	αναμνησις	μνημοσυνον	μνεια	μνημη	others
זכר		Ex 3:15 17:14 Dt 32:26 Est 9:28 Job 18:17 Ps 9:7 34:16 102:12 109:15 112:6 135:13 Hos 12:5 14:6	Ps 111:4 Isa 26:8	Ps 30:4 97:12 145:7 Prv 10:7 Eccl 9:5	ονομα Dt 25:19 ο μνημονευων Ps 6:5 αρσεν Isa 26:14
זכרון	Num 10:10	Ex 12:14 13:9 17:14 28:12-29 30:16 39:7 Lev 23:24 Num 5:15 :18 16:40 31:54 Jos 4:7 Neh 2:20 Est 6:1 Isa 57:8 Mal 3:16		μνημα Eccl 1:11 2:16	αγαυριαμα Job 13:12 ψαλμον Zec 6:14
אזכרה	Lev 24:7	Lev 2:2 :9 :16 5:12 6:15 Num 5:26			
Apocrypha	Wis 16:6				

TABLE F

GREEK AND LATIN TRANSLATIONS OF *kipper* AND *kippur*

	orare	exorare	precare	deprecari	impetrare	fundere preces	rogare	rogare et expiare	expiare	expiatio	piaculum	placare	placabilis	mundare	emundare	propitiare	propitius esse	propitius fieri	dimittere	redimere	delere	offerre	ritus sacrificii	OMIT IN VULGATE
ιλασκεσθαι																1	1	1						
εξιλασκεσθαι	12	1	1	8	1	1	17	1	14	5	3	4	1	1	1	2				1	2	1		7
ιλασμος										1														
εξιλασις										1														
ιλεως γινεσθαι																1								
καθαριζειν									1			1												
εκκαθαριζειν																1								
περικαθαριζειν														1										
αποκαθαιρειν																				1				
καθαρον γινεσθαι									1															
καθαρισμος									1															
αφαιρειν																				1	1			
αγιαζειν									1			1												
αφιεναι																				1				
αδφουν																1								

TABLE G

ENGLISH TRANSLATIONS OF *kipper* AND *kippur*

A V \ D V	make atonement	accomplish atonement	be atonement	atoning sacrifice	make atonement and pray	pray for	entreat	pour out prayers	be merciful	show mercy	forgive	pardon	cleanse	expiate	expiation	pacify	appease	redeem	keep off	not stand	abolish	offer	rite of the sacrifice	omit in Vulgate
make atonement	7	1	1	2	1	36	1	1	1			1		3	7	1						1	1.	7
make reconciliation	1													1	1						1			
be merciful								2																
forgive											2													
reconcile	1												1		1									
pardon							1																	
cleanse														1										
purge											2	1	3	1				1						
pacify																2								
appease																	1							
put off																			1					
disannul																					1			

INDEXES

Arabic numerals refer to pages.
Roman numerals refer to chapters.
Roman numerals followed by arabic refer to notes. E.g., xi:60 refers to note 60 to Chapter XI.

1. GENERAL INDEX

Including transliterated Hebrew words. Words beginning with Hebrew *ayin* are listed under the second letter preceded by an apostrophe.

2. INDEX OF GREEK WORDS

3. INDEX OF LATIN WORDS AND PHRASES